BETWEEN
TWO EMPIRES

By R. J. Mitchell and M. D. R. Leys

A HISTORY OF THE ENGLISH PEOPLE

BETWEEN TWO EMPIRES

A History of French Politicians
and People between 1814 and 1848

M. D. R. LEYS, M.A.
Fellow of St. Anne's College, Oxford

LONGMANS, GREEN AND CO
LONDON · NEW YORK · TORONTO

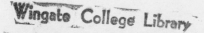

LONGMANS, GREEN AND CO LTD
6 & 7 CLIFFORD STREET LONDON W I
BOSTON HOUSE STRAND STREET CAPE TOWN
531 LITTLE COLLINS STREET MELBOURNE

LONGMANS, GREEN AND CO INC
55 FIFTH AVENUE NEW YORK 3

LONGMANS, GREEN AND CO
20 CRANFIELD ROAD TORONTO 16

ORIENT LONGMANS LTD
CALCUTTA BOMBAY MADRAS
DELHI VIJAYAWADA DACCA

First published 1955

Made and printed in Great Britain by
William Clowes and Sons, Limited, London and Beccles

With gratitude to
MAJA SERING

PROLOGUE

THE story of France between the First and the Second Empire has a double fascination. It was then that the consequences of that great climax in French history, the revolution of 1789, were worked out in peace; though Frenchmen fought in Spain, in Greece, in Belgium, in North Africa, they were not engaged in any great national war. Men and women had the opportunity to think over and to express in art, in literature, in science, ideas and emotions which, all over Europe, had been leading to a new approach to the fundamental questions of the relation of Man to God, to Nature, to the State. How their thoughts would be translated into action depended on politics; on the practical framework of the institutions through which law was made, duties prescribed and rights protected or limited. Herein lies the second interest of the period; it followed and it gave birth to a system which signified the predominant influence of one man as the leader of the nation.

The first Napoleon had ruled through a bureaucratic machinery, and it survived him because it could ensure the day-to-day functioning of the government of the people. Politicians could freely form groups and parties, overthrow cabinets or even kings, work out patterns of parliamentary practice knowing that, though the personnel might change, the machine would continue to work. As was the case all over Europe before 1848, politics were the concern of a small privileged class, which represented not only noble birth but wealth, often gained in the new ways of industry and finance. Property always seeks protection, and the reappearance of an Empire after the revolution of 1848 can be ascribed to the desire for order, deeply embedded not only in the rich, who were few, but also in the peasant landowners, who were very many, greatly outnumbering the workers of the towns.

In this study the foreign policy of successive governments has been ignored save where it seemed to exercise a direct influence on the people and the politicians of France. There are many excellent books in which it can be studied. What has led me to read the voluminous memoirs written by so many people who played an active part in the politics of those thirty-four years has been my wish to discover the results on France of the failure to establish a system of constitutional monarchy. It seems to me that it was then that the divisions in modern France became clear and permanent.

Fears and hatreds, patterns of thought and action, have survived. A strong centralised administrative machine and a weak political executive; a dread of organised Catholicism powerful enough to lead to a denial of liberty by men who believe in freedom; an individualistic independence which leads to instability in political alliances; all of these developed between the Empires. To understand the people and the politicians of France between 1814 and 1848 leads, I believe, to an understanding of the France of to-day.

CONTENTS

	PAGE
Prologue	vii
Maps	
Central Paris in 1848	x
Environs of Paris	xi

CHAPTER

I	The New France	1
II	The Bourbons Return	12
III	The Charter and the People	23
IV	The Flight of the Bourbons	37
V	The Second Restoration	46
VI	France Afraid	58
VII	The Matchless Parliament	68
VIII	The King and the Charter	81
IX	The Sofa Party and the Press	96
X	Plots and Politicians	108
XI	War in Spain	123
XII	Royalism Triumphant	136
XIII	Church and State	147
XIV	The Royal Revolution	157
XV	The Monarch of July	176
XVI	The State and the Workers	188
XVII	The Citizen King	202
XVIII	Thinkers and Teachers	213
XIX	France is Bored	223
XX	The Gathering Storm	236
XXI	Farewell to Monarchy	247
XXII	The Empire is Made	261
Books for Further Reading		271
Index of Selected Subjects and Places		272
Index of Important People		275

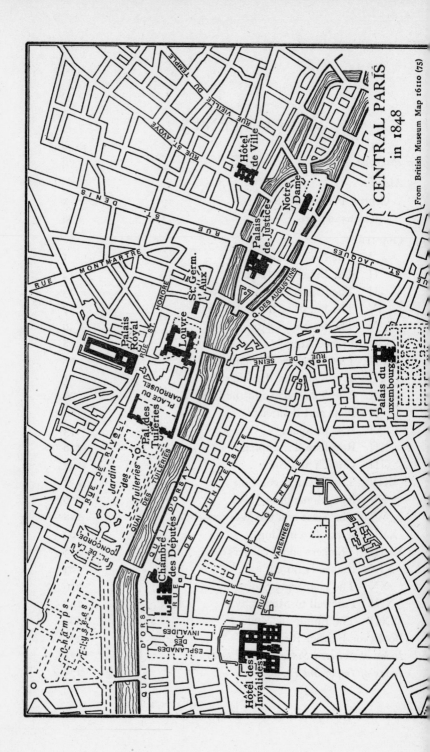

CENTRAL PARIS
in 1848

From British Museum Map 16110 (75)

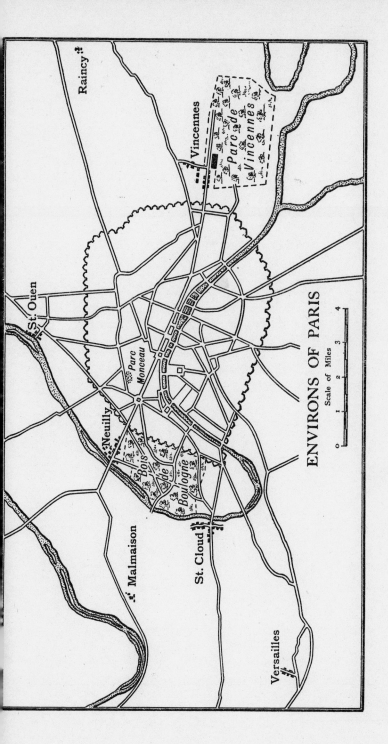

ENVIRONS OF PARIS

Scale of Miles

0 1 2 3 4

Raincy

Vincennes

Parc de Vincennes

St. Ouen

Parc Monceau

Neuilly

Bois de Boulogne

Malmaison

St. Cloud

Versailles

Chapter I

THE NEW FRANCE

FRANCE in 1814 was invaded. The state which had been mistress of Europe under her great Emperor now suffered the fate which her sons had inflicted on nearly every European country save England; on the south-west her men were retreating from Spain before Wellington; on the north and east Napoleon was fighting a brilliant but hopeless campaign against the great forces of the allies. Another and different type of invasion was also going on; from England and the Rhineland and the Low Countries Frenchmen long exiled were returning: men who had fled before the Revolution or had been driven out because of their noble families or their opposition to the Revolution, and churchmen who had refused to conform to the nationalisation of their Church; men who had served foreign governments, or lived as best they could, some in comfort, some scraping a living by teaching. They had been offered a chance to return by Napoleon and many exiles had accepted it, but these were the men who had never given up hope that one day the usurper would fall and the King return to the throne of his murdered brother.

They could hardly realise how much they were strangers to their own country. So much had happened in the twenty-five years since the Revolution; so much blood had been shed; so many experiments in government had been made; so profound had been the social revolution; so ignorant were the exiles and their sons, often born in a foreign land, of the depth to which new ideas and new habits of living had penetrated, that they had little idea that the mass of the people had wholly forgotten what to them seemed a natural way of living and thinking. There were many royalists in France itself with whom some sort of correspondence had been spasmodically maintained, but their numbers had diminished with the years and many had loyally served Napoleon. These men, too, hoped for a return of the monarchy, but they could not share the expectations of their exiled kinsmen and friends.

Three aspects of the nation's life had been too deeply altered for any simple restoration to be possible—the government, the Church and the ownership of land. France was, as she still is, a nation of farmers. Before 1789 a growing population had led to a great demand for foodstuffs, and agriculture was prosperous. Great estates were owned by the Church and the nobility; the revolutionaries seized all the lands of the Church, including those of the religious orders, and much of the land of the nobility. By 1814 some land, mostly forest, was still in the hands of the Government, but the bulk had been sold; speculators had bought much, but generally for resale to the men who worked on the land and who bought it eagerly. Much had been sold far below its true value, so the peasants were not crippled by debts and mortgages, and farming is the one industry which in times of disturbance and war is bound to prosper. At the worst, a landowner could live on what he grew: at the best, he could sell his surplus at high prices. Most of the farms were small; even to-day the majority of French farms are worked by the family, with little hired labour. Under Napoleon agriculture was fostered and new techniques and new crops were introduced; one of these, sugar beet, was at first grown only under direct compulsion from the Government, but in some areas it proved a very valuable addition to the old established grains and roots and fruits.

Under the Empire the peasant made money, but he had suffered badly from the endless wars which conscripted his sons for the army. In 1814, therefore, he was passionately anxious for peace. In the early years of the Revolution he had resented the laws which re-organised the Church in France and interfered with his traditional worship, but Napoleon's agreement with the Pope in 1802 had satisfied his piety by restoring the accustomed ways and his interests by leaving him free of tithes to be paid to the Church. He now wanted two things from any government: security in the ownership of his land and freedom from the threat of war. He cared little who ruled, so long as the taxes were not too heavy, and the prices of his crops were good, for he had not been asked to play more than a nominal rôle in the running of the State.

So placid, on the whole, was life in the country that politicians were apt to forget the peasants. Yet they remained the majority of the French people, even though, as time went on, some of their children were moving into the growing towns to work in the developing industries. These, too, were mainly on a small scale even when compared with their counterparts in contemporary England, let alone modern industry. In most trades the organisation was still 'domestic'; a few men worked alongside their employer, himself a master craftsman. There were few large towns; Paris was exceptional in industry as in everything else; she had no conceivable competitor. Near Paris and in the north and east heavy industries had greatly developed, especially mining and the manufacture of armaments. Under the Empire actual munitions of war were a Government monopoly, and mining was closely controlled by the State. As a result, conditions in French mines were probably a good deal better than in the English; precautions were taken against accidents and injured workers had a right to compensation.

The old gilds of craftsmen had been abolished, and all combinations of workers were prohibited by law. In spite of this, *compagnonnages*, 'companionships' of men working in the same craft, were constantly reappearing, but they were very small in membership and purely local in organisation. Under the Empire a system of controlling workers had been introduced, the *livret* plan. Craftsmen were sometimes given an advance on their wages by their employers, and in unsettled times a man might leave his job before this had been fully paid off. This was the excuse for the law of 1803 by which every hired workman had to have a 'little book', a sort of passport, with his name, age and place of birth, and a certificate that he had duly completed his apprenticeship. Whenever he changed masters, he had to show the police this book, signed by his old employer, as a proof that he was not in debt. During the Empire, demand for labour was so great that little attention was paid to this check on a worker's movements; later in the century it became a useful means of control by employers or by the Government.

Another imperial law was more favourable to the workers. In 1806 *Conseils de Prud'hommes* were set up, which acted as courts of arbitration between masters and men over wages, piece-rates, conditions of work and so forth. Representatives of both sides attended and the agreements come to were enforced by law. The system, on the whole, worked very well.

Both wages and profits tended to rise under Napoleon; his was for the most part a period of full employment, and the workers shared in the somewhat artificial prosperity of a war-time economy. In some respects, French urban workers were better off than their English contemporaries; they certainly had a better and more varied diet. Their housing was probably slightly worse; even in the mid-nineteenth century it was rare for a workman to have more than a single room for himself and his family.

Great fortunes had been made by speculators during the Revolution, when metal coins disappeared and the paper notes that replaced them were issued in such quantities as to lead to a tremendous inflation of prices. Even when gold and silver were restored in 1797, the shortages due to war gave great chances to enterprising and unscrupulous men. Anyone who could secure some of the goods in short supply, such as sugar and coffee which came from overseas, could make a fortune. The Bank of France was founded in 1799 to help provide short-term loans for business men at moderate rates, and was brought under State control in 1806. The provinces made little use of the bank, but it proved very valuable to Parisian traders. Alongside this central bank were a number of private banking firms, again all centred on Paris, and, like the English banks of the same period, not always wisely managed.

A certain amount of the bankers' activity was concerned with dealing in the *rentes*, the national debt of France. It was the size of the debt of Louis XVI which had forced him to summon that meeting of the States General which developed into the revolution of 1789. Each subsequent government had been forced to borrow, and though a part of the loans had been repudiated, Napoleon's wars had added enormously to the outstanding liabilities. Shares in the debt were bought and sold by investors through the Bourse, the Stock Exchange, and speculators forced the price up or down according to their guesses about the political prospects of the time. The price of *rentes*, therefore, became a sort of political barometer, indicating the views of the business world on the policy of the Government.

Men who had made a fortune could hope to become members of Napoleon's new nobility, alongside his civil servants and his out-standing generals. His marshals, as is still the custom here, were given titles commemorating their victories, but civilians, too, drew their titles from conquered lands. The notorious Chief of Police, Fouché, became Duke of Otranto, and Talleyrand, so long Napoleon's adviser in foreign affairs, was made Prince of Benevento, although he belonged to one of the old noble families of France. Not all of Napoleon's courtiers were men who had lately risen; several of the members of the old aristocracy who had not emigrated or who had returned to France held positions of importance and of honour. When the emigrants returned in 1814 this new nobility greatly offended their sense of what was right and proper. Class distinction in the old France had been very rigid, and the man with a dozen quarterings on his family coat of arms and accustomed to the elaborate manners of the eighteenth century was very contemptuous of the lowly birth and lack of polish of many of Napoleon's peers. They, in their turn, thought the old-fashioned style purely comic, and resented fiercely the social slights to which they, and still more their wives, were exposed. This purely superficial difference made co-operation between the old and the new France very difficult in the Court and society, and so had an important influence on politics.

More serious, for it went far deeper and affected the majority of the people, was the cleavage over the Church. By the Civil Constitution of the Clergy the Church in France had been separated from

Rome, and its property seized. Napoleon had made a Concordat with the Pope in 1802 which confirmed the loss by the Church of its lands and tithes and made the State responsible for paying regular salaries to the clergy and maintaining the fabric of churches and buildings. In many ways this new plan was beneficial to the Church; the peasant no longer cast envious eyes on the priests' or monks' fields or grudged the payment of tithes of his crops. The parish priest had fewer worries and on the average a better income than in 1789. On the other hand, he had lost a common interest with his flock, and was less integrated into the community. The Church was also inevitably brought into politics, for the payment of clerical stipends was an annual item in the national budget. As years passed, people forgot that the money voted was a compensation for the nationalised lands, and looked on it as a burden on the taxpayer. The freedom of the Church was also restricted; for instance, more bishops were needed, but they could only be given sees if more money were available.

Napoleon had to a certain extent cheated the Pope; the Organic Laws, passed nominally to enforce the Concordat, in some respects modified it. The Government's consent was required for the publication of any Papal Bull, or the holding of any synod or formal meeting of clergy, and the State had control over the seminaries where young men were trained for the priesthood. No foreigner could hold a position in the Church without Government leave, and the Protestant clergy, who also received State salaries, could have no organised relations with their brethren in other countries.

The priests and bishops in France in 1814 included some men who had stayed with their people, hiding during the persecution; some who had submitted to the Civil Constitution but had been reconciled to Rome; many younger ones who had been ordained since the Revolution and had grown up under the shadow of Imperial control. All of them seemed, to the clergy who had emigrated, to be traitors to the faith. 'The Little Church' was the name given to the bishops and priests who returned to France in 1814. Certainly there were not very many of them, but their influence was disproportionately large, for most of them belonged to the old noble families. All of them sincerely believed that it was essential for the Gallican Church to regain its independence and therefore to own property, not to have to ask for money from the State. France, in their view, had apostatised and must now demonstrate her penitence. They deeply regretted that the Pope should ever have come to terms with the usurper Napoleon; they had rejoiced over the quarrel between Pope and Emperor in 1811. But they were not Papalists, or to use a commoner term, Ultramontane, seeking direction from

Italy across the barrier of the Alps. They wished France to be as independent of the Papacy as was compatible with membership of the Roman Church. Only the monarchy, they believed, could restore the ancient freedoms, and at this juncture only from the Church could the monarchy get solid moral support.

These exiled clergy saw, perhaps more clearly than the men who now occupied the sees and parishes which had once been theirs, that France was ready for a revival of religion. As often happens after a period of war and strain, a renewed fervour was being shown all over Europe. New religious orders were being founded and old ones reformed; in the Protestant countries the Evangelical movement was at work in both the national and the free Churches. Not all of the demonstrations of piety in France that antagonised the free-thinkers were political or hypocritical; many expressed a genuine upsurge of religious emotion.

Sincere churchmen have always held that the proper training of the young is a major duty for those who have a 'cure of souls'. There was a great deal to be criticised in the French educational system as Napoleon had left it. The theorists of 1789 had had wonderful plans for universal education which had only very partially been carried out when the great soldier and administrator took control. For Napoleon, education of the citizens, especially in science, was essential, but free development of the minds of the young might be extremely dangerous. Therefore, in 1806, he regimented education; he established a single national university in Paris with full control over all provincial universities and over all kinds of colleges and schools. Its professors and administrators were appointed by the Government, and only those persons whom it authorised were allowed to teach. All educational establishments were inspected by the Civil Service to see that the university's regulations were fulfilled. The Church as a teaching body was not wholly excluded, though nearly all the secondary schools were entrusted to lay masters. In 1808 the Salesians, known as the Christian Brothers, were permitted to teach in elementary schools, and some orders of nuns were established to manage schools for girls. Whether Napoleon's system meant complete regimentation of education, or whether academic and religious freedom could thrive within it, would obviously depend on the character and quality of the men in charge of the university.

Education, like every other aspect of French life, had been profoundly influenced by the continuous wars. Men were called to the colours at an ever earlier age, and secondary education suffered accordingly. The army offered great chances to men of ambition; no social barriers stood in the way of the rapid promotion that accompanied long casualty lists. Many of the officers in 1814 had known no other life than that of arms; they had shown off their uniforms in half the capitals of Europe; often they had helped to administer large districts. To many of them the prospect of peace stood for release from danger and discomfort; but to a very large number it meant the end of a career and the seeking of a living without any money behind them or any qualifications for civilian posts.

Whatever government should be in power, it was unlikely to be very generous in the way of pensions, half-pay or gratuities. For some time the State's revenue from all sources had not been enough to meet the annual expenditure; the taxes were as fairly levied as could be expected, but were heavy, and the payers would hope for a reduction in the burden when wars were ended. Napoleon's soldiers, so long victorious but now being driven back over the Pyrenees and fighting on the defensive on the eastern frontiers, had a gloomy prospect before them.

The civil servants were more hopeful. Under Napoleon a very efficient and highly centralised bureaucracy had been established. Every department had a prefect, under whom the local officials did their work. These men, as well as the Ministers of State and heads of Government departments like the Police and the Post Office, were appointed by the Emperor and worked under the control of his Council; they had no security of tenure but could be dismissed or moved about at will. They had immense power; they reported on all local affairs to Paris; they supervised all activities, political and economic. Many of the more patriotic and thoughtful of them were wondering what would happen to their country; they knew well that Napoleon had lost his popularity, but they also knew that no strong body of men had formed any plan for a modification of his rule or for an alternative government. They were very well aware of the political passivity which so astonished foreign observers in 1814, for it was they who had helped to prevent any spontaneous political life.

Napoleon's government was a façade of representation concealing a highly organised despotism. The Council of State was the real organ of power; the nominated Senate and the elected deputies were often by-passed. So long as all went well, there was little trouble, but it was being felt more and more, especially since the disastrous Russian campaign of 1812, that the hero had thrown away France's opportunity of becoming the leading Power in Europe by his personal and insatiable ambition. Criticism was becoming sharper; men were demanding not merely equality and the fraternity to be found mainly in the army, but some genuine liberty. Even Napoleon's own counsellors were coming to believe that he must be deposed; Talleyrand, the renegade bishop and courtier who had conducted

foreign business with him in his most successful period, had parted
from him and had long been intriguing with Alexander, the Tsar of
Russia.

Probably, had it been possible to ask them, most Frenchmen
would have preferred to keep Napoleon if he would accept the position of a king, and would grant more liberal institutions. He was only
forty-five; though his health was suffering from his incessant
activity, he might be expected to live for many years yet. He had a
son to succeed him, born in March 1811. The men who knew him,
though, could not believe that he would settle down as a ruler of a
limited nation and with limited power. Some of the allied states
would have been ready to come to terms with him, but the men
whom he himself had placed in power in France were convinced that
he must be deposed.

What solution could there be for France's future? One plan,
Napoleon's own, that he should abdicate in favour of his baby son,
would raise a double problem. Should the child's mother, Marie
Louise of Austria, act as Regent? Would the Emperor of Austria be
agreeable to an Austrian princess occupying so delicate a position,
even if the other Powers—and the lady herself—were willing? And,
secondly, was it at all likely that Napoleon would really retire into
private life, abandoning his wife and child? The plan, though it
would have pleased many Frenchmen, was not a practicable one.

No one seriously thought of a republic. There were still a number
of theoretical republicans in France, but the failure of the experiments between 1789 and 1799 had made the Powers and the
majority of Frenchmen highly suspicious of this form of government. What had been hoped for in 1789 was still desired, a king who
would not only represent the past glories of France and also give an
element of stability to the State, but who would consent to exercise
his powers in genuine co-operation with representatives of the
people. English politicians and writers had for the last twenty years
been exalting constitutional monarchy as the ideal form of government. For the next twenty their influence was to be used whenever
possible to impose this system on every state that was dissatisfied
with its existing government, whether in fact its traditions and social
structure were really suited for an organisation copied from England
or not.

The choice of a monarch for France was not wholly a foregone
conclusion. Few people believed that the Bourbons were really
suited for the delicate task they would have to undertake. One
suggestion was to choose a successful and popular soldier, one of
Napoleon's marshals, and let him found a new dynasty, as Bernadotte was doing in Sweden, as the accepted heir of the old king.

Such a man, though, would certainly be looked on with jealousy by his fellows; no one was able to occupy the position Napoleon's friends had made for him in 1799. More serious was the suggestion that Louis-Philippe, Duke of Orleans, the head of the younger branch of the Royal Family of France, should be given the throne. To those who know what did, in fact, happen, it looks as if this plan might have saved a great deal of trouble, including a revolution in 1830. It is probable that he himself had some hopes, but he, too, was an exile, though an unwilling one; he was as little known to the ordinary Frenchman as were the brothers of Louis XVI. He had no party in France, whereas for years the royalists had been hoping and plotting for the return of the men they looked on as their rightful rulers.

Reluctant though they were to admit it, Frenchmen and allied victors both came to the conclusion that a restoration of the Bourbons was the only plan for France. As Talleyrand said in his *Mémoires*: 'The legitimacy of a sovereign power results from the ancient status of possession, in the same way as the right of property for private people.'[1] Napoleon himself, according to Talleyrand, had expected that if France were to be reduced to her old frontiers, it would be 'the sort of peace that only the Bourbons could make'.[2] Nearly every one realised it was inevitable that Louis, brother of the king who died on the guillotine, should be the new ruler of France; only those few who had waited and prayed for this ending to the long drama of the Empire rejoiced.

In Paris early in 1814 Joseph, Napoleon's brother, and his ministers felt the reins of his government slipping between their fingers. In February the wounded from the battlefields began to arrive in large numbers, and for the first time Parisians saw with their own eyes the terrible aftermath of war. Hasty preparations were made; sick people, even those with infectious diseases, were turned out of the hospitals and sent to their homes; the city authorities appealed for bedding and clothing, threatening if gifts were insufficient to billet the wounded in private houses. New municipal slaughterhouses, not quite finished, were hastily fitted up as hospital wards.

At first Paris society ignored the situation; on Sunday, 13 February, 'the promenades', a lady recorded in her diary, 'are covered with people; finery and elegant carriages; the theatres are full.'[3] But

[1] Talleyrand, Prince de: *Mémoires*. Ed. de Broglie. Paris, 1891, Vol. II, p. 160.
[2] Ibid., p. 161.
[3] Marigny, Madame de: *Journal Inédit*. Ed. de Lacharrière. Paris, 1907, p. 14.

already wealthy people were beginning to leave. The passport office was reported to have issued 1,300 passports in a single day, and the Mont de Piété, the official pawnshop, refused to advance more than twenty francs, less than a pound sterling, on any single object, so great was the number of people trying to deposit their valuables there to ensure their safety. As the armies drew nearer, cattle and little carts piled high with goods began to block the narrow streets, as the peasants left their villages and took refuge in the city. Day by day the confusion grew; the Council of Regency appointed by Napoleon left Paris, taking the Empress and her child to a safer place. On 30 March, 1814, an armistice was arranged between the local French commanders and the allied invaders, and next day Alexander of Russia made his triumphal entry.

For some time the royalists inside France had been trying to organise a rebellion against Napoleon. In January 1814, when the conscripts were called to the colours, there had been a good deal of resistance, especially in Brittany, but the parish priests were opposed to a rising, and the royalists' hopes of large-scale demonstrations in the north and in the old royalist stronghold of the Vendée were shattered. Round Bordeaux and Bayonne, which was besieged by Wellington in December 1813, the royalists tried to persuade the people to clamour for a restoration, but they had little success. Peace was passionately wanted, but not a change of ruler. Propaganda, including some blatant falsehoods, failed to convince Wellington that the return of the Bourbons was the heartfelt desire of the French people.

Perhaps if the local leaders had been less divided among themselves they might have done better. Three different and rival groups were at work in Bordeaux, but no demonstrations of any size were made until the British advance guard entered the city. Far from being impressed, Wellington was thoroughly annoyed with the royalists, for the agitation in the streets made it harder for him to keep order.

Rumours, sometimes exaggerated, of local risings reached Paris and made it clear that, unless a definite plan for governing France were quickly made, a complete breakdown of administration was possible. On 1 April, Napoleon's Upper Chamber, the Senate, held a very thinly attended meeting and set up a provisional government whose duty it was to produce a draft constitution, presumably to be imposed on Napoleon or on some other person. Two days later it solemnly deposed the Emperor, who in his turn abdicated in favour of his son on 4 April. The Senate's acts were confirmed by a skeleton Legislative Assembly.

Talleyrand, who had been appointed with four others to form the provisional government, rapidly produced a draft constitution. All Paris was alive with rumours; busy consultations were going on with the victors. Alexander made it clear to Talleyrand that he did not want the Bourbons, for he had at this time vague sentiments for liberty and popular government. Talleyrand persuaded him to accept the Bourbons, but only bound by a constitution. The question was: Would the Bourbons agree?

Chapter II

THE BOURBONS RETURN

LOUIS XVI had died on the guillotine, and his son had vanished in the dark recesses of the prison. That he was dead there was no reasonable doubt; but so impenetrable was the mystery surrounding his fate that pseudo-Dauphins continued to appear for many years after 1814, sometimes causing the Royal Family a good deal of trouble. The dead king's brother was now his heir, and though he was childless another brother had two sons to carry on the line.

Would these men be willing and able to rule in co-operation with some sort of representative assembly? That was the question the politicians were asking, and on the answer depended the future of France. Constitutional monarchy, as we know it to-day, did not exist; even in England the King still had great influence over policy, and the unreformed House of Commons by no means represented the people. No one expected the monarch to be an impartial figurehead, but how extensive his influence could be would depend on his own character and his capacity for judging events and seeing what was possible for him to do and when he would be wise to yield. Above all, the success of the restored monarchy would depend on its popularity.

Louis XVIII took that title to emphasise that his brother had, in fact, been succeeded by the dead child, even if no one had ever acknowledged him as King. He was a widower, born in 1755, and his heir presumptive, known as Monsieur, was Charles, the Duke of Artois, who was two years younger. Louis was by no means wholly unsuitable for the very difficult part he would have to play. He had a strong vein of common sense; he realised from the first that he would have to come to terms with a France very different from the one he had left. He was easy-going and affectionate, very loyal to those to whom he had given his trust, and honestly determined to work hard at his royal duty. He had disapproved of the endless intrigues of the exiled royalists and had a profound distrust of his brother Charles and all his friends. But he was a Bourbon; he had a tremendous sense of his dignity and a tremendous belief in his inborn and hereditary rights; he was keenly interested in all the elaborate ceremonial of a historic court.

In person he was not at all suited for public appearances. He was far from strong physically and was so fantastically stout that he walked with great difficulty and had to have help to rise from his arm-chair. A greater contrast to the active Napoleon could hardly be imagined. He had been living for years in peace at Hartwell, in England, surrounded by his friends, and he refused to move away until the situation in France was clear. Also, he had no money for the journey; he was in debt and had to borrow from the Rothschilds' bank in London before he could at last make his painful, slow progress to take up his throne. His lethargy and his peculiar appearance were a very real handicap; the envoys sent from Paris were dismayed when they saw him, and the soldiers in France when they saw their King made great fun of him.

Monsieur was in almost all respects different from his brother. Where Louis was slow, Charles was impetuous; he could see no reason for any hesitation, for he could not believe that any change in the pre-revolutionary government of France was right or necessary. For years he had been active in conspiracies for the restoration of the monarchy, in touch with the plotters inside and outside France. In his earlier years he had been a notorious libertine; now in later middle age he had repented, and so great was his parade of piety that he was thought, probably very unjustly, to be insincere. He cut an excellent figure, especially on horseback; unlike his brother he could act the king very well indeed. Both men were obstinate; but Louis could listen to reason and could be convinced; Charles could never believe he was wrong. To gain his ends he did not disdain subterfuge, and if it suited him to go back on a promise, he had no qualms.

His elder son, the Duke of Angoulême, was in many respects unlike his father. He had been born in 1775 and had married his cousin, the daughter of Louis XVI. He had bad manners and was very clumsy and shy; he was obviously, indeed surprisingly, stupid. Occasionally he gave way to fits of rage when he wholly lost control of himself, but normally he behaved more like a dull loutish schoolboy than a grown man and a prince. His wife could have found little in her husband to compensate her for the agonies she had suffered over the death of her father and mother. Her eyelids were permanently reddened, and this was popularly ascribed to her girlhood of weeping. She was extremely conscious that she was the daughter of the kindly king who had tried to help his people and whom they had with the basest ingratitude destroyed. It revolted her to come in contact with the 'regicides', a term which for her included everyone who had played an active part in the revolution. Her only consolation was her religion; hers was a most fervent but a rather narrow

and puritanical piety, which by no means excluded a passion for revenge. Her strength of character led her to be called the only man of the family. In appearance she was awkward and far from attractive; her rigid leather corset and old-fashioned clothes greatly amused the fashionable ladies of Paris, in their light and elegant Empire-style dresses. Still, no one could fail to respect her, and those who knew her had a deep sympathy for this woman of tragic memories.

Her brother-in-law, the Duke de Berry, provided the light relief in this strange Royal Family. He was born in 1788 and was still unmarried in 1814. He had no interest whatever in politics; he would accept any system that would save trouble. He wanted to have his debts paid off, and to have enough money to enjoy a really good time. His temper was quick and easily roused, but he was usually courteous and soon became popular with the people whom he met.

The younger branch of the Bourbons was headed by the Duke of Orleans, Louis-Philippe. His father had been suspected of planning to become king in place of Louis XVI, and of fomenting riots during the Revolution; he had publicly associated with the revolutionaries and took the name of Égalité as a symbol of his opinions. But he, too, had fallen on the guillotine in 1793. Louis-Philippe, his eldest son, born in 1773, had had a strange childhood, for his father had taken him and his brothers and sisters away from their mother and placed them in the charge of his mistress, Madame de Genlis. When revolution came in France, the boy of sixteen was enthusiastic to help; he joined the army and was present at the Battle of Jemappes, where he showed courage of a quality to make him popular with the troops.

He was unlucky in his commander; Dumouriez, after winning the first critical battles for France, went over to the enemy, and all who were associated with him were in danger. Louis-Philippe and his sister had to fly the country. For years he wandered about, seeking employment as a schoolmaster, trying in vain to find some way of life. When the Spaniards revolted against Napoleon, he asked leave to join them, but the English politicians feared to embroil themselves with a man detested by the elder branch of the Bourbons. In November 1809 he married Marie Amélie, the daughter of the King of Naples, and proceeded to acquire a large family. His early poverty made him anxious to get money; as soon as he could he laid claim to what remained of the family estates, and used his capital in wise speculation to build up a good inheritance for his children. Not unnaturally, perhaps, he was regarded with the deepest suspicion by the royalists; he associated, when he got back to France, with the rich bankers who could help him, and almost ostentatiously avoided the splendours of a court where, in any case, he was unwelcome.

It was the energetic Charles who followed the victorious allies into France; while his son, Angoulême, went down to the south-west, Monsieur went to Nancy. There he was met by the agents of Talleyrand. One of these was the Baron de Vitrolles, a member of an old noble family, who had married an heiress related to Metternich, the virtual director of Austria's foreign policy. Vitrolles had happened to be in Switzerland in 1789, so, although he had served from 1791 to 1794 in the so-called army of the émigrés, he had not been a technical émigré and was allowed to return to France in 1797 and live quietly on his estates. He was a convinced royalist, but compromised with the new governments so far as to hold small local offices. He might, had he been an abler man, have formed a very useful link between the old and the new France. Talleyrand hoped for this, but his choice was not a good one; de Vitrolles was an active, bustling person but had far too high an opinion of his own capacity and an immense ambition. 'Neither his character nor his ability seemed to fit him for the important part which one saw him play at all the critical periods of the Restoration.'[1] De Villèle, the royalist politician who said this, was no friend to de Vitrolles, but his judgement seems to have been sound.

The aim of this embassy to Nancy was to persuade Artois to agree, in the name of his brother, to a draft constitution. It needed a man of much greater weight than de Vitrolles to accomplish this. The Bourbons had at Nancy the first of the great opportunities which they missed. A proclamation, issued by Artois apparently spontaneously, at the first possible opportunity when he entered France, and before he had met the politicians in Paris, would have been a very popular and reassuring gesture. The Senate's draft constitution, which stressed the point that the King had been 'freely' called to the throne by the people of France, was not at all acceptable to Artois, who never believed in constitutions even when he was King. Nor would he yield on a minor but still important point. Frenchmen, and especially the soldiers, cherished the tricoloured flag which had flown in triumph over so much of Europe. To Artois and his friends it was a product of revolution, and must be eliminated. Wherever they went they distributed white cockades and the lilies of the Bourbons; the French must return to their old allegiance and of this the white flag was the symbol. By pure accident, the allied generals helped the royalists. Troops of all nations were converging on Paris, intermingled with scattered units and with deserters from Napoleon's armies. To help in the maintenance of discipline, the

[1] Villèle, Comte de: *Mémoires et correspondance*. Paris, 1888, Vol. I, p. 265.

invading troops were ordered to wear a simple distinguishing mark in the form of a strip of white cloth, white because that was the only colour both conspicuous and easily obtained. It looked, therefore, as if the allies supported the wearing of the white cockade, and waverers were more ready to display it.

Down in the south-west, Angoulême reached Toulouse. The royalists had prepared a welcome for him, and he promised, in return for the cheers, that Napoleon's heavy taxes would no longer be levied. This partly compensated the local people for their distress when the National Guard were ordered to tear off their tricoloured cockades. Later on, when they discovered that the prince had no right to make such a promise and that the tax collectors were just as busy, there were serious riots.

Monsieur, moving slowly towards Paris, was also collecting cheers by saying 'No more conscription, no heavy taxes.'[1] On 12 April he made a solemn entry into the capital, being met with ceremony by Talleyrand and some of Napoleon's generals. The soldiers did not succeed in hiding their feelings. 'Their dark and embarrassed faces made one think of those defeated kings who followed the chariots of a Roman triumph',[2] wrote an onlooker. The members of the National Guard made up for the army's lack of enthusiasm. They cheered and waved their weapons, crying *Vive le roi, vivent les Bourbons!* till the crowd took up the shout. It took an hour and a quarter for the procession to reach Nôtre Dame, so many clergy and officials blocked the way, offering their respects. At the cathedral the prince was received under a magnificent canopy, which had been presented by Napoleon at the time of his coronation. A *Te Deum* was sung, and the prayer 'Lord, save the King'; then the procession returned to the Tuileries palace, which was reached shortly before six.

Artois had made a good impression during these hours. His excellent horsemanship, his obvious happiness, pleased the people. When asked if he were tired, he answered: 'Why should I be? It is the first happy day I have had for thirty years.'[3] He came to the palace windows to acknowledge the cheers of the royalists. But he had made no promise for the future. Talleyrand and Beugnot, the Prefect of Police, put their heads together, and in the *Moniteur*, the official newspaper, next day appeared a speech supposed to have been uttered by the prince. It ran, 'Members of the Provisional Govern-

1 Viel-Castel, L. de: *Histoire de la Restauration*. Paris, 1860–78 (20 vols.). Vol. I, p. 297.
2 Vitrolles, Baron de: *Mémoires et Relations Politiques*. Paris, 1884. Vol. I, p. 405.
3 Viel-Castel, op. cit., Vol. I, p. 305.

ment, I thank you for all you have done for our country. My emotion prevents me from expressing all I feel. No more division; peace and France; I see France again and nothing is changed, save that there is one Frenchman more.' This 'speech' suggesting reconciliation was so popular that Artois accepted it as his own.

For the next two days Alexander of Russia argued with Charles, while Talleyrand tried to keep the alarmed senators quiet. Finally, Fouché, the revolutionary who had been made, by Napoleon, Duke of Otranto as a reward for his work as the head of the police, worked out an acceptable formula to regularise the position. Artois was declared to be the Lieutenant-General of the kingdom and head of the Government until 'Louis Francis Xavier, called to the throne of France, has accepted the Constitutional Charter.' Fouché also wrote, and Talleyrand revised, the speech in which Monsieur was to acknowledge his new position. In this speech he accepted in his brother's name certain bases on which the new régime was to be founded, so the Bourbons were to be constitutional monarchs, and the kingship of France rested on a contract, not on pure hereditary right.

The bases which formed the foundation of the Charter of 1814 were twelve in number: 1. There was to be a two-chamber legislature. 2. All taxes were to be voted by the Chambers. 3. Political and personal liberty was to be secured. 4. The Press should be free except for such restrictions as were essential for public order. 5. Freedom of religion was guaranteed. 6. Property rights were inviolable, and the sale of the confiscated lands recognised as valid. 7. The Ministers were to be responsible to the Chambers. 8. Judges would be immovable and independent. 9. The existing national debt was acknowledged. 10. All soldiers were to retain their military rank and pensions, and the Legion of Honour should be maintained. 11. Every Frenchman was to be eligible for any office, civil or military. 12. No one should be liable to prosecution for his opinions or his vote.

Under the name of the Council of State a new Government was at once set up; it included Talleyrand, the Abbé de Montesquiou (1756–1832), who had been acting as Louis' agent, three other members of the now defunct Provisional Government, three generals, and de Vitrolles (1774–1854) as Secretary. Artois ignored this official council; he took advice from a small group of his personal friends. His period of power did not, fortunately, last very long, but the mistakes that he made had permanent results.

De Vitrolles suggested that special Extraordinary Commissioners should be appointed to take charge of provincial government. De Montesquiou, who was acting as Minister for the Interior, opposed

2

the idea, but Vitrolles was now firmly established in the friendship of the Lieutenant-General, and he got his way. To show his intention of uniting the old France and the new, Charles chose about half these Commissioners from Napoleon's soldiers and the other half from his own friends. Their functions were vague; they had no explicit instructions; and their powers were enormous. They had the right to set free any political prisoners; to supervise the general administration; to appoint or dismiss any official, civil or military. It was impossible for them to have any common policy, so their procedure was contradictory; though they sent reports to Paris no one sent them any instructions. So some of them left things as they were; some of them organised royalist demonstrations that led to riots; one went so far as to remit all taxation in his district. The old officials carried on as best they could wherever they could, and all local councils tried to secure themselves by drawing up loyal addresses and sending them to Paris.

Distrusting the official channels of information, Artois set up a secret police of his own. Here he acted against the advice of de Vitrolles, who was shrewd enough to realise that the use of paid spies could do much harm and no good. According to the usual custom of informers, Charles' agents sent in alarmist reports and got well paid for their vigilance. Even after Louis' arrival, these men continued in his brother's pay, to the natural indignation of the King.

The newspapers were filled with obsequious flattery of the new Government, and 'the old royalists hastened from the four corners of France, while the servants of the Empire rushed to be beforehand with them'.[1] The higher rose the hopes of the royalists, the greater were the fears of all the men who had played a part in the Revolution or who had served Napoleon. All over France there was uneasiness and fear.

The confusion in Paris during these critical days was fantastic. Foreign troops were billeted in private houses and encamped all around the city; great houses were being requisitioned for the use of the foreign princes and their suites; those turned out could find no lodging, for the crowds coming up from the provinces filled every corner. Only people like Napoleon's own relations were leaving the city.

The departure of one of them, the Queen of Westphalia, led to a great sensation. Napoleon had created a new state along the Rhine—the Kingdom of Westphalia—installed his brother Jerome there and secured his marriage to Catherine of Wurtemburg, a daughter of an

[1] Broglie, Duke de: *Personal Recollections*. Trans. Beaufort. London, 1887, Vol. I, p. 245.

old princely house with which Alexander of Russia was on friendly terms. On 21 April, 1814, Count Nesselrode, a man high in the service of the Tsar, wrote to de Vitrolles complaining that the Queen had been arrested and her property seized. A man called Maubreuil and some others were named as responsible for the outrage. De Vitrolles ordered the arrest of these people, and gave instructions that any property they had seized should at once be brought to him. Six cases were taken to the room he was occupying in the palace of the Tuileries; he was told there should have been seven and two bags as well. In the night he was woken up to receive two bags, which contained only small change, and another badly broken box.

Next morning he interviewed Maubreuil. The man declared that the Queen was removing crown jewels of Napoleon and that he had been given orders to recover all such jewels; he added that he had also been told to assassinate Napoleon. He produced documents giving him the right to ask for the assistance of all civil and military authorities in 'a secret mission of the highest importance'. These had been signed by ministers of the Provisional Government. Later he claimed that Alexander himself had approved the plan of assassination.

The whole story sounded very peculiar. Maubreuil was a man of an old Breton family, who had held a position at Jerome Bonaparte's court but had been dismissed; the rumour was that he had tried to make love to the Queen. De Vitrolles decided to test his story by opening the cases; they were locked and new keys had to be cut, but when they were opened in the presence of one of the Queen's ladies, the jewels were gone. Maubreuil was arrested, but he had powerful friends among the royalists and was merely detained in the official headquarters of the Prefect of Police.

In December 1814 a man employed by the prefect offered two diamonds for sale. His room was searched, and a plaster bust of Homer struck the police as a rather peculiar ornament for a man of his type. He declared it represented his grandfather. It was broken open and inside it was found a diamond comb, part of the missing jewellery, from which the two diamonds had been removed. Maubreuil's correspondence had been closely watched; in one of his letters were clues which led to the bulk of the jewels being recovered; they had been packed in a box and sunk in the Seine.

Every attempt was made to hush up the story, but Paris was full of rumours. Some believed Maubreuil to be the hero of a romance of thwarted love; others that he was just a highway robber; but most people thought that some dark conspiracy of the royalists lay behind the treatment of Jerome's wife. The weakness of the Government was clearly shown by their unwillingness to bring Maubreuil to open trial; he was a plausible speaker and it was feared that his story would be believed by the public. He was simply kept in confinement and when the Bourbons left Paris in 1815 he was released, and even given a small pension on condition that he left France and never returned.

Scandals like this did little to help France's cause with the victors. Relations between the Lieutenant-General and the allies were often strained. It was humiliating to Artois to have the Tsar holding his Court in Paris; it was infuriating for Alexander to feel that Russians had died for the restoration to power of men who seemed so wholly absorbed in their own personal plans and so unaware that but for the sacrifices of foreigners they would never have returned at all. The Tsar wanted Charles to see that he must come to terms with Napoleon's experienced advisers as well as working with Talleyrand, obviously reluctantly. Alexander, during his temporary alliance with Napoleon, had made friends with French diplomats, and he invited one of them, Caulaincourt, created Duke of Vicenza by Napoleon, to a dinner party at which Artois was to be present. The selection might have been better, for the royalists believed, quite unjustly, that Caulaincourt had played some part in the death of the Duke of Enghien in 1804. When the Tsar brought him forward to present him, Artois, very angry, turned his back and left the room without saying a word. Everyone was terribly embarrassed and the Tsar was furious.

Such incidents merely showed how intolerable the situation was becoming. There were in practice two governments in France, the official Cabinet and Artois' private circle, while the representatives of the victors were constantly interfering. Talleyrand was anxious for the King to come and end his brother's regency; he also wished Louis to be impressed with his view of the situation of France. Once again, as in the case of de Vitrolles, he made a mistake in his choice of a liaison officer. He chose the Duke of La Rochefoucauld-Liancourt (1747–1827), one of the vast noble family of La Rochefoucauld, who had been Louis XVI's Grand Master of the Wardrobe. After the execution of his king the Duke had left his country, but instead of joining the other émigrés he decided to study social reform in England and America. Louis XVIII considered this most improper, and asked him to resign his official post. The Duke, very much hurt, also resigned his *cordon bleu*, the French equivalent of the Garter. This contempt for etiquette bitterly offended the King, and when the Duke arrived as Talleyrand's emissary at his house in England, Louis refused to see him.

The Duke soon discovered that the King had a very close friend and adviser, the Count de Blacas. Talleyrand had not suspected the

existence of a royal favourite, and was alarmed. Much more serious
was the King's refusal to give his formal assent to his brother's
acceptance of a constitution. After recovering from a fit of the
gout, he moved very slowly towards his country; in London he
received the first public acknowledgement of his sovereignty at a
fête given by the Prince Regent. Louis made a speech; he attributed
his restoration to Providence and 'this glorious country and the
confidence of its people'. This ignoring of not only the other allies,
including Alexander, but of the French nation itself, caused immense uneasiness among the constitutionalists in Paris. Alexander
sent his able Corsican adviser, Pozzo di Borgo, to travel with the
King and give him good advice, but Louis still refused to commit
himself. Talleyrand thought of going himself to meet him at Calais,
but he did not dare to leave Paris, where he was steadily keeping up
his efforts to persuade the victors that France was still strong enough
to turn them and the Bourbons out if the peace they offered was too
severe.

An incident at Compiègne was a better augury for the anxious
politicians who got daily reports from their representatives travelling
with the King. Louis gave an audience to some of Napoleon's
marshals, sitting as was usual in a big arm-chair. When he wished to
rise, he waved away his usual attendants and beckoned two of the
marshals to assist him. 'It is on you, gentlemen, that I always wish
to lean,' he said; 'come near to me and keep close to me; you have
always been good Frenchmen. I hope France will never need your
swords again, but if ever, which God forbid, we are forced to use
them then I, gouty as I am, I shall march with you.'[1] This little
spontaneous speech greatly reassured the chiefs of the army, who
had felt the surrender very bitterly and were very doubtful about
their new rulers.

When St.-Ouen, not far from Paris, was reached, Talleyrand was
there to see the King. Louis was determined to show that he did not
consider the ex-bishop essential to the monarchy, so he kept him
waiting two or three hours. Even then, Talleyrand had to ask de
Blacas to persuade the King to see him, which was a bitter pill for
the man who expected to be hailed as the king-maker. When they
did meet, Louis was far from cordial, and refused to give any
definite answer about the promise of a constitution.

Even the Tsar, who also came out and was received with most
elaborate ceremonial, failed to get a pledge from Louis. Delay was
really dangerous in this case, for some sort of proclamation must be
made at the formal entry into Paris. Talleyrand drafted one in which
Louis promised to maintain the Charter which would be drawn up

[1] Viel-Castel, op. cit., Vol. I, p. 351.

by the representatives and accepted by the people of France. Louis promptly altered this phrase; de Blacas and de Vitrolles further amended it, and Talleyrand accepted the final draft. This proclamation became known as the Declaration of St.-Ouen.

'Louis, by the grace of God King of France' accepted the principles of constitutional monarchy, rejected the plan already passed by the Senate, and enumerated the 'bases' of his brother's proclamation. The opening phrase had some importance, for it allowed the royalists to say that Louis was King by divine right, and the Charter was a gift that he could revoke.

On 3 May the King's procession entered Paris. It was rather an anti-climax. It was the third formal entry that the Parisians had watched, and those of the Allies and of Artois had been more impressive. Monsieur had ridden; the King sat heavily in a carriage drawn by eight white horses, his portly figure clothed in an odd mixture of garments of the pre-Revolution style and of the English fashion. Beside him sat his niece, the tragic-eyed Duchess of Angoulême. Facing him were the Prince of Condé and his son, the Duke of Bourbon, both old men, and the Prince so frail and strange in his appearance that he seemed like a ghost of 1789.

'There were few demonstrations of joy, either on the part of these august personages, or on the part of the people. . . . Astonishment . . . seemed the dominating emotion in the crowd.'[1] The spectators, according to the Duke de Broglie, were 'composed of two quite different elements. One, by far the more considerable, was formed of persons like myself, curious, sad and resigned; the other was composed of ardent loyalists, limited in number but ardent in demonstration.' To the majority of Frenchmen, the delay of two months between the capitulation of Paris and the arrival of the King indicated clearly that the restored monarchy was the consequence of the defeat of the armies of France. Had it been possible for Louis to have appeared immediately the armistice was signed, he would have had his share in the universal joy at the ending of the long-drawn wars. His hesitation and his brother's errors had robbed him of the strongest of his claims on the affection and loyalty of the new generation: that of being the King who had brought France peace.

[1] Underwood, T. R.: *Journal*. Bound with Marigny, op. cit., p. 288.

Chapter III

THE CHARTER AND THE PEOPLE

LOUIS XVIII might be ill and ugly, obstinate and ceremonious, but he was an honest man. He had seriously doubted whether a formal constitution was wise; now he had accepted the idea he meant to carry out his pledge. He would be a monarch with limited power, but he did not think the limits need be drawn too closely. He saw that at present he must be prepared to accept as his ministers men whose history and capacity fitted them for the immediate duties of making peace with the foreigners and order in France, but he would have as the officials of his Household his own friends.

It was on 13 May, 1814, that the first list of ministers of the restored monarch was published in the *Moniteur*. There was no President of the Council, who would be a copy of the English Prime Minister; all members were supposed to work directly under the King. In practice, Talleyrand, the Minister for Foreign Affairs, was looked on as the head of the Cabinet, though the highest titular rank was that of the Chancellor who, like the English Lord Chancellor, presided over the Upper House. This office was given to Dambray (1760–1829), who in 1789 had been a judge of some distinction. He had not emigrated but had retired to his country estate and lived there quietly all through the Republic and the Empire. De Villèle, a shrewd royalist, thus described him: 'By his loyalty, his devotion under every trial, his noble and imperturbable integrity, and his judicial capacity, he always commanded respect; but his activity in the sphere of politics showed, unfortunately, a deplorable incapacity.'[1] By the formality of his manners he often gave offence, and his recognition that he had no experience of politics made him unwilling to play an active part.

The Ministry of the Interior was a key post. The Minister was responsible for the appointment of the prefects, who controlled all local administration. The Abbé de Montesquiou kept this position, which he had held under the Provisional Government. He had acted as Louis' agent in Paris during the tense days before Napoleon's abdication, and was a shrewd and level-headed man who thought it best to leave things alone as much as possible.

---

[1] Villèle, Comte de: *Mémoires et correspondance*. Vol. I, p. 267.

The Finance Minister was Baron Louis (1755–1837), a banker, who seemed to think wholly in terms of the counting-house. The royalists disliked him. 'His ideas were straightforward because they were limited; and an English routine was the depth of his wisdom,'[1] said de Vitrolles; while de Villèle called him 'Taxation and Speculation personified'.[2] Able and clear-headed in his own department, he could not give the ministry any width of vision or help to formulate any general policy.

The Minister for War would have to deal with complexities of the disbanding of Napoleon's armies. For this important office a very bad choice was made. The Count Dupont had been one of Napoleon's generals, but was known to the general public as the man who had had to capitulate at Baylen in 1808 and been imprisoned by the Emperor. He was thus for ever associated with the first conspicuous disgrace to the French armies in Spain, and however capable he might be he could not hope to be popular. He, too, had been in the Provisional Government.

The navy was confided to another of Artois' ministers, Malouet. He had made a name in the Constituent Assembly of 1791, and it was hoped that his appointment would show that ex-revolutionaries were trusted. He had served in the navy under Napoleon, but had been disgraced and exiled in 1812. Now he was old and ill and quite unfit for the duties which he did not long have to fulfil, for he died in August 1814.

De Blacas was, of course, the Minister responsible for the King's Household. The special Ministry of Police was suspended for the time, and a Director of Police appointed, Beugnot. He was a clever man, who intensely disliked the spy system associated with the management of the police at this time, but he was always offending people by his lack of tact.

Such a group of men could have no cohesion, no sense of joint responsibility. They never met even formally; each one saw the King individually about the business of his own department. De Vitrolles had been Secretary to Artois' Provisional Government, and believed that the suppression of this office was a fatal error. No doubt a Secretary could have summoned meetings, but it is hard to imagine that this curious group of able men and of incapable, with different outlook and divergent experience, could have agreed on any general line of policy. De Vitrolles had really lost his place because he was notoriously Artois' man, and Louis was most suspicious of his brother's friends.

Alongside the Ministry, a Council of State was created whose

[1] Vitrolles, Baron de: *Mémoires*, etc. Ed. Forgues. Paris, 1884. Vol. I, p. 43.
[2] Villèle, op. cit., Vol. I, p. 269.

functions were at first purely nominal. It became the custom to appoint to membership of this Council any minister who resigned his office, often with a pension. These appointments, and even those of the ministers, interested Louis far less than appointments to offices in his Household. All the ancient dignities were restored—Grand Huntsman, Grand Master of the Wardrobe, First Gentleman of the Bedchamber and so forth; whenever possible, these were given to the men who had held them in 1789 or to their direct heirs. The old ceremonial was restored, the old elaborate uniforms reappeared. The pleasure of the King was tremendous, but the emphasis on the past and the enormous expense shocked a good many people, while the old nobles and their ritual seemed to men of the new order purely comic.

Far more serious was the reinstitution of the Royal Guard, the old cavalry guard in which every private ranked as an officer. Louis XVI had cut down this corps, which was practically useless, for the protection of the King and the palace was done by Swiss and French guards, but Louis XVIII restored it to its former magnificence. Its members were wholly recruited from the royalist nobility; some were elderly émigrés, some hot-headed young men, proud of their birth, active and gallant, but wholly untrained as soldiers. Their gorgeous uniforms pleased the crowds and this they thought meant that the Guard was a popular institution, but their complete inexperience and the peculiar old-fashioned drill they used roused the mockery and contempt of the veterans of the Empire.

Louis had once again missed a great opportunity. He felt that he must be surrounded by men whom he could trust, and must reward his faithful friends. Had he been braver and more clear-sighted, he would have appointed Napoleon's famous Imperial Guard as his Royal Guard, and probably won their personal loyalty as well as giving a striking proof of his desire to reconcile the new France to the monarchy. Instead, the existence of this Imperial Guard was a problem for his Government. If it was not trustworthy, it ought to be disbanded; but the unpopularity was too great to be faced and it was sent into barracks in the country, where the proud men had nothing to do but recall past glories and grumble at the new system.

An attempt was made to reorganise the whole army on pre-Napoleonic lines. Old military titles were revived in place of the modern ones, which were much more convenient and which everyone understood. Malouet tried to please the officers by a wide distribution of medals, but, so far from pleasing them, this degradation of honours that had only been given for distinguished service irritated the new as well as the old recipients. The soldiers had been losing faith in Napoleon; during March 1814 80,000 men had deserted; now they began to think of him again as their 'Little Corporal', and remember their pride in his victories.

Earlier memories were revived when all over the country the royalists arranged solemn requiem masses for those who had died during the Revolution. Sometimes the sermons turned into diatribes against all the aspirations and theories of 1789. It seemed as if the worst fears of those who had dreaded the return of the émigrés were justified. One writer said: 'I shall be happy about the future of our lawful princes when they believe that they have returned to our country, not to their country.'[1] It did not seem that this hope would be fulfilled.

No one could be certain of his future prospects until the Bourbons had shown what was really involved in the vague promises made first by Charles and then confirmed by Louis. The English constitution, the only model which was available, was largely unwritten; the French one would have to translate into definite terms what precisely were ministerial responsibility, royal prerogatives and so forth. A group of obscure people set to work on this attempt to produce something sufficiently French and logical from such authorities as were available. By Louis' definite order Talleyrand was kept wholly in the dark; he was, in fact, very busy with his interviews with the representatives of the foreign Powers. The senators and deputies of the Empire were summoned to meet, not as representatives of the country to bargain over constitutional rights, but as 'notables' to advise the King on the draft he laid before them.

On 14 June they assembled in a joint session. Louis addressed them in an excellent speech which he had written himself. Dambray spoke as President of the Senate and struck an inharmonious note by referring to the Charter as a gift from the King. The preamble, too, which had not been submitted to the drafting committee, emphasised the hereditary rights of the monarch.

That it was modelled on England and not on the only working constitution that France had recently known, that of the Empire, was quite clear. De Vitrolles represented a good deal of French opinion when he wrote: 'No one questioned whether this coat which had been cut for another would suit us; nobody troubled himself about the difficulty of transplanting to a new soil the ancient British oak.' The preamble, too, indicated that this imitation might well be due to outside influences, for it referred to 'a free and monarchic constitution' that would 'fulfil the expectations of enlightened Europe'. Two most distasteful points to the ordinary man were, therefore, stressed: that the Bourbons believed they

[1] Véron, le docteur L.: *Mémoires d'un Bourgeois de Paris*. Paris, 1853, Vol. I, p. 208.

ruled by divine right, not the will of the people, and that England and Russia, not France, had settled the limits of their rights.

According to the Charter,[1] the King held supreme power in the State. He commanded the army and navy, made treaties, appointed officials, and, by Article 14, which was to be invoked by Charles X, made regulations for the exercise of the laws and the security of the kingdom. He proposed, sanctioned and promulgated all laws; he nominated the members of the House of Peers. His income was to be a sum fixed for the whole reign, not voted annually.

But though the King's powers sounded like the eighteenth century, the citizens' rights recalled the Revolution. All were to be equal before the law; the old privileges were gone and though the nobility was to remain as 'a truly national institution' no individual would be exempt from taxation. There was to be no conscription, and all citizens had the right to 'free expression of thought'.

Legislation, as in England, was the joint work of King, Lords and Commons. In theory the King alone through his servants could introduce a law, and he had the right to reject any amendments made by the Chambers. In practice, as in England, the Cabinet planned legislation, and very rarely was the right to reject amendments invoked.

No limit was fixed to the number of peers, who were to be nominated by the King to sit in the Upper House either for life only or as hereditary peers. No man could enter the House till he was twenty-five, or vote till he was thirty. Princes of the blood royal must have the King's leave to attend. The peers had the right to discuss and amend all laws, including the budget. They were to act as a High Court of Justice for their own members, whatever offence they might be charged with, and for all persons accused of treason. They were to debate in secret. A law passed in 1817 made it necessary for every peer to have an entailed estate.

The election of the House of Deputies was reserved to the middle class, for electors had to pay 300 francs a year in direct taxes, which was a considerable sum. They also had to be at least thirty years old. The method of election was to be fixed by a later law; at the moment this seemed a wise provision in a country where no genuine elections had taken place for a long time, but it left room for frequent changes to be made later on as suited the party politicians. The number of deputies for the first election was fixed at 262. Only men paying 1,000 francs a year (the equivalent of £40) in direct taxes were eligible and they must be forty years old; at least half the members for each department must genuinely reside there. To secure both

---

1 See Simon, P.: *L'Élaboration de la Charte Constitutionelle de 1814*. Paris, 1906.

continuity of policy and the representation of current opinion, it was decided that one fifth of the House should be elected each year, the deputies sitting for five years.

The budget had to be introduced first into the Lower House, otherwise the legislative powers of both Houses were the same. All taxes were to be voted for one year only.

The President of the House of Deputies, the equivalent of the English Speaker, was to be chosen by the King from a list submitted by the House. Debates were to be public, unless five members demanded a secret session, and a summary would be printed in the *Moniteur*. The ministers, nominated by the King, had the right to speak in either House, whether they were members or not. This was an ingenious plan, for it did away with the need for a government to have members in both Chambers. A minister accused of treason or of extortion could be accused by the Deputies and tried by the Peers.

The Catholic, Apostolic and Roman Church was declared to be the religion of the State, but every citizen had the right to belong to any Church or to none. Christian ministers of religion, whether Catholic or Protestant, were to receive stipends from the State.

The existing judicial system was maintained, and all judges were to hold office for life. New appointments were to be made by the King, who also had the right of pardoning offenders or diminishing penalties inflicted by the courts. All existing legislation was to remain in force, unless repealed or modified by new laws.

All Constitutions depend very much more on practice and precedent than on written documents. It was clear that, in spite of the elaborate balancing of power, the elected Lower House would be the vital part of the new system. Although in the early days France had to look to the English House of Commons as a model, for she had as yet had no genuine Parliament of her own, the Chamber of Deputies soon developed a very different procedure, which has had a fundamental influence on French political life. At the beginning of each session the selection of names for the office of President of the Chamber of Deputies led to a trial of party strength. As five candidates were chosen, the selection of men who were leaders of groups rather than colleagues in a united party led to a good deal of manœuvre and the stiffening of personal animosities. Normally, though not always, the King chose the man who had received most votes. The English Speaker, once elected, is recognised as above faction and is usually re-elected. The President of the French Chamber often had to vacate office before he had really learnt the very difficult job of successful chairmanship.

All bills were introduced by Government spokesmen, but then they went to a 'bureau' whose members were chosen each month by drawing lots. This plan was taken over from the Legislative Body of the Empire. The bureau appointed a committee to report on the measure, and the selection of this committee often decided the fate of the bill. The Government thus at once lost charge of its own measure, for the committee picked one of its members to act as a Reporter and inform the House of its views—that the bill should on the whole be accepted or amended or rejected. Ambitious men tried to get chosen as Reporters and to make the most of any adverse views; there was always the hope that, should the Government fall, they might be chosen for ministerial office. After the Reporter's speech, the whole Chamber discussed and voted on the bill three times; the first debate was on the general principles on which it was based, then the text was discussed clause by clause, and finally the bill as a whole. No measure could be carried over from session to session; if a bill were not passed by both Chambers before the end of the session, the whole procedure had to be repeated when it was reintroduced.

Each deputy or peer who wished to speak on a bill had to give in his name as a supporter or opponent, and when his turn came he left his seat and mounted the tribune, a sort of pulpit. No doubt it was easier to hear the speakers thus set on high, away from the crowded seats right, left and centre, but it made debating almost impossible. Everyone prepared his speech beforehand, not knowing what points would already have been made, and most read their orations; the tendency for each was to aim at impressing the House by long and ornate sentences, with carefully balanced periods. The natural result was that the debates were very lengthy and the same issues were raised again and again; the stenographers, whose duty it was to take down the speeches in full, must often have been very bored. Only condensed reports were published in the *Moniteur*; but if a speech were greatly admired, the deputies ordered it to be printed in full. This was an honour at which all politicians aimed.

After the first debate, and in the second debate after each clause of the bill, a vote was taken. The first vote was made by members sitting or standing up; if it were clear that there was a great majority for or against a measure, this was sufficient. If there were any doubt, the 'nominal appeal' took place; then written votes were placed in an urn. Some timid deputies left their voting papers blank, and as no division lists were published their constituents could not know how they had voted. This method of semi-secret balloting led to a lack of responsibility and an encouragement of intrigues.

Each session opened with the King's Speech, and this soon was recognised as the programme of the Cabinet. Formal Replies were made in both Chambers, and the terms in which they were written were closely debated. The tone of the Reply indicated what measure of support the Government could expect in both Chambers. Not all of the parliamentary time-table was taken up by bills; each House had the right to receive petitions, and these were freely used as a rough equivalent to the English Question Time. If it were desired to draw the Government's attention to a grievance, a petition was presented; if the ministers themselves wished to raise a point of policy they would see that a suitable petition appeared.

It would have seemed natural that a new Chamber of Deputies should be elected to accept and to work the new Constitution. In the summer of 1814 this was hardly practicable. A new electoral roll would have to be made if the suggested property limits to the suffrage were accepted; many possible voters were still under arms; whole areas were occupied by foreign troops. For the time being, the Chambers of the Empire continued to act; the only differences were that the deputies discharged three of their officials who had sat in the revolutionary Chamber that voted for the execution of Louis XVI, and that several new peers were added to the Senate.

The Charter of 1814 was debated and passed by both Chambers. The next urgent task was to get a budget passed. Money was needed for day-to-day expenditure; Baron Louis anticipated that in 1814 this would come to 827 million francs or about £33 million sterling; this included 63 million francs for interest on the *rentes*, the national debt. He also announced that Napoleon was owing well over a thousand millions; in fact the debts were nearer 750 millions, but it was to the new Government's advantage to blacken the Emperor. He declared that for 1815 he hoped for a very considerable drop in expenditure.

He reckoned that if all the existing taxes were levied they would bring in about 520 millions in 1814 and more the next year. Ignoring all the promises the Princes had made that the burden on the people would be lightened, Louis asked for all of Napoleon's taxes to be kept in force, and he got his way. The Empire's fiscal system formed the groundwork of the finances of the restored monarchy.

Of great political importance were the direct taxes, for they served as an electoral qualification. They were levied on land, on houses (the doors and windows tax), on personal property, and there were the *patentes*, a sort of registration fee paid by professional men and manufacturers. All were voted on a standard rate with, if necessary, additional centimes. In a normal year, Louis expected 291 millions from the direct taxes.

Indirect taxes fell on wines and spirits manufactured inside France, and there were customs duties on practically all imports. These, together with the profits of the State tobacco monopoly, should yield 86 millions. Stamp duties on legal documents, profits of the Post Office, and other items came to another 27 millions.

The Finance Minister was counting on a deficit of 307 millions in 1814, but hoped for a surplus of 70 millions next year which would partly meet it. The remainder, and all Napoleon's current debts, the Baron proposed to pay by issuing Treasury Bonds bearing interest at 8 per cent and repayable in three years' time, by increasing the permanent debt by an issue of 5 per cent *rentes*, and by selling the confiscated lands still in the possession of the State.

This budget of 1814 was very important. It set the pattern for future finance; it pleased the men of the new France who sat in the Lower House by its recognition of the continuity of the old government and the new, and the acceptance of responsibility for the debts of the Empire. There was little opposition; the budget was carried by 140 votes to 68. The moneyed classes showed their relief by buying *rentes*; the price of the 100-franc certificate rose from 60 to 78 francs. The ordinary small taxpayers were horribly disappointed; they had hoped that peace meant an immediate reduction in taxation. The royalists were furious; they felt that the monarchy was being crippled by paying the debts of a usurper.

Baron Louis' rather optimistic estimates depended on reducing expenditure drastically. The army vote was heavily cut, and an immense number of officers were put on half-pay. The expenditure on roads and public works was also greatly lowered; this was a very short-sighted policy, for the roads were in a bad state and repairing them would have given employment to some of the discharged soldiers. The grants made to the monarch formed a sharp contrast. Louis XVIII was voted an income of 25 million francs a year for life, and an extra 30 millions was set aside to pay the debts of the Royal Family. This last sum was badly misused; there was no proper investigation of the claims, so many legitimate creditors went unpaid while other payments of very doubtful validity were made.

All over France the returned émigrés were trying to regain their property. Many of them had not lost their rights, but when estates had been legally taken over and sold, the Government held firm to the promise made at St.-Ouen and recognised their new purchasers as the owners. In the south there were riots when some nobles tried to expel the men in possession of their former lands; two lawyers published a pamphlet declaring that the rights of the landowners of 1789 or their heirs over-rode all other claims. These men were prosecuted, but not punished. More moderate royalists proposed that the new owners should give up the land but receive in compensation the sums they had paid for it. Such a plan was quite impractical, even had the Government had immense resources at its disposal, for much land had been bought for nominally large sums in depreciated paper money, and some estates had changed hands several times.

In an attempt to reassure the country, the Government got a petition presented to the Chamber by a lady asking for confirmation of her rights as an owner of confiscated land. A resolution was passed saying that her rights were guaranteed by the Charter. The royalists, however, proposed that the lands still in Government hands should not be sold, but given back to their original owners. This caused a great sensation; the *rentes* fell; the debates were stormy. A bill to this effect was carried in November 1814, but never put into force. The suggestion was obviously most unjust, for it was often pure chance that the lands were still unsold; either all past landowners should have been compensated or no restitution made to any. But this question of the royalists' lands was raised again and again; after all, it was only natural that men who thought they had done right to follow the Royal Family into exile should resent seeing their old family estates in the hands of those who had gained by the Revolution.

The outburst of books which had followed the promise of freedom of the Press was troubling the Government. A law was passed which submitted all books except pamphlets of under twenty pages to censorship. More general indignation than that caused by this limit to the liberty of authors and readers was caused by the Royal Ordinances of 7 and 14 June, 1814. Something approaching the English Sunday was introduced into France by these regulations; all shops, cafés and inns had to be closed during the hours of divine service. On the Feast of Corpus Christi a solemn procession passed through the streets of Paris, and all traffic was stopped between 8 a.m. and 3 p.m.; every householder on the route had to hang out decorations, whatever his own religious views might be. De Berry was very much annoyed at his royal uncle's piety. 'I'm happy in France,' he said to Beugnot, the Director of Police; 'I don't want to go back where we came from, and that will certainly happen if we give these Puritans a free hand.'[1]

Everyone was conscious that the new Government had no clear line of policy, but dealt with things as they came. This was probably inevitable; the outstanding man in the Cabinet was Talleyrand, and he was in Vienna, attending the peace conference and doing his best to sow discord among the victors. When Malouet died in August, Louis could have reorganised his ministry, but he wasted the chance. In December Dupont was removed from the War Office, so there were two vacant offices. Beugnot, who had become friendly

[1] Viel-Castel, op. cit., Vol. I, p. 487.

with Artois, was taken from the police and made responsible for the navy; this should please the royalists. To satisfy the Bonapartists, Soult was made Minister for War. The idea of giving one of Napoleon's marshals responsibility for the army was excellent, but the choice was unfortunate. Soult's military reputation was high, but he was unpopular and known to be ambitious. To secure his position at Court, he affected an extravagant royalism which disgusted the soldiers, already antagonistic because of the quite necessary discharge of men and retirement of officers.

Open opposition to the Government began to appear, both in the Deputies and in the Press. On 21 November the Government introduced a bill which would have allowed the King to dismiss some of the judges in the *Cour de Cassation*, the Court of Appeal. The opposition succeeded in passing amendments which so altered the proposed law that the ministers withdrew it. On 30 December both the Chambers were prorogued.

It was not so easy to get rid of opposition from the Press. Two newspapers were prominent, the *Censor*, which was moderately liberal in tone, and the *Yellow Dwarf*, which divided its columns between exaggerated adulation of the monarchy, in caricature of the royalist papers, and bitter jests at the clergy and the old nobility. The police in vain tried to stop the flood of pamphlets which appeared all over France ridiculing the new Government.

When the Chambers were prorogued, Louis took the opportunity of issuing another ordinance. In theory, these exercises of the royal prerogative were merely for the enforcement of the existing law. This one seemed to do rather more: it remodelled the University. The highly centralised Napoleonic system was to end, and its place be taken by seventeen separate universities which had been colleges of the University of Paris. Over them all was to be a council, whose president was a bishop. This suggestion of clerical control of education naturally alarmed all non-Catholic teachers; the moderate Catholics were also very much afraid of so direct an intervention of the Church in what was sure to be a highly controversial political problem.

On 21 January, 1815, the bodies of Louis XVI and Marie Antoinette were solemnly reburied. The Bishop of Troyes preached the sermon at the requiem mass. He was the most famous preacher of the day, but his sermon was so fierce an attack on the principles of the Revolution that the *Moniteur* did not reproduce it. A few days later a popular actress died and, as she was not a practising Catholic, was refused church burial. An indignant public rioted in the streets of Paris.

Hoping to please the people, Artois and his sons set out on tours

3

of the provinces. It was felt that the Royal Family ought to show it-self to the country, and Louis was not strong enough to travel around. Too many incidents unfortunately occurred which led to annoyance rather than admiration. At Besançon, Monsieur refused to receive the Archbishop, because he had submitted to the Civil Constitution of the Clergy and then been reconciled to Rome. Charles even went so far as to prohibit the Bishop from leaving his house, lest they should meet by accident in the street. On several occasions de Berry lost his temper and irritated people, especially the soldiers. During one procession, the Prefect of the Department fell off his horse and was killed. The Prince seemed completely in-different, and this created a very bad impression.

Everywhere they went the princes tried to buy popularity by making local worthies members of the Legion of Honour. This institution had been created by Napoleon to give public recognition to men who had given outstanding service to the State, whether military or civil; a few privileges were attached to it, and it was a really great honour to be a Legionary. Those who held it were very angry; those who received it had no real satisfaction.

There were greater causes for discontent than the mistakes of the royal princes. Peace, everyone believed, meant prosperity. In France it was bringing a good deal of unemployment, and a slowing down of trade. The war industries closed down, and some manu-factures were having to meet foreign competition. Speculative pro-duction was discouraged by the high rate of interest; the Govern-ment itself was borrowing most of the available capital.

The army was the most dangerous centre of discontent. Even had Napoleon remained King of France, he would have found it hard to disband his forces without social dislocation. When the men were embittered by defeat, and the Government was a strange one, the situation was full of peril. Arrears of pay were due, and it was hard to find money for them; so Soult decided to recall 60,000 men to the colours to have them under control. By the end of February 1815 only 35,000 had reported for duty. Those who did often refused to wear their new white cockades; when de Berry had reviewed some troops in October 1814 nearly all the men of one company had paraded wearing the tricolour. The officers put on half-pay found it extremely difficult to supplement their minute incomes; lieutenants only got 44 francs a month and captains 73. It was galling for them to read in the *Moniteur* the names of the wholly inexperienced royalists who were given their commissions.

The marshals and generals had most of them recognised that Napoleon's fall was inevitable, and were sincere in their promises of loyalty to the Bourbons. But they, too, had suffered severe financial losses; several of them had been given estates in Italy and other countries, and they had now to be surrendered. Murat, King of Naples, and Bernadotte, adopted as the heir to the King of Sweden, were the fortunate ones; the rest had only the titles of their dukedoms.

At the Court they were treated with deliberate rudeness by the royalists. A foreigner at a reception once asked the name of a charming lady. 'Oh,' said the royalist to whom he spoke, 'we don't know those women; they belong to the marshals.' And it was scarcely tactful of an old duke to say to Ney, after a long conversation, 'What a pity it is that you have not, like one of us, that quality which cannot be acquired.'[1]

Most of the marshals and generals were proud men, treasuring their honours because they had risen from obscurity through their bravery and skill. They were contemptuous of the stiff formality of the émigrés, and of their antique style, particularly when it entered their own military sphere. The manœuvres at a sham fight between troops commanded on one side by Angoulême and the other by de Berry seemed merely ridiculous to the veterans of Napoleon.

There was no conspiracy for the overthrow of the Bourbons. There was much grumbling, and a vague sense of insecurity, and questioning whether Orleans would not have made a better king. A sentimental feeling for the Emperor in exile led men to treasure portraits and mementoes; a roughly-shaped bust of Louis XVIII was made to open and disclose one of Napoleon. The royalists called Louis le désiré, the desired, but his common nickname was 'the pig', owing to his unfortunate figure. The artillery men counting their shots said 'Sixteen, seventeen, pig, nineteen'[2]; and the king in the suits of playing cards was referred to in all military circles as the pig of spades, etc. These facts were reported to the Government by the police.

Nor were the royalists contented. The close friends of Louis and his brother received handsome gifts and valuable offices, but the smaller people found, as had the royalists of the English restoration in 1660, that the King's memory was short and his purse limited. Wellington reported to his Government that 'the émigrés are as annoyed with the King as the Jacobins and Bonapartists'.[3] In December 1814 a fair number of disappointed men returned to England to resume their work as teachers.

The year 1815 opened for the new reign with heavy clouds on all sides save the east, for at Vienna Talleyrand was raising France's

[1] Viel-Castel, op. cit., Vol. II, p. 95.
[2] Houssaye, H.: *1815*. 11th edition. Paris, 1894. Vol. I, p. 50.
[3] *Wellington to Castlereagh, Oct. 4th, 1814*. Despatches. Supplement.

prestige by his amazing diplomatic skill. It was impossible for the ordinary Frenchman to know what was happening at the Congress, so the ability of the one first-class politician in the Cabinet was of no practical advantage so far as the situation in France itself was concerned.

Chapter IV

THE FLIGHT OF THE BOURBONS

On his abdication Napoleon had been exiled to Elba, a tiny island between his native Corsica and Italy. The victors had made many mistakes in dealing with their great antagonist. Elba was far too accessible for it to be safe to leave him there, nominally an independent ruler, and there were rumours, which reached Napoleon, that he would be transferred to some more distant home. He had been guaranteed an income of 50,000 francs a year, but through incredible stupidity it was not paid regularly. Still worse, he believed, not without some justification, that he was in danger of assassination.

There was enough contact between Elba and the mainland coast for Napoleon to hear a good deal about the failures of the men who had supplanted him. That he should dream of returning to France was inevitable, and when on 26 February, 1815, the guard on the coasts of Elba was temporarily relaxed, he snatched at his chance. There were no real preparations; the whole attempt was that of a gambler. His hopes were based on two things: he knew the French people were dissatisfied with the Bourbons, and he believed that the allies were divided over their plans for the reconstruction of Europe. What he failed to realise was the intensity of the fear of himself, which was the one cementing element in the alliance.

He had a brig, the *Inconstant*, at his disposal. With the four hundred-odd men of his personal guard he set sail; he had little money and no uniforms for his men. Light and contrary winds delayed progress; the time was spent by the soldiers in copying out by hand the proclamations of the Emperor. At length the French coast was reached on 1 March and the expedition landed; little enthusiasm was met with, but no resistance.

The news quickly reached Paris, where it roused very mixed feelings. The middle classes were alarmed; they were sure that the allies would not accept Napoleon as ruler in France and that a renewal of war was certain. The out-of-work soldiers and the republican theorists were delighted. The royalists were at first not displeased, for they hoped for an immediate victory which would show to all the world that France was loyal to her ancient line of kings. The princes of the blood were given commands of armies to repel the invader.

Artois was sent to Lyons to capture Napoleon. He found the troops garrisoned in that area so obviously hostile that he lost heart and returned to Paris. De Berry's army melted away in a trickle of deserters. From confidence, Louis' government went to an extreme of fear. The Chambers were summoned to meet in Paris, but it would take some time for the members to assemble. Meanwhile, the ministers were each one blaming the others for allowing Napoleon to land and for the unpopularity which made the armies unreliable. The marshals were flattered till they were sickened. But it was not the generals who first abandoned the Bourbons; it was the rank and file who flocked to their old commander and were often followed by their officers.

The Civil Service was no more reliable. As Beugnot said, 'It is impossible to count on the officials; the old ones, those who served under the Empire, are all against us, the new ones have all the world against them.'[1] There was a wild idea of forming a new ministry of a character so liberal as to win the support of the ex-republicans, but the royalists got this dropped. Soult was dismissed from the War Office, for he was notoriously unpopular in the army; but instead of making Ney or Macdonald or some other distinguished fighting man responsible for organising the resistance to Napoleon, Louis and his advisers chose Clarke, the Duke of Feltre, who had been Minister for War under the Empire but whose sycophancy since the restoration had disgusted the men with whom he would have to co-operate.

Ney and most of the other marshals were convinced that their duty to France conflicted with their old loyalty to Napoleon. They knew enough of the strength and the resolution of the allies to be certain that there was little hope of a permanent return of the Emperor. They knew that, though the Bourbons were unpopular, enthusiasm for Napoleon was not strong enough for the common people to sacrifice themselves gladly in a national rising. Their professions of loyalty to Louis were honestly made, but it was with heavy hearts that they prepared for war.

It was Ney, the impetuous and gallant, who was selected to lead the main force against Napoleon. He had quarrelled with his Emperor in 1814 when he tried to persuade him to abdicate, and when he vowed to bring him captive to Paris, he meant what he said. It seemed to him essential that the advance up the Rhône valley should be halted before Napoleon could occupy Lyons. But when on 13 March, 1815, his army reached a town a few miles away, he found

[1] Viel-Castel, op. cit., Vol. II, p. 314.

he was too late. Too much time had been wasted by the politicians in Paris, and Napoleon held the city.

As the moment for action drew near, the emotion of the marshal grew; it was a terrible thing for him to fight the man he had served so well. Then, at night, a messenger brought him a personal letter from Napoleon. The appeal to their old affection and the flattery which called him the bravest of the brave were too much for Ney. With the letter came copies of Napoleon's proclamations. 'They don't write like that now,' he said. 'The King ought to write like that. That is the way to talk to soldiers.'[1] He recalled the slights his wife had suffered at the Bourbons' Court.[2] He hated the idea of leading an army, which would have to depend on foreign help, against an army of Frenchmen freely following their great Emperor.

Next morning he sent for his staff officers and told them that he personally was going to join Napoleon; they could act as they thought right. Then he paraded his troops and spoke to them. 'The cause of the Bourbons is lost for ever,' he said. 'The sacred cause of liberty will suffer no more from their baleful influence. They tried to disparage our glory. . . . The time is past when a people can be governed by extinguishing its rights. Liberty will triumph in the end, and Napoleon will secure it for ever.'[3]

The men, who had been restless and unhappy, cheered themselves hoarse. The tricoloured cockade reappeared; Ney rode off to join his old master, but his heart was full of doubt and sadness.

Oudinot was in command of the famous Old Guard, and was bringing them by forced marches from Metz to defend Louis' person. At Troyes the men mutinied. In vain the marshal tried to win them over; they were resolved to join their Emperor. Victor's men from Mézières also deserted the lilies of the Bourbons, and as news of these defections reached Paris the Government grew panic-stricken. Louis produced a proclamation on 18 March addressed to the rebellious troops in which he called them his 'wandering children' and bade them return to his paternal arms, reminding them that an invasion of France was certain and the consequences would be disastrous. Napoleon's appeals had been far more eloquent as well as invoking an older loyalty. It was too much to expect men to join their old enemies to fight their old hero, for the sake of a King whom they held responsible for the slights and disappointments of the last year.

A Paris wit posted a placard on the column of Vendôme which

---

[1] Houssaye, op. cit., p. 304.

[2] Ibid., p. 312.

[3] Viel-Castel, op. cit., Vol. II, p. 349.

read: 'Napoleon to Louis XVIII. My good brother, it is no use sending me any more soldiers. I have enough.' The Government's frantic attempts to get recruits did more harm than good; soldiers ignored their calling-up notices.

An appeal to the liberals was attempted. On 16 March a special joint session of the two Chambers was addressed by Louis in person. The spectacle of the rather feeble elderly man was touching, and his speech was cheered. Artois and the princes swore fidelity to the Charter, but their enthusiasm for the constitution came rather too late. The liberals, many of them, felt that there was more hope of freedom under frightened Bourbons than under a victorious Napoleon, but there were not enough of them to give much practical help. The genuine royalists were, of course, distressed by this appeal to former revolutionaries. They wanted to reorganise the peasants in the Vendée and the Chouans who had resisted the forces of the Revolution. To appeal to Napoleon's deputies seemed to them an error of principle.

Artois made a desperate attempt to carry out this new plan of reconciliation; he demeaned himself by interviewing Fouché on the night of 15 March and offering him the Ministry of Police. This unscrupulous man, ex-cleric, extreme revolutionary, and under Napoleon so able a director of police that, in spite of his profound distrust of him, Napoleon employed him again and again—this Duke of Otranto was far too astute to take any responsibility for a falling Government. It was then decided to arrest him, but he got away from Paris in safety.

Fouché was not the only person to leave Paris. A new emigration was beginning. The passport offices were besieged; the price of *rentes* was falling, though not to panic level. It was impossible to conceal Napoleon's advance. The cry of '*Vive l'Empereur!*' was heard again; his portraits reappeared. It was perfectly clear that the restoration Government was not governing.

Louis felt inclined to stay in Paris. Marmont, who had stayed with the King when his fellows had gone to Napoleon, agreed with him that if he stayed in the Tuileries it would be awkward for Napoleon; 'the victim', as the King had said to the Chambers, 'would be greater than the executioner'. But so romantic a rôle was not really appropriate, and in the end de Blacas persuaded Louis that it was his duty to leave.

Where he should go was not easy to decide. De Vitrolles was anxious that he should go to the west and raise a royalist movement. But, as de Vitrolles wrote in his memoirs: 'The thought of exile did not disturb him. The part which I wished him to play seemed to him the beginning of a course of action and of uncertainties which wearied his imagination.'[1] It was too much to ask of an elderly and disillusioned man that he should play the gallant hero. Moreover, as the Abbé de Montesquiou pointed out, de Vitrolles' plan would inevitably associate the Bourbons with the Vendée and alienate all the rest of France, to whom the civil war started by the royalists in the Vendée in 1793 had seemed a treachery and not a crusade.

Finally, the King decided to go north-east. The Duke of Orleans had already gone to the frontier provinces hoping to organise a resistance to Napoleon which could co-operate with the expected invasion by the allies. About midnight on the night of 19 March, 1815, the disheartened Louis, leaning on de Blacas, walked with difficulty down the staircase of the Tuileries and entered his coach. An hour later his brother Artois followed him, and the second flight of the Bourbons had begun.

The journey to Ghent was no solitary adventure; many prudent men of all parties followed the King, and in later years to have been with the Court in Ghent was a title to promotion and favour. Nor did Paris rejoice when the news of the King's departure became public. Some of the crowds drifting about the streets raised cheers for Napoleon, but on the whole the city was quiet and gloomy. On 21 March General Excelmans proclaimed Napoleon, the tricolour reappeared, and people crowded into the streets to await the Emperor, who did not arrive until eight o'clock at night on 23 March.

The Hundred Days were a curious interlude. The drama was a sort of postscript to the story of Napoleon though inevitably it affected the period between the Empires. On the whole, so far as the internal life of the country went, there was little change. 'The peculiar power of the machinery and formalism of our administration, which goes on like a piece of mechanism when once it has been started'[2] was demonstrated at Versailles, where the redecoration that had been ordered by Louis went on uninterrupted. In the throne room of the Tuileries lilies had been sewn on to the carpet to cover the Napoleonic emblem of the bee which was woven into the design. The ladies of the old Imperial court set to work on hands and knees, taking out the stitches and revealing the original fabric. This typified what was happening everywhere.

Letters of congratulation came to Napoleon signed by men who had written almost identical letters to Louis. The Emperor found the earlier ones, and realised that his faith in his hold on the hearts of his people had little foundation. To one of his former ministers he said: 'The people let me come as they let those others go.'[3] Louis,

[1] Vitrolles, op. cit., Vol. II, p. 351.
[2] Ibid., Vol. II, p. 458.
[3] Viel-Castel, op. cit., Vol. II, p. 381.

too, recognised that France would obey whomever was in power. To the commander of the garrison at Lille he said: 'You must act as circumstances dictate. If they make you put another cockade in your hat, do so; but you will always keep my colours in your heart, and I am sure you will wear them again when the occasion comes.'

It soon became clear that there would be no general civil war. There were royalist risings in Brittany and the Vendée, but a combination of force and persuasion scattered the peasants. The Duke and Duchess of Angoulême had been at Bordeaux when the news of Napoleon's landing reached them in the middle of a ball in their honour. The daughter of Louis XVI made an impassioned appeal and organised local forces, but when General Clauzel appeared with a small force he met little resistance. Clauzel had been made much of by the Bourbons, and his immediate support of Napoleon was a bitter blow; still worse was it to see that the local people and the garrison were not willing to offer any serious opposition although the forces sent by Napoleon were very small indeed. In vain the Duchess tried to persuade the soldiers to resist. 'Oh God!' cried the unhappy woman. 'After twenty years of misery it is hard to have to leave one's country. I have never ceased to love France, for I am French; but you are no longer Frenchmen.'[1] As she turned to go, the men shouted '*Vive l'Empereur!*' after her. She left the district, but her husband, who stayed, was taken prisoner and sent, by Napoleon's orders, to Spain.

The Duke of Orleans went back to England. Before he left he showed a friend a tiny tricolour cockade and said, 'It has never left me. Isn't it hard that I have to leave without wearing it again?'[2] But for the moment the tricolour stood for Napoleon, and fifteen years were to pass before the man who prided himself on having fought at Jemappes was to wear in public the symbol he carried in secret.

It was the Great Powers, not France itself, who decided the future of the country. The dismay and consternation of the diplomats, who had for months been negotiating at Vienna, was naturally great. Napoleon had hoped that the divisions between the victors would prevent further co-operation. Their armies had been disbanded; they were still burdened by the cost of past wars; the King they had enthroned had been turned out of his country; would they resume war to replace him?

Alexander of Russia was doubtful. He had been extremely annoyed by the royalists, and spoke of Orleans as a better King for France. The English radicals in the House of Commons protested against making war for an unpopular dynasty. But in March 1814

[1] Ibid., p. 415.
[2] Ibid., p. 400.

the allies had made the Treaty of Chaumont, by which they had pledged themselves to act should Napoleon again disturb the peace of Europe, and Talleyrand was active for the restoration of Louis. On 25 March the Powers agreed on their respective contributions for war, and Louis was officially recognised as still legitimate King of France.

The money difficulty was met by advances from the great bankers, especially the Rothschilds. This remarkable firm of five brothers, established in different European cities, was able to arrange transfers of cash or credit with great ease. Nathan, in London, was on very good terms with the English Government, and arranged for a transfer of English credits to Vienna, and Solomon took £200,000 in cash to Berlin for the use of Prussia.[1] They had lent Louis money in 1814 and knew very well which side it would pay them to support. Their prompt provision of money where it was needed had a good deal to do with the speed of the reassembling of the allied armies.

In France, Napoleon was aware that the collapse of the Bourbons did not mean that his own position was strong. The soldiers were his, and most of the peasants and workers, but to hold them he had to make promises of political liberty and to appear, at any rate, to outbid the Bourbons in constitutional guarantees. He summoned Benjamin Constant (1767–1830), a theoretical republican philosopher, to advise him and discussed the situation with him. 'Everything is changed,' he said. 'The wish for constitutions, debates, speech-making, seems to have returned. However, it is only a minority that wants them, don't deceive yourself. The people want only me . . . I foresee a struggle, a long war. To maintain it, I must have the support of the nation, but as a reward I believe it will demand liberty. It shall have it. . . . The place of a constitutional king might suit me. It will certainly suit my son.'[2]

Constant helped to draw up a revised constitution, known as the Additional Act, and this was submitted to the people for their approval on 22 April. More than half the people entitled to vote refrained, from indifference rather than because they were royalists. The results were proclaimed to an assembly on 1 June; there was, of course, an overwhelming majority in favour. But this support was not of much practical value. If Napoleon were again to rule France, he must once more win his throne by victory in war.

Napoleon created a ministry and summoned a Council of State. He himself had to command his armies; he had no one on whom to rely to govern during his absence. He badly wanted Talleyrand, but

[1] Corti, Count: *The Rise of the House of Rothschild.* Trans. Lunn. London, 1928, p. 173.
[2] Viel-Castel, op. cit., Vol. III, pp. 14 ff.

had to fall back on Fouché, whom he rightly distrusted. Several of the able younger men refused his offers of posts, and were ordered to leave Paris. The Emperor was depressed and vacillating; although he was only forty-five, his health was giving way, and he had no longer that superb confidence in himself and his fortune which had given him audacity and determination. His only ally was the gallant Murat, King of Naples, who was defeated in Italy and forced to come to France on 25 May. His letters to the sovereigns of Europe were formally rejected; his couriers were arrested on the frontiers.

Some military historians regard Napoleon's last campaign as one of his finest. The allied forces outnumbered his army, but his strategy was magnificent. That he should be defeated at Waterloo was by no means inevitable, but that he should continue the campaign after that defeat was virtually impossible. He had summoned an assembly to meet on 3 June; many of the deputies were old republicans. Hoping for their support, Napoleon hastened back to Paris after the defeat at Waterloo on 18 June. He reached Paris on the 20th; it is conceivable but not very probable that if he had at once addressed the Chambers he might have roused their enthusiasm. But the deputies were from the wealthier classes and not the type to be willing to risk a long and desperate war to keep Napoleon as a constitutional king.

The ablest and most active of his ministers was Fouché, and he had determined that Napoleon must go; he was in touch with the royalists. Time was wasted in long-drawn discussions both in the Cabinet and the Assembly. Napoleon realised his danger and ordered a dissolution; both Houses passed votes refusing to be dismissed. The Emperor said to Constant: 'If I chose, in an hour the rebellious Chambers would cease to exist. . . . But I did not come back from Elba that Paris should swim in blood.'[1]

Short of raising what might become a civil war, there was nothing he could do; his choice lay between deposition and abdication. As before, he abdicated, on 22 June, nominally in favour of his son, though he was well aware that the boy's chances of succession were practically nil. Yet even now he could not bear to go; he hesitated and delayed. He could perfectly well have escaped to the United States, but to the irritation of both his friends and his enemies he left for the coast only a few hours before the Prussian cavalry entered Paris. On 25 June he left for Malmaison, full of memories of Josephine, his divorced wife, who had died there just over a year before. On the 28th he sent a large sum in gold to Laffitte, a Paris banker, for transfer to America. Part of the delay was due to Fouché; he hoped to be able to hand over Napoleon to the allies, so delayed

[1] Ibid., p. 228.

the preparation of the ships Napoleon had ordered. Then the former police chief began to fear that the soldiers would persuade the Emperor to stay, so he sent messages which induced Napoleon to leave for Rochefort. He reached it on 5 July; even then he could have escaped, but eventually he surrendered to the captain of the British ship *Bellerophon*.

As soon as he was gone, Fouché had a free hand. To get rid of the republicans to whom Napoleon had given offices, he sent them to negotiate with the allies, while he, through de Vitrolles, carried on a correspondence with Louis. The only real obstacles to an immediate restoration of the King were the soldiers, who were quite prepared to go on fighting, and Fouché himself, who wished to make it appear that he had immense difficulties to overcome, and so be sure of his reward. The rapid approach of the Prussian and English troops put an end to the confusion. Wellington knew that the Prussians were anxious for revenge on the Parisians; he himself was afraid that too harsh action would make Louis' position quite intolerable, and leave the French determined on revenge. He therefore insisted on Louis being once again proclaimed King before he would accept the capitulation of the Paris garrison.

The 1815 terms of surrender left out two points which had been granted in 1814. Then it had been promised that the contents of the national museums and art galleries should remain intact, although they were full of precious things taken from collections all over Europe, and, secondly, that soldiers should not be billeted in private houses. The allies now promised to protect the Government and officials and private people and their property; the French troops had to withdraw beyond the Loire.

The Chambers realised that Louis would return, but hoped to get him to revise the Charter. They went on discussing constitutions till they were forcibly expelled by the Prussian soldiers. Wellington wrote to Talleyrand that Louis' return would depend on two things —he must take Fouché, Duke of Otranto, as a minister, and he must accept the tricolour as the national flag. Louis accepted the minister, but not the flag—as he said, a man can be got rid of but a symbol is permanent.

The Bourbons, therefore, returned once more to Paris without any change in their legal position, and it seemed as if the only results of the Hundred Days had been the heavy loss of life in the Waterloo campaign and a temporary disturbance of the country. This view most people recognised as superficial; brief though the interlude had been, its consequences were enduring.

Chapter V

THE SECOND RESTORATION

O NCE again the troops of the allies were occupying Paris, and the peace negotiations had to begin all over again in a much worse atmosphere for the French. In 1814 Talleyrand had been able to use the genuine desire of the various governments for a settlement that would leave the French people contented. He had been able to play upon the fears of the allies that Napoleon might be recalled; now the people had shown that they were not willing to serve the Bourbons loyally and whole-heartedly. Their passivity, their apparent lack of interest in the form of their government, shocked and puzzled foreign observers. If they were willing to let Napoleon return, would they not also be willing to accept any republican or other leader? If the men would renew the war at Napoleon's word, could they be trusted to keep the peace? The Germans in particular had held that the only safety for Europe lay in a France so weakened that she could not be an aggressor; the English and Russians had been more sympathetic, but they could not feel so friendly now. The war had cost them all heavy sums and had disrupted their plans; France must pay the bill. It was impossible that the Treaty of 1815, made in Paris, a conquered city, could be so favourable to France as one made in 1814, no matter how skilful were her diplomats.

Within the country the cleavage between the old and the new France was widened. On both sides it was felt that the constitution was not secure; changes were possible. The royalists ascribed the collapse of the monarchy to its weakening by Louis' acceptance of the detestable Charter, and his continued employment of men who had been trained by the usurper. Infuriated by what they considered the ingratitude of the nation, the royalists returned for the second time determined on revenge. The men who had profited by the Revolution must be stripped of their lands, their honours and their offices, and France be ruled once more by her king and her ancient nobility.

The middle-class liberals ascribed the failure of the first restoration to causes precisely opposite. It was the employment of incapable émigrés and the attempt to restore what had gone for ever

46

that had made Louis unpopular. If he would act frankly as a constitutional king, with experienced administrators and a genuinely representative parliament, then the people would settle down. If he would not, then he would have to go and be replaced by someone who would, for instance Orleans.

On the whole Louis himself held the second view. He recognised that he must, by a genuine acceptance of the changed conditions, make it clear that his interests and those of the people were identical. These views were constantly urged on him by the representatives of England and Russia; for one of the results of the Hundred Days was the intervention of foreigners in the domestic politics of France. It had not been easy for the King to accept these ideas; at first, during his journey from Ghent, he had issued a very ill-judged proclamation, in which he spoke of 'the powerful efforts of our allies in scattering the satellites of the tyrant', and of punishing the guilty. He had also allowed his detestation of Talleyrand to be obvious. Wellington's intervention led to a change of attitude; Louis checked Artois when he upbraided the Foreign Minister in his presence. More important, he agreed to the issue at Cambrai on 28 June, three days after the first proclamation, of a second drafted by Talleyrand, in which he admitted that his Government might have made mistakes, reassured those who feared a reimposition of tithes and the seizure of the confiscated lands, and promised forgiveness to all but 'the instigators of this horrible plot'.

As Louis advanced into France, the portraits of Napoleon and the tricoloured flags once again vanished from sight. They were hidden, not destroyed. For the moment Bonapartism went entirely underground; but as the months went by the Napoleonic legend began. With the hero safely out of the way, the romantic view which he himself had tried to paint of the great man, Father Violet returning in the spring, the Little Corporal come to liberate his people, took more and more hold on the imagination of the older men who had known the Empire and of the young men who heard their tales of glory. The seed of the Second Empire had been planted, though its growth was very slow and often checked.

Louis' first duty was to appoint a new Cabinet. He agreed to the demand that he should dismiss his dear friend de Blacas. He wept bitterly at the parting; he loaded him with gifts and had him appointed Ambassador to Naples. Then he took an even more distasteful step; he made Talleyrand, the ex-bishop, his Prime Minister. To strengthen the ministry someone had to have authority, and the man in close touch with the allies was the only possible choice. The new Cabinet could have no moral influence, for it represented no national feeling, and the duties it had to perform

were difficult and delicate. There was still a French army beyond
the Loire, while foreign troops were marching in and occupying the
eastern departments. Disorder was to be expected, yet both the
foreigners and the French themselves must be convinced that the
return of the monarch meant the return of peace and happiness.

The men chosen to help Talleyrand were a most peculiar combination. Dambray, the Chancellor, had served in the first Cabinet,
not very successfully. He was a man of fifty-five, greatly respected
but severe in manner and never popular, even among his colleagues.
He had drawn up the unfortunate proclamation of 25 June, 1814.

Finance, too, remained in the same hands, those of the banker
Baron Louis. He followed the correct routine; he had strength
enough to resist the temptation of easy popularity, either with the
Court by making funds available, or with the people by reducing
taxes. But he, too, could contribute nothing to a general political
programme.

Pasquier (1767–1862) was one of the 'new' men. He had been
trained under Napoleon, though he had refused office during the
Hundred Days, and knew how to work the government machine; he
was clever and tactful; but he detested the ultra-royalists and was
hated by them. He was given, for the time being, two very important
offices, the Ministry of the Interior and that of Justice. He had to
co-operate closely with Beugnot (1761–1835), who had been Prefect
of Police in 1814 and was now the head of the Post Office. This was
an important office, for it was well known that in their passage
through the post letters were opened and read, often copied,
occasionally suppressed. This clever, witty man could give the
Minister of the Interior very valuable information.

The most sensational of the new appointments was that of
Fouché, Duke of Otranto, as head of the police. He was almost
universally disliked, but he had managed to convince not only the
allies but also many of the royalists that he was essential. He had
saved many of those whom he was supposed to be pursuing when he
was in power during the Hundred Days; his emissaries, sent to
Louis at Ghent and to the foreigners fighting his nominal master,
Napoleon, had kept them in touch with events in Paris. Everyone
knew that to Fouché his own interests came first, but at this juncture
it seemed that his and the King's interests were identical. To add
him to Talleyrand in the Cabinet would indicate, so it seemed, that
Louis sincerely meant to forget the Revolution and employ the
ablest men no matter what their past history had been.

Two men who were to be leaders in the future were given minor
posts. Armand-Emmanuel, the Duke of Richelieu (1766–1822), was
a member of a famous family. He had been forced to emigrate, but

had not hung about the exiled Court; he had gone to Russia and had been in charge of the Crimea under Alexander. He was appointed head of the King's Household. Élie Decazes, a lawyer, a man of thirty-five, was of the middle class; a royalist called him a 'Gascon usher' and spoke of his 'vulgar, peremptory effrontery'.[1] Talleyrand said he had 'something of the charm of a fairly handsome young hairdresser'.[2] He was a friend of Baron Louis, who got him appointed Prefect of Police. One of Napoleon's marshals, St. Cyr, was made Minister of War.

The new Cabinet was, on the whole, detestable to the royalists. It seemed as if the King had wholly abandoned his natural advisers, and was slavishly following the advice of foreigners. By a royal ordinance issued in July, procedure was brought closer to the English model, for the Cabinet Council was to meet as a body to advise the King. The Council of State, which resembled the English Privy Council and was attended by the princes of the Royal Family and people appointed to it by the King, including former ministers, was to meet only on special occasions.

On 13 July another ordinance dissolved the Chambers which were still nominally in existence, and laid down regulations for elections in August. The system was that of indirect election. The franchise was slightly widened from that suggested in the Charter; 300 francs paid annually in direct taxes was still the qualification, but a man had the vote at twenty-one instead of at thirty. In each of the *arrondissements*, the subdivisions of the departments, the voters were to meet and choose members of the departmental electoral college. They were also to draw up a list of candidates, equal in number to the deputies to be elected in the department. Eight days later the departmental colleges would meet to make the final choice.

The number of deputies was raised from 258, as in the Charter, to 402; they had to pay 1,000 francs in tax and be twenty-five years old. When the departmental electors met, the prefect of the department produced the lists of candidates sent in by the district colleges, and at least half the deputies elected had to be on these lists. The prefect was also empowered, if he thought it necessary, to add ten nominees to the voters in the district colleges and twenty to the departmental college.

This elaborate system was copied from Napoleon's scheme of 1803; it was believed that excitement would be reduced and a more detailed examination of the qualifications of candidates would be possible. The nomination of extra voters was a safeguard for the few cases where the Government wanted extra support for its candidates.

[1] Frénilly, Baron de: *Recollections*. Trans. Lees. London, 1909, p. 276.
[2] Vitrolles, op. cit., Vol. III, p. 127.

4

The tax qualifications meant a very small electorate; it was calculated that only about 90,000 men would have the vote and only about 16,000 be eligible as deputies.

The arrangements were avowedly tentative, for the ordinance stated that the system would be revised by the Chambers. Yet another alteration by royal prerogative modified the Council of State. It was now to be divided into an Ordinary and an Extraordinary Council. The existing Council, full of inexperienced royalists, was to be the Extraordinary Council, which in practice never met, but whose members could receive a salary. The Ordinary Council was modelled on Napoleon's; it was to contain thirty Counsellors and forty Masters of Requests, appointed annually. These seventy men were divided into five committees, presided over by Ministers of State, and were to help in drafting laws and administrative regulations. On the request of a Cabinet Minister all five committees could meet for joint consultation. This was the real working body; as its members were not permanent, it would be in political harmony with the Cabinet. The thirty Counsellors were appointed at once; they were all men of experience and distinction. The Masters of Requests were to be, as it were, in training for full membership, and they were appointed by degrees. The help the Council could give to inexperienced ministers could be enormous; if its members were not changed too often, they would resemble to some extent the heads of departments of the modern British Civil Service.

The first elections of the Restoration were held in August 1815. Circumstances were far from normal; many districts were occupied by foreign troops; at least a third of those qualified did not vote, not daring to express their real political opinions, or being unable to attend. The Government appointed the presidents of all the electoral colleges, but even without their influence the new Chamber was certain to be royalist. Nearly all the deputies elected were younger sons of the old aristocratic families or country squires.

The Upper House, too, was modified. All the peers who had sat in the Chamber during the Hundred Days were expelled. Only a few nominations had been made in 1814; Louis nominated seventy-four new peers on 14 August. Nearly all of them came from the 'new' France; they were officials of the Empire or wealthy men who had made their money since the Revolution. Talleyrand persuaded the King to make peerages hereditary; he was afraid of the fluctuations in membership which could result if they were for life only.

Harmony in the Government was thus practically impossible. Two 'regicides' were the leading figures in the Cabinet; the Chamber of Deputies was ultra-royalist; the House of Peers con-

sisted mainly of men trained in the Napoleonic tradition; the permanent administration was staffed by officials and judges practically
all of whom had been in office under the Empire and had been
willing to give Napoleon during the Hundred Days the same service
they had yielded to the Bourbons.

That the Talleyrand–Fouché ministry could be a success was
really impossible. Louis sincerely meant to play the constitutional
King, but he could not conceal his dislike at having to co-operate
with men whom he distrusted. No one, indeed, did trust them; the
only real support they had came from the victors, who thought the
composition of the Cabinet offered some guarantee that there would
be no persecution of the republicans and Bonapartists.

The first actions of the Government seemed to justify this view.
There was no wholesale dismissal of the officials who had served
during the interregnum. The loan which Napoleon had floated
during his brief period of power was recognised as valid, though it
had been raised on extremely bad terms and most people had
expected it to be disavowed. The investing classes were greatly reassured, and the Government securities rose in value. A new
forced loan, each department having to subscribe a stated sum,
raised 100 million francs with very little opposition. The censorship
of books was raised, though a close check had to be kept on newspapers because of the extreme violence of the royalist Press.

An urgent and delicate task was the disbandment of the armies.
St. Cyr persuaded Louis to cut down the numbers of his Royal
Guard and to suppress altogether that of his brother. The real
fighting men had most of them to be sent home; the largest group
was the army beyond the Loire, where, in spite of desertions, Davout
still commanded over a hundred thousand men. For some days
Davout tried to negotiate for terms, but on 14 July he recognised
that simple submission was necessary. He summoned his officers and
told them that 'only the Government of Louis XVIII can prevent
the devastation and partition of France. That is why the army must
support him.'[1] The officers agreed, and told the men once again to
wear the hated white cockade. Rather than do this, about half the
soldiers quietly deserted, but there was some rioting and some
attacks on local royalists before the rest submitted. The pay of many
regiments was in arrears, and the Government had to borrow from
Laffitte the gold Napoleon had deposited with him to meet the
demands for pay.

Davout had expected that his remaining troops would be kept as
an indication that France was not powerless. Talleyrand, without
consulting St. Cyr, promised the allies that they should be

[1] Houssaye: *1815. La Seconde Abdication.* Paris, 1905, p. 413.

disbanded at once. St. Cyr indignantly resigned, but was persuaded to remain in office by a promise that he could organise a new army, from which the more conspicuous imperialists could be excluded.

All over France, therefore, Napoleon's soldiers were going home, bitterly conscious that not only defeat but what they held to be treachery had led to the dashing of their hopes. The officers were in a dangerous position, especially the generals who had deserted the King to follow the Emperor. They tried to take confidence from the Cambrai proclamation which promised an amnesty, and from the fact that so many of them were involved that the King would have to execute or imprison practically all the experienced soldiers in France if they were to be held to be traitors.

Everyone was anxious to know who would be the men selected for punishment as the authors of the 'horrible treachery' referred to in Louis' proclamation. It is possible that the King himself would have preferred to take no vengeance, but he was pressed from three sides to take some action. Naturally, his royalist friends were crying for revenge, and a public punishment would be better than the private attacks which might be multiplied if no outlet were given officially for the outraged feelings of the legitimists. Then Fouché was determined that if any prosecutions were to be made, he himself should be responsible for them. Too many of his own friends would be involved if any other prosecutor investigated the history of the Hundred Days, and his own conduct would not bear too close a scrutiny. In a list of public enemies he could include those whom he personally feared. The allies, too, were saying that if everyone escaped it would be thought that Louis was too weak to dare to punish traitors. As de Vitrolles wrote, 'It was a curious contradiction that the foreigners who in 1814 . . . were uneasy lest we should be severe and revengeful, were now accusing us of weakness.'[1]

No other member of the Cabinet was anxious to undertake so unpleasant a task as drawing up the list of those who were to be excluded from the amnesty, so Fouché had it his own way. When his catalogue was produced before a Cabinet meeting, it seemed to be of names 'chosen haphazard from the highest ranks as well as the most obscure'.[2] De Vitrolles, who had attached himself to the Government without any official appointment, and resumed his office of Secretary to the Cabinet, demanded that those accused should be divided into two categories, those who had plotted with Napoleon before he reached Paris, and those who had supported him after 23 March. Even with this discrimination, the list was an absurdity. The truth was that very little proof could be found of any conspiracy

1 Vitrolles, op. cit., Vol. III, p. 146.
2 Ibid.

preceding Napoleon's landing in France, for there had been no plot; and that almost every official in the country could have been included in the second category.

There is some doubt as to how many names were included in Fouché's original list. De Vitrolles says 60, Talleyrand says over 100, another source gives 300. Ministers set to work deleting names, and the final list, as it appeared in the *Moniteur* of 24 July, contained the names of nineteen generals who were to be tried by courts martial, and of thirty-eight others who were to remain under police supervision until the Chambers had met and decided what action should be taken.

The appearance of the list gave a distinct shock to the public. By the Declaration of Cambrai, Louis had said that it was the Chambers who were to decide who were the traitors, and had promised to pardon 'all that had occurred after 23 March'. Thirty-one of the men on Fouché's list had supported Napoleon in his march on Paris or accepted office from him before 23 March. The other people accused included nine men whose only public offence was that they had been elected to the Emperor's Chamber of Deputies; an official who had stayed at his post, as had practically all the others; and a journalist who was suspected of writing for the republican newspaper, the *Yellow Dwarf*.

Davout, on St. Cyr's assurance, had advised his subordinate commanders to remain at their posts. When he found their names included in the list of traitors, he wrote to the War Minister saying that they had merely obeyed his orders, and his name should replace theirs. The only answer he got was his dismissal from the army. Macdonald, who succeeded him, delayed the arrests and allowed the proscribed officers to escape.

Before the official prosecutions began, a terrible unofficial vengeance was taken in many parts of the country. It was in the south-east that matters were worst. Sometimes the disbanded soldiers began the trouble by attacking royalists, but more often it was the other party which was responsible. Not all the murders were the work of genuine royalists; as Hyde de Neuville, a legitimist, wrote, 'These excesses were committed to the cry of " *Vive le Roi!* ", and that was sufficient for all royalists to be included in the same hatred.'[1] In Marseilles some Egyptian refugees, who had lived on a pension from Napoleon, were murdered. Among the assassins was a man who had been a Jacobin in 1793. 'After killing in the name of the people, they killed in the name of the King. The pleasure was the same.'

Some of the worst trouble was in the Rhône valley. Political

[1] Neuville, Baron Hyde de: *Mémoires.* 3 vols. Paris, 1888–92, Vol. II, p. 134.

hatred, combined with traditional religious enmities, led the people of Avignon and Nîmes to burn Huguenot churches as well as to kill and wound republicans and Bonapartists. On 18 July the women of Nîmes attacked the Protestant women with the wooden bats they used for beating the linen when they washed it in the river.[1] Nails stuck into these bats made them formidable weapons, which they called 'royal bats'. At Uzès a scoundrel called Graffand, who had been employed by Angoulême, took six people out of the prison and shot them, saying 'no one can blame us, for three were Protestant and three Catholic'.[2] Three weeks later this man was actually given a job by the prefect.

It is impossible to say how many were the victims of what soon was called the White Terror; it was never so extensive as the Terror of 1793, but it had less excuse. It is probable that in the south-east between two and three hundred people were killed. In other districts there were few deaths, but much rioting and damage. The most serious and lasting effect was that, in the minds of many, the Church was associated with injustice and cruelty. Persecution of the Church had weakened the Republic; connection with the royalists in 1815 did harm to the Church in France which has never been repaired.

One particular organisation, known as the Congregation, has long been blamed for the close connection between the Church and a political party. A minor historical problem has been that the records of this body showed that it had never had a membership large enough to be as effective as its contemporary opponents and later historians both believed. Recent research has explained the mystery.

The Congregation of the Virgin was one of a number of secret associations set up by groups of Catholics during the revolutionary persecutions; many of them were simply pious societies which had existed before 1789. The Congregation was started in Paris by a Jesuit priest, and was a society for young men who met for prayer and mutual spiritual help at the time when any public exercise of religion was dangerous. Similar organisations were set up in the provinces and survived even when the reconciliation with Rome took place; there were about ten Congregations under the Empire, some started by men who had been members of the one in Paris, some independent. Organisation was quite informal; in Bordeaux the Congregation proper had about 400 young men as members, but a society of older men and associations for married women and for girls were connected with it. One main aim of these groups was to keep in touch with Rome after Napoleon had quarrelled with the

[1] Houssaye, op. cit., p. 466.
[2] Ibid., p. 473.

Pope; they circulated in secret Pius VII's Bull excommunicating the Emperor. The police discovered this and four young men were arrested, but did not betray the other members of the organisation. Napoleon called it a 'choirboys' conspiracy', but was sufficiently alarmed to order the suppression of all 'mystical associations and congregations'. There was now inevitably a tinge of political conspiracy attached to the Congregation, which perhaps made membership more attractive to young men of good family and education. The priests who directed the associations were concerned with the spiritual life of their charges, and indignantly denied that their aims were political, but under the circumstances it was inevitable that the young men should be opposed first to the republic and later to Napoleon, when he, too, denied them religious freedom, and that they were, as a result, royalists.

An active man of twenty-seven, Ferdinand de Bertier,[1] decided in 1809 to form a political society aiming at the restoration of both Church and King. Freemasonry was strong in France, and Bertier copied its organisation. The name he chose for his associates was Knights of the Faith, though they were also called the Ring. There were three grades of membership. The outer circle was called the Associates of Charity; these men simply promised to say prayers and do good works, and pay a small annual subscription. From among them, unknown to the other members, Bertier and his friends chose suitable young men and invited them to join an inner circle, the Squires. After careful observation, some Squires were invited to become full Knights. The accolade was given and a binding oath of secrecy taken; the very existence of the Knights of the Faith was not to be betrayed. There were elaborate ceremonies and chivalric titles, all very attractive to young men who felt honoured by being chosen. Only the Knights knew that the real aim of the association was the restoration of the Bourbons; the outer circles believed it existed merely to help those who had suffered for their faith and to maintain contact with Rome.

Naturally, Bertier chose his Knights from among men of his own class and upbringing; they belonged to the old noble families of France. They plotted endlessly; they raised a number of futile local risings. The year 1814 saw, they thought, the fulfilment of their prayers, but they were enraged by the issue of the Charter; they wanted no concession to the Revolution. Indeed, they wanted all traces of 1789 removed; the convenient new departments abolished and the old unwieldy provinces restored; all of Napoleon's prefects immediately dismissed. It seems surprising that men who actually

[1] Sauvigny, G. de Bertier de: *Le Comte Ferdinand de Bertier et l'Enigme de la Congrégation*. Paris, 1948.

lived in France should be so wholly unrealistic, until one remembers that the Government had been their enemy and that they had lived in a self-supporting world of dreams and desires.

In 1814 and again later on the Knights tried to get official approval of their organisation from the Pope, but, according to long custom, Rome would not approve any secret society which imposed a binding oath upon its members. Secrecy was the very atmosphere of the Knights, and not even the Pope could make them abandon it. The membership grew, and by 1826 there were 48,000 fully-enrolled Knights. All of them were by profession if not in spirit ardent Catholics, but above all they were ardent royalists.

It was these men who were responsible for the political intrigues for which the Congregation bore, and has since borne, the blame. They took part in many outrages during the White Terror; one of the most sensational and revolting was the murder of General Ramel. He was the commander of the troops in Toulouse, where the Knights had a strong 'Banner', as the local groups were called. During the Hundred Days the Knights had tried to rouse local royalists to resist the Emperor, but they were not very efficient, and Ramel's men easily broke up their forces. The General's aim was merely to prevent civil war; he knew that his soldiers were strongly for Napoleon. On the news of the second abdication, bands of armed men threatened to assault the local Bonapartists, and once again were scattered by Ramel's orders.

Ramel himself was then attacked and severely wounded. He was carried to his house, and was lying in bed in his doctor's charge when his enemies broke in. The doctor told them he was dying, but they battered him to death as he lay there helpless. So far as is known no Knight was personally guilty of this vile murder, but the Knights had armed the men who carried it out and they had instigated the clamour for revenge. Worse still, they condoned it; they terrorised witnesses into refusing to give evidence to the police, and when at last three men were brought to trial they used their influence to get one acquitted and the other two sentenced to only five years' imprisonment.

That a secret society of some kind was behind this case was obvious, but though the prefects were ordered to dissolve all such societies, the Knights escaped. They kept their secrets better than the many loose Bonapartist and republican groups; they had powerful friends in high places. The blame for their actions fell not on them but on the Church and the party to which they belonged, and especially upon the Church.

The Knights were active in seeking Government posts, and a good many of them became prefects. They organised requiem masses for the souls of those who died under the guillotine; some of them did very useful work in starting new charitable organisations and reviving and reforming the old. They and the bishops who returned from emigration were too often responsible for giving a political tone to such activities; in some places parish priests who had conformed to the Civil Constitution of the clergy and had been officially pardoned by the Pope were forced to climb into their pulpits and publicly confess their error. 'Missions' were organised all over the country; they took the form of a series of sermons urging the people to penitence and were usually followed by a great procession and the erection of a crucifix. This method of reviving religious activity is common to many kinds of Church and to all periods; it was popular in France in the eighteenth century and still is to-day. Like the Salvation Army in England, the missionaries set hymns to popular tunes; like the Wesleyans, their emotional sermons sometimes led to religious hysteria. Where politics were kept out of the missions under the restoration Government, it is probable that a great deal of good was done; people enjoyed the resumption of traditional pilgrimages, and the processions and hymn-singing gave an outlet for emotions. But too often the association of the Church with counter-revolutionary propaganda led to serious rioting, and drove the men who believed in the principles of 1789 or—and they were far more numerous—had loved Napoleon, to detest the priests and look upon them as wholly reactionary. Anti-clericalism became a political creed. It has often been said that the Bourbons suffered for being too kind to the Church. It was the Church that suffered from trusting too much to the Bourbons, or rather to the royalist politicians.

Chapter VI

FRANCE AFRAID

THE official prosecution of the men held responsible for the Hundred Days was not a great success. Many of those on the list escaped, and when others were brought to trial, the Government's prestige suffered as a result.

A man particularly detested by the royalists was Marshal Ney. He had attempted to escape to Switzerland, but found his way blocked by Austrian troops near Lyons and took refuge with some relations who lived in the château of Bessonis in Auvergne. When any stranger came to the house, he hid in an attic, and but for a piece of amazing carelessness he might well have escaped detection. Lying in the sitting-room he left his sword, a magnificent weapon which Napoleon had given him. A visitor caught sight of it and remarked on it to his friends, who told him that only Ney and Murat possessed swords like that he described. Local royalists arrested him without the knowledge of the Prefect of Police.[1]

Ney, sick of his virtual captivity, surrendered, to the secret dismay of the Government. Louis exclaimed, when he heard the news : 'He has done us more harm to-day by letting himself be taken than he did on 13 March',[2] when he joined Napoleon. For the trial of the famous Marshal offered all sorts of problems.

As a soldier, he was entitled to trial by court martial, and by military law his judges must be of his own rank. Most of the marshals of France had also served Napoleon during the Hundred Days, and many of them refused to act as judges. Finally, seven were nominated, and of these five had fought for France during the Waterloo campaign. It would have been almost impossible for such men to condemn him. But the friends who were helping Ney in his defence made a cardinal error; they claimed that Ney, as a Peer of France, had a right to be tried by the House of Peers, not by court martial. The marshals were immensely relieved, and after rather long-drawn-out discussions declared themselves incompetent to act as his judges.

On 11 November, 1815, the Peers were officially informed that they were to act as a court for the trial of a peer accused of high

---

[1] Véron, Dr. L.: *Mémoires d'un Bourgeois de Paris*. Paris, 1853, p. 254.
[2] Viel-Castel, op. cit., Vol. III, p. 524.

treason. The correct procedure was long discussed, for there were no precedents; in the end it was decided that all the peers must be present and that the trial should be public. When Ney was brought before the House on 18 November the excitement was intense. The galleries were crowded, and the revengeful royalist ladies who attended this and other trials were nicknamed the '*brodeuses*', the 'embroiderers', as a parallel to the '*tricoteuses*', the women who knitted round the guillotine during the Terror.

Ney was charged not only with his defection to Napoleon, but with plotting to bring him to France. His case was really a strong one, but his lawyers spoilt it by bringing up legal objections to his being tried at all. They claimed that, by the terms of the capitulation of Paris, the inhabitants of the city, and Ney among them, had been promised that they would not be proceeded against for their opinions or their actions. Wellington was consulted as to whether this plea was justified; he had to reply that the phrase had been intended to cover only the normal inhabitants of the city, and certainly not soldiers who happened to be within the walls. This was common sense, though many people wished that the Iron Duke could have given an answer that would have saved his distinguished enemy.

The Peers were most anxious that the trial should be conspicuously fair. Against the wishes of the prosecution, they adjourned until 4 December so that time should be given for the preparation of the defence.[1] The Government was disturbed by this delay, for public excitement was so great that they wished the whole business quickly over. The adjournment was of little service to the Marshal; for Ney's real ground of defence was that his treachery was purely personal. He had had no previous correspondence with Napoleon; his troops were about to desert; he had not ordered anybody to change sides. He could argue that to resist Napoleon meant civil war, and he had to do what he thought best for France; he could say that practically all the other generals had done the same, so that if his act were treachery they should stand beside him in the dock.

Still trying to avoid any trial, the defence lawyers denied the competence of the Peers by claiming that he was not French, for the town he was born in had been taken from France by the peace treaty. This plea shocked the Marshal, and he was furious. 'I am a Frenchman, and I will die a Frenchman!' he exclaimed.

There could be little dispute about the facts of his actual change of sides. Three questions were put to the Peers. The first was: Did Ney receive Napoleon's emissaries on the night of 13 March? The

[1] A full account of Ney's trial is to be found in Viel-Castel, op. cit., Vol. IV, pp. 299 ff.

only proof that he did was his own admission. Forty-seven peers considered that there should have been independent witness, and so voted 'No', but the other 113 said 'Yes'. The second question, Had he read a proclamation to his men advising them to join Napoleon, and had he himself led them in doing so?, could only be answered in the affirmative. The third was: Was Ney guilty of high treason? Only one man said 'No', the Duc de Broglie, for he held that Ney's act was not really treason. The rest voted 'Yes'. The Marshal was found guilty.

A vote had then to be taken as to the penalty to be inflicted. Five peers refused to vote at all; seventeen wished him to be exiled. A hundred and thirty-nine condemned him to death, five adding a recommendation to mercy. At three o'clock on the morning of 7 December the death sentence was signed.

Ney had hoped for an acquittal. Convinced in his heart that he had acted rightly, he found it difficult to believe that he, who had served France with all his force, could publicly be declared a traitor. At half past three on this winter morning an official came and read the sentence to him, beginning with a recital of all his titles. Ney interrupted him. 'Say: Michel Ney, and soon a little dust.' He asked when the execution would take place, and was told that it would be that very day at nine o'clock in the morning. Then he requested that his wife and children should come and see him in two hours' time, and went to sleep till that sad interview.

He had refused the consolation of religion, but one of the soldiers guarding him said simply, 'Marshal, oughtn't you to think about God? It's always a good thing to be reconciled with God.' Ney answered, 'You are right. One ought to die like an honest man and a Christian.' A priest was sent for, and the last rites performed.

To the last the Marshal kept his gay courage. When he entered the carriage which was to take him to the place of execution, a priest was with him. Ney waved him to enter the carriage first. 'You go first now, father; I shall go up above before you.' Faced by the firing party, he refused to allow his eyes to be bandaged. In a resolute voice he said, 'I protest before God and my country against my condemnation. I appeal to mankind, to the future, to God. *Vive la France!*'

He had not told his wife that his death was imminent, and she went to beg the King to be merciful. She was told that it was impossible for an interview to be granted, as now it would be without an object.

There was less excitement than had been expected when the news of the execution was published, for everyone had anticipated Ney's death. Only one newspaper, the *Constitutionnel*, dared to say anything at all friendly about the Marshal. The phrase was used in their account, 'He had twenty years of glory and one day of error.' It was in later years that the name of Ney was used to stimulate opposition to the Bourbons.

It was perhaps possible to justify the execution of Ney, but another sensational trial, that of de Lavalette, was a first-class mistake on the part of Louis' government. De Lavalette had been a general, but had left the army in 1800, yet his name appeared on the list of treacherous soldiers. His sole offence was that he had taken charge of the postal service before Napoleon actually reached Paris. His friends urged him to escape, but he was determined to show his innocence and actually wrote to the King on 14 July asking to be brought to trial. The wiser members of the Cabinet had hoped that he would fly, but after this letter they had to send the police to arrest him. They reached his house early in the morning while he was still asleep, so they went away, no doubt hoping that when they came back he would have gone. When they returned four hours later, he was quietly eating his breakfast.

It was obviously absurd to try him as a soldier, so he was brought before an ordinary court, which condemned him to death on 21 November. One ground for his condemnation was a letter which he had written to Napoleon for the New Year of 1815, an ordinary polite letter of good wishes which had never even reached Napoleon in Elba. There was no proof whatever that he had shared in any plot against the Bourbons. Most of the respectable people summoned as witnesses spoke highly of his character, and even though the foreman of the jury was his personal enemy, and all the jurymen royalists, it was only by eight votes to four that they found him guilty.

It was with confidence that he appealed, but on 14 December the Court of Appeal confirmed the verdict. His friends begged the King to pardon him, but the Cabinet refused to ask for mercy, so Louis felt that he must support his ministers and would not intervene. The execution was fixed for 21 December.

On 20 December his wife learned that there was no hope of a reprieve. She was visiting her husband every day in prison, and now determined to arrange his escape. She went in a sedan chair to the prison and as usual left it outside. She persuaded her husband to put on her clothes and walk out of his cell, burying his face in a handkerchief. After some narrow shaves he reached the sedan chair, and to his horror found that the porters had gone off; they had purposely been kept waiting a long time, so that darkness should have fallen. Fortunately, others were found, who carried the chair with the supposed disconsolate lady to a hackney coach. Then he was driven by a roundabout route to the refuge that had been planned—the Foreign Office.

The head of the Accounts Department of the Foreign Office had been proscribed during the Revolution and had been saved; his wife had made a vow that if ever she could she would help someone in danger for his politics. Now Bresson fulfilled her pledge; he hid de Lavalette in his rooms, where he stayed some days while the police were searching all Paris for him after his wife had been found replacing him in his cell. An Englishman named Bruce and two friends brought him an English uniform,[1] and in this disguise he rode out of Paris on 7 January, 1816, and made his way to Holland. But, though he was only forty-seven, he was a broken man, and his wife, always a delicate woman, was so shattered by the strain that she lost her reason.

This dramatic escape was a serious blow to the prestige of the Government. It leaked out that it had been made possible by the co-operation of public servants and Englishmen, and the anger of the royalists grew as they realised that such assistance for a man condemned as a traitor involved a moral condemnation of their policy of reprisals.

While Paris was thrilled by trials, and while some areas of France were panic-stricken by the White Terror, other areas suffered from the brutality of the exasperated victors. The Prussians, in particular, wanted the revenge they had been denied in 1814. The Prussian general Blucher determined to blow up the bridge in Paris which commemorated the defeat of the Prussians at Jena in 1806. Talleyrand heard of his plan and protested; Blucher's response was to say: 'The bridge will be destroyed, and I hope M. Talleyrand will first take up his place upon it.' When Louis heard of this, he wrote to Talleyrand on 8 July saying that he himself would go and sit on the bridge in his arm-chair. In spite of this gesture, the Prussian engineers went on with their preparations and on 10 July some mines were exploded under the bridge, but did little damage. When the King of Prussia arrived he, urged on by Alexander of Russia and by Wellington, stopped the destruction which Blucher had planned as a suitable revenge for French violation of the tomb of Frederick the Great.

Round about Paris whole villages were laid waste by the invaders. English soldiers picketed their horses in a field of ripe corn; Prussians stopped carriages on the road and robbed travellers; houses were broken into and furniture destroyed. Allied soldiers were billeted on private citizens, who had to feed them well for five pence a day. The royalist feelings of the ordinary Parisians soon

[1] Bruce, I.: *Lavalette Bruce*. London, 1953, pp. 177 ff.

disappeared and between 19 and 23 July forty-five people were sentenced in the police courts for 'seditious manifestations', such as crying 'Down with the Bourbons!' One joker tied a fleur-de-lis to the tail of a pig, in reference to the soldiers' nickname for the King, and led it round various cafés.

Provocation came from both sides; the royalists declared that the red carnation was a Napoleonic emblem, and assaulted people who wore these flowers or displayed them in their windows. Members of Louis' Royal Guard were continually fighting men of the National Guard. It was not safe for any soldier of the allied forces to go about alone at night; several were murdered. Paris was full of disorder and the ordinary people went about afraid.

Foreign armies were quartered in no less than fifty-eight of the eighty-six departments of France, and Castlereagh estimated the cost to France as one and three-quarter million francs a day. The prefects were responsible for the lodging and feeding of the troops, and in areas occupied by the Prussians were arrested and sent off to Germany if they did not give satisfaction to the local commanders. Between 20 August and 20 September, 1815, twenty prefects and sub-prefects, and many minor officials, were deported to Germany.

On 6 August the allies asked for 50 million francs in cash to pay their men during August and September, and promised to stop making local requisitions of money and seizing private property. Rations and clothing were still to be supplied by the French local authorities. But bitter complaints still came in of ill treatment and brutality. A highborn lady was forced to wait on non-commissioned officers and even to pull off their boots for them; a mayor was killed by an Austrian captain because he could not supply him with coffee; a carter was killed for not getting his cart out of the way of some troops quickly enough.[1] The Government felt powerless; it ordered the prefects not to interfere in such cases, so in several places villagers deserted their homes when allied troops were quartered on them. It was calculated that over 7,000 people had taken refuge in the forest between Troyes and Bar.

Wellington realised that, unless the occupation of France was put on a proper basis and these acts of brutality and pillage were stopped, there would be a general rising. Of course, not all the soldiers behaved badly; in some places they were comparatively popular and had helped to prevent clashes between the royalists and their opponents. But even if they had all behaved with perfect discipline, the presence of a million and a quarter foreigners, who had to be paid, housed, fed and clothed, was a tremendous drain on the country.

[1] Houssaye, op. cit., pp. 492, 493.

The final settlement of peace terms was thus urgently needed. Talleyrand found that his negotiations had to be carried on in a very different atmosphere from that of Vienna. In 1814 Alexander of Russia had been sympathetic to France and to Talleyrand; now the Tsar was irritated and suspicious. In 1814 he had been at a safe distance from his fellow politicians and the King; now he had to meet them daily. He had no real friend in the Cabinet; he and Fouché were both hated by the royalists, although Fouché was trying by flattery to ingratiate himself with Artois. In a Cabinet council Fouché, as Minister of Police, produced a most alarmist report about the condition of the country and the unpopularity of the armies of occupation. When the representatives of the allies heard of it, they protested, and Talleyrand took the opportunity of asking the King to dismiss the Duke of Otranto. Fouché, however, persuaded the English that he was an essential member of the Government, and at their request Louis withdrew his threat of dismissal. In a despairing attempt to win over the royalists this man of fifty-six married a young girl of good family, but this horrified rather than flattered the aristocrats, who continued to ignore him. The King never saw him if he could avoid it, and did business with his subordinate, the Prefect of Police, Élie Decazes.

Decazes was quick to use his opportunities, and clever enough to see that his influence must be used to check the extremists. It was to him that reports from the prefects came in, and he extracted passages and read them to the King. He charmed the monarch and began to have his confidence, so by careful selection from the reports he was able to persuade him of the danger of the policy of revenge pursued by the ultra-royalists.

When the election results came in, it was obvious that the Talleyrand–Fouché cabinet would have great difficulty in getting any support in the House of Deputies. Louis was extremely glad of the solid reason he could give the English for getting rid of the man whom he, and indeed most people, hated and feared, so Fouché was dismissed from office on 11 September, 1815. To smooth things over, he was made France's representative at the Court of Saxony, but was allowed to hold the post for only three months. He was ordered never to return to France, so the Duke of Otranto passed the years till his death in 1820 in the banishment which he himself had inflicted on so many others.

Talleyrand had hoped to improve his own position when Fouché fell from power, but he quickly found that it was being taken for granted that he, too, would soon be dismissed. In his memoirs he said that he had resigned because the allies' peace terms were so harsh as to undo all his work at Vienna, and that though the foreign diplomats urged him to remain in office, he was determined to resign. Vitrolles' account of his fall is probably more accurate than Talleyrand's own. He says that the Foreign Minister asked Louis to assure him that he would give his full support to his ministers; 'if this cannot be, then we must ask the King this very day to choose other advisers.' 'Very well,' Louis answered calmly, 'I will form another Cabinet.' It seems very likely that Talleyrand had hoped to keep in power and believed he was indispensable, and that he was greatly taken aback when his threat of resignation, meant to strengthen his position, was immediately taken seriously and accepted.

With the fall of the Talleyrand–Fouché ministry, the new royal Government really began to function. So far, policy had been decided from day to day by men whose title to office had been either practical experience gained under a different form of government, or personal association with members of the Royal Family. Now, with a new Chamber of Deputies and a new ministry, the believers in monarchy had their great opportunity. Many of the royalists were able and sincere, and though their ideas were not those of the bulk of the people, with the Church and the bankers behind them they might possibly have produced a government in some ways well adapted to French conditions and traditions. Their difficulty was to find a political programme based on something more solid than emotions.

The Chambers had been summoned for 22 September, but their opening was postponed until 6 October to give time for the formation of a new Cabinet. This was looked upon as genuinely the King's own prerogative and duty; there were no organised parties, for there had until now been no free parliament. Louis' choice was, however, limited by two factors. He dreaded his brother's intrigues and was, therefore, suspicious of his friends, the extreme royalists or ultras, as they now began to be called; and the urgent need of placating Europe meant that his advisers must be men who seemed to offer stability in France.

He chose as his President of the Council, the equivalent of the English Prime Minister, the Duke of Richelieu, who had held a minor post in 1814. He hoped that this man by his aristocratic birth would be acceptable to the royalists, and that his friendship with Alexander of Russia would commend him to the allies. Richelieu was nearly fifty, and a man of the utmost personal probity; he abhorred anything in the way of intrigue or insincerity. He was often deceived by those with whom he had to work, and if he discovered this he was implacable in his resentment. His honesty and courage were great, but his absence in Russia meant that he had few friends, and no

5

personal knowledge of the post-revolutionary men and institutions. This made it very difficult for him to choose his colleagues.

The only man in politics since 1814 whom he knew at all well was Decazes, Louis' new friend, whom he had employed as his lawyer in an attempt to recover some of his property. Those of the Artois party who had hoped to fill the office given to Richelieu said that the Prime Minister had been appointed owing to Decazes' influence; others said that he had been forced on Louis by the Tsar. Certainly Alexander had a great respect for him, but if one can believe de Vitrolles, who certainly knew a great deal about what was going on at Court, the Tsar did not suggest the appointment. He merely 'hoped that he would be great enough to deal with the difficulties of our situation, but the hope seemed to indicate the presence of a doubt'.

The thankless and difficult task of Minister for War was given to Clarke, Duke of Feltre, one of Napoleon's marshals who had served him in that capacity, but had decided to go to Ghent with Louis in 1815. His duty would be to disperse and not to train armies. A former minister of Louis XVI, Dubouchage, was given the Navy, to prove the continuity of the new with the old monarchy. Richelieu wanted Pasquier as Minister of Justice, but he was not willing to take office, so the duties were laid on a man of seventy, Barbé-Marbois, who had served both Louis XVI and Napoleon. Decazes, as Minister for Police, would clearly have a much greater influence on affairs than the Minister of Justice. Baron Louis also refused to remain Finance Minister, and was replaced by Corvetto, who had been a distinguished member of Napoleon's Council of State and had great knowledge, both theoretical and practical, of finance.

To satisfy the ultra-royalists, de Vaublanc was made Minister of the Interior. A man of fifty-nine, he had been a royalist during the Revolution, but had served the Government under the Directory and the Empire. During the Hundred Days he had followed the Bourbons to Ghent and now expressed the most ardent royalism. He had a gift of oratory, but was both stupid and conceited. His appointment was a serious error; the ministry of which he had charge was, with the possible exception of the Foreign Office, by far the most important for the good government of France.

One man was bitterly disappointed when the new Cabinet's membership was announced. De Vitrolles had acted as Secretary to both the last cabinets and believed himself to be indispensable. But he had associated himself too closely with Artois; Richelieu would not have at the council board a man who would be certain to report every incident to the King's brother. For some time Vitrolles kept in touch with Louis. 'I was received every three or four days in his

Cabinet,' he wrote. 'I told him about the attitude of the Chambers, of their feelings of loyalty, of the way to use them in the King's service. At first I was well attended to and fairly well understood. But, according to his habit, the King sought rather to escape business than to understand it. He preferred anecdotes to discussion, and the anecdotes he told himself to those which others could tell him.'[1] De Vitrolles' view of Louis had a great deal of truth in it; but it is also probable that the King did not want to discuss politics with an unofficial adviser, who was a friend of the brother and heir whom he distrusted, as well as with his ministers. Soon de Vitrolles ceased to have any influence, except as an active leader of the extreme royalists.

Richelieu advised the King, who was delighted at the suggestion, to reward his outgoing ministers, with the exception of Fouché, by making them Ministers of State and members of the Extraordinary Council. Those who had not already been given the highest rank in the Legion of Honour now received it, and Talleyrand was made Grand Chamberlain, a sinecure Court appointment, with a salary of 100,000 francs a year. Macdonald and Oudinot, the marshals, and some others who had served Louis in 1814, were also made councillors. All these people got 20,000 francs a year salary, so the position was practically that of receiving a pension of £800 a year as well as an honour. Ministers of State could be dismissed at will, and during the restoration men who incurred the government's displeasure knew that they ran the risk of losing a nice income.

The new Cabinet pleased the royalists, for there were enough 'ultras' in it to satisfy them. The representatives of the allies were dubious; the English, in particular, regretted the fall of Talleyrand. To consolidate the ministry and make it effective would be, Richelieu knew, not at all easy, but he could not at the time realise all the weaknesses. A major one was that only Decazes was a deputy, only Richelieu, Clarke, and de Vaublanc peers. Harmony between the Cabinet and the Chambers could not be maintained unless they were closely in touch or unless, which the composition of the ministry itself made most unlikely, there was an agreed and practicable programme of political action.

[1] Vitrolles, op. cit., Vol. III, p. 340.

Chapter VII

THE MATCHLESS PARLIAMENT

IN the autumn of 1815 the great experiment of constitutional monarchy really began in France. The Lower House was not intended to be a democratic assembly, but it represented the upper and middle classes more accurately than did the English House of Commons. The King was not a clever or an active man, but he was perhaps all the better suited for the peculiar rôle of a monarch with limited power. The Prime Minister was a man of the highest character. The success or failure of the system depended on the political capacity of the royalists.

Their programme had to have a long-term policy as well as the immediate objective of restoring order and making peace with Europe. Very few of the new deputies were really pleased with the Charter as it stood. Apart from the extremists, who still dreamed of an impossible return to the France of Louis XIV, many of them were thinking of modifications. One group wanted the franchise extended, for at present power lay in the hands of the men who had made money out of the Revolution; for the time being they were for the King, but it was felt they could not be trusted. The strength of conservatism usually lies in rural areas, and to enfranchise the richer peasants would have given an appearance of democracy while giving a wider basis to the party. Another set wished to diminish the power of the centralised administrative machine created by Napoleon. As soon as an attempt was made to work out definite plans, however, difficulties began. The former landowners thought of the peasants as men who had robbed them of their property; the royalists, who had themselves become prefects, realised how immense was their influence and feared to abandon so powerful a support for the Government.

To help them in the clarification of their ideas the royalists had brilliant writers, among whom Chateaubriand stood first. He was twenty-one when the Revolution broke out in France, and was then travelling in America. He returned to his country in 1792, but stayed only a few months, during which he married. After joining the émigrés in the Rhineland, he, like so many others, came to England and taught in a school. In 1800 he returned to France and made an immense reputation by his writings. He was an erratic person, always falling in love, extremely attractive to women, wildly extravagant and always in debt. He was singularly lacking in common sense; when Louis was in Ghent he was there, too, and was practically invited to be the King's confidant when his favourite de Blacas was dismissed. 'I am going to part with M. de Blacas,' said Louis; 'the place will be vacant, M. de Chateaubriand.'[1] Yet when the return to Paris took place Chateaubriand lingered, so that all the official posts were filled when he arrived and he got only the sinecure position of a Minister of State. Perhaps it suited him better to have a regular salary with no duties rather than to be called on to exercise the patience required from those in daily contact with Louis. One cannot but speculate on the change it might have made had he, and not Decazes, been Louis' personal friend and counsellor.

He was made a peer, but found that he could have exercised more influence as a deputy. Debates in the Upper House were not reported, and he himself said that the Chamber was full of old men with ear trumpets who fell asleep. He tried in his speeches to praise the Charter to gain the support of the moderates and the allies, but the whole business bored him. His fellow royalists admired him, but some were jealous and others felt, with some justification, that he was too vain and too impetuous to be counted upon.

Chateaubriand was a great romantic, and an outstanding example of the impact of the romantic movement on French politics. The revolt from the classical tradition in literature and art had begun in Europe before 1789; the storms and stresses of war and revolution made it spread more widely and penetrate more deeply. In politics it led the conservatives to look back to an idealised vision of a society where authority in Church and State harmonised the discordant elements in society. The novels of Disraeli are an English example of this tendency. The men of the Left wing looked forward, not backward, for their golden age. Utopian socialism, which influenced many young men between 1814 and 1848, was their form of romance; dreams of liberty as well as practical discontent lay behind many of the conspiracies of the restoration period. Both sides laid stress on symbols, the lily and the violet; the white flag and the tricolour and later the red; songs old and new were chanted. Never was a period richer in poetry and drama, and not only in France much of it was shaped by politics.

The essence of the romantic movement was freedom and experiment. Political action needs cohesion and discipline, so both the Right and the Left wing were weakened by the very richness and diversity of their emotions. No sooner did the royalists gain power

1 Bérenger, H.: *Chateaubriand*. Paris, 1931, p. 168.

than divisions appeared. The Royal Family itself was disunited, and Louis' dislike and perhaps jealousy of his brother was a major factor in the division of the royalists into groups which, in turn, prevented the appearance of effective parliamentary parties. Richelieu was naturally a conservative, but he was Louis' man and hated the intriguers who surrounded Artois. It was his principal duty to make peace with the allies; demonstrations of extreme royalism in the White Terror had not only shocked them but had given them an excuse for retaining large forces in France. Though he himself had lost his lands, he was deeply opposed to the idea of revenge. There could be no real harmony on the Right.

The men of the Left, whether liberals or Bonapartists, were in 1815 in a very weak position in Parliament, but they were well aware that their support among the unenfranchised majority of the nation was far greater than that of the royalists. The liberals found their backing among the middle classes and the professional men, so they had the means to play an active part in politics. Decazes, now a powerful influence in the Government, was definitely in favour of a liberal policy. But in what did that policy consist?

In these early days it could only be empirical. The Charter must be maintained in spirit and in letter; order maintained without injustice or oppression; the Press allowed as much freedom as was compatible with stability; a firm line must be taken in support of those who owned confiscated land, and the national debt. Such a programme was one of administration, of day-to-day decisions, not one to evoke enthusiasm. When a theoretical liberal group did appear, that known as the 'Doctrinaires', it proved as impractical as the ultra-royalists. The moderate Left was too divided.

Those who still believed in a republic, or in a restoration of Napoleon, were forced willy-nilly to be conspirators. Plots are the most romantic of all forms of political action, and the least likely to lead to stability of purpose. Political conspiracy was endemic in France between the Empires, and its inevitable consequence was the formation of groups, not of solid political alliances. Parties are formed from combinations of groups, it is true; but the circumstances of the restored monarchy were against any permanence of combination. The group system, not the party, became the tradition of French political life.

Richelieu himself was too preoccupied with peace negotiations to spend much time over discussions with his colleagues. With the Tsar's support he secured a slight modification in the claims of the allies, but even so the treaty was so disadvantageous to France that he hated having to sign it. France, with the exception of some border towns and part of Savoy, retained her frontiers of 1790; she thus lost practically all the gains made by her armies during the Revolution. An army of occupation of 150,000 men was to remain for five years; the cost of food and lodging was to be met by the French and in addition 50 million francs a year was to be paid towards the soldiers' pay. If all the allies agreed, the army might be withdrawn after three years. An indemnity of 700 million francs was to repay the allies for the costs of the campaign of the Hundred Days, and all private claims on the French Government made by foreigners were to be satisfied. The sum of 140 millions in *rentes* was to be set aside to meet these payments; actually this amount proved to be inadequate.

Payments under the treaty came, therefore, to not less than 1,540 millions of francs, allowing 700 million for the cost of the army of occupation. France's total revenue from taxation was in the neighbourhood of 600 millions, out of which her own normal expenditure had to be met. The allies' claims could only be met by borrowing, and to raise so enormous a sum meant inevitably that the terms of the loan would be very disadvantageous. The allies meant France to be weakened financially. They also meant to keep an eye on her and all other possible disturbers of the peace; before they left Paris the Powers made the Holy Alliance for the protection of legitimate governments—only England refusing to join formally—and planned a series of meetings for consultation.

The peace was the main theme in the King's Speech to the Chambers when they met on 7 October, 1815, in a joint session. He warned the Parliament that it would involve a very heavy cost. He promised to sacrifice a portion of his personal revenue and to reduce the salaries of his private staff to alleviate the financial burden. He then spoke of the Charter 'which I thought over with such care before I granted it, to which daily, as I reflect on it, I feel more attachment, and to which all of you, beginning with my own family, will swear obedience. Doubtless, like all human institutions, it is susceptible of improvement, but no one of us must forget that besides the advantage of revision there is danger in innovation.' He asked the Chambers to 'found liberty on respect for the laws' and to 'heal the wounds which have only too deeply lacerated the breast of our country'.

After the King's Speech, and in his presence, the Peers and deputies, beginning with the princes of the blood, took an oath of fidelity to the King, the constitutional charter, and the laws of the kingdom. Two of the ultra-royalist Peers added the proviso 'except in so far as concerns the Catholic religion'. De Vaublanc, who called out the names of those who were members of the Chambers, omitted that of the Duke of Otranto, for he believed that to name Fouché as a Peer of France would lead to a scene.

The new House of Deputies, called by Louis *introuvable* or 'matchless' because of its fervent royalism, was happy and excited. Most of the members thought that the fall of the Talleyrand–Fouché cabinet was a proof that the King had given up his foolish alliance with the men of the Revolution and the Empire. They hated the memory of the Hundred Days, and many in their hearts feared another revolution. Most of them had no political experience, and believed that a restoration of absolute monarchy was not only possible but desirable.

In a letter written to his father on 12 November, 1815, de Villèle, who soon became the leader of a group of moderate royalists, described the Chamber in which he sat. He said there were three main groups; the royalists, who were numerous but not organised; the ex-revolutionaries and Bonapartists; and the pseudo-royalists, who were really in sympathy with the revolutionaries. This last group, he thought, was under the influence of Talleyrand, and included the ministers. 'This party has succeeded in getting itself adopted by the foreign Powers by painting the royalists as extremists and, above all, by stressing their intolerance towards the Protestants in the south. . . . It tries with difficulty to conceal its real scheme, which is to substitute the Duke of Orleans for the lawful heir of the King.'[1] It is interesting to note that this rumour, for which there seems to be no foundation, was already prevalent. Against these intriguers he felt the true royalists to be in a weak position, for they would get no support from the Cabinet or even from the King himself.

It may well be argued that it was this very weakness of the royalists which allowed the constitutional monarchy to survive. At first it seemed as if the pressure of the deputies for revenge would be overwhelming, and had it been successful there might have been disorder amounting to civil war. In the formal reply to the King's Speech, the Chamber of Deputies said: 'It is our duty to ask for your justice against those who imperilled the throne. . . . Those who, even now, are not afraid to parade their rebellion must be delivered to the just severity of the courts of law. . . . We will not speak, sire, to your Majesty of the need of confiding the different branches of your authority only to men whose hands are pure; your ministers' . . . vigilance on this essential point will be all the more easily exercised as events have revealed men's sentiments and thoughts.' To this demand, which in practice meant the dismissal of all officials who had served Napoleon, the King simply replied that the laws which assured public order would be maintained with firmness.

[1] Villèle, Comte de: *Mémoires et correspondance*. Paris, 1888, Vol. I, p. 387.

The tone of the formal reply indicated to the ministers a point of which they were already aware, that their views did not harmonise with those of the majority of the deputies. They tried to make a show of meeting the demands for punishment of 'rebels' by introducing, on 16 October, a bill imposing penalties on people who by seditious cries or other means disturbed public order. The penalties were very mild, and the deputies were indignant, especially as Portalis, a man of seventy who had helped draw up Napoleon's Civil Code, was the Government spokesman in favour of the law. De Villèle made his first parliamentary success when he spoke against it, and the Cabinet withdrew it rather than have it rejected. Decazes then introduced in its place a bill which would allow the arrest and detention without trial of anyone suspected of offences against the persons of the King and his family, or against the security of the State. The vagueness of the offences and the extent of the power given to the Government alarmed moderate men, but limiting amendments introduced by Pasquier were rejected and the bill was passed.

The weakness of the Cabinet was further shown when a bill it introduced to define treason was made much more sweeping by the committee of the House which reported on it. The mere expression of opinions in favour of a radical change in the Government, without any action or any plot, could lead to the writer being deported. The Government was forced to accept the changes, but succeeded in adding to the list of offences the voicing of rumours that the Government intended to violate the rights of holders of confiscated land. This brought the ultra-Right under the ban of a law which made fines, imprisonment and the loss of civil rights the penalties for sedition.

When the bill came before the Peers, Chateaubriand made an impassioned speech against this clause, which, he said, aimed at 'stifling the murmurs which were inseparable from an act of gross injustice, at imposing a silence which would be broken, if men might not speak, by the very stones which served as landmarks for the estates whose new possessors were to be reassured'. As Chateaubriand had lately been rewarded by being made a member of the Council of State, his speech was very imprudent. In spite of it, the Peers carried the Government's bill.

Yet a third penal law set up courts martial (provosts' courts) in the departments, which were empowered to deal with robbery under arms, acts of rebellion, or any menace to royal authority. The judges were army officers and local justices acting together, and there was no appeal from their decisions. Barbé-Marbois, the Minister of Justice, detested this measure, and when before its introduction the King asked when the bill would be ready, he replied: 'Sire, I blush to inform you that it is already prepared.'[1] The passage of this law gave a chance for fierce imprecations against the Bonapartists.

These three acts seemed wholly to do away with the personal liberty of political opponents of the Government. Decazes told the prefects to take no action except in cases of real necessity, though some royalist officials used their powers to persecute their enemies. There were an enormous number of accusations and trials; very many of the accused were acquitted, but the number of people charged was so great as to lead in some areas to a sort of legal White Terror.

Yet Artois' party did not consider the Government nearly active enough in punishing those implicated in the Hundred Days. Clarke, at the War Office, was urged to exclude all Bonapartists from active service. To have done so would have been to leave the army with practically no experienced officers, so an attempt was made to draw up categories in which officers were to be placed according to the date at which they had joined Napoleon and the activity they had shown in his service. There were no less than seven of these classifications, and the distinctions between them were so subtle as to be almost incomprehensible. A commission was set up to make the final list, but after two years it was still struggling and the whole affair was allowed to drop. The only result had been to increase the unrest and discontent in the army, and to destroy any hope that might have been entertained of rapidly and effectively winning for the Bourbons the genuine loyalty of the soldiers of France.

Clarke, the Duke of Feltre, continued the reorganisation of the army which had been begun by St. Cyr, but slowly and with hesitation. He re-established Monsieur's private guard; he made many young royalists officers, but the strength of their regiments was so far below normal that many corps were mere skeleton organisations. The excuse for not enrolling men was that of expense, yet a very costly Swiss Guard was established.

De Vaublanc, as Minister of the Interior, extended the power and strength of the National Guard, of which Artois was made Commander-in-Chief. Local officials were nominated by the Prince, and the members were practically all royalists. He, therefore, had a large number of armed men under his orders, scattered all over the country. Many of the experienced prefects were dismissed and their posts given to men like Bertier, the leader of the Knights of the Faith, who were quite inexperienced in this type of administration. Some of them did good work, but nearly all of them dismissed their subordinate officials, and all over France local functionaries who had lost their posts spread indignation against the Government.

[1] Viel-Castel, op. cit., Vol. IV, p. 202.

The split between Richelieu's government and the majority in the deputies was emphasised by the demand of the royalists for a further list of persons to be excluded from the Cambrai amnesty and the Government's wish to take Fouché's list as final, with the addition of all members of the Bonaparte family who were to be excluded from France. The debates, which went on during November and December, were made much more bitter by the escape of Lavalette. The deputies proposed enormous exceptions to the Government's amnesty, and the 5 per cent *rentes*, that useful political barometer, which had risen to 64 francs for the 100-franc certificate, fell to 59.

On 5 January, 1816, the royalists' amendments were carried, in spite of the Government's opposition. Richelieu suspended the sitting, saying that the King must be informed. After an hour and a half the session was resumed, and the minister reported that, as was his constitutional right, the King would not accept the amendments save for one or two trifling points. In the end the Chamber did reject the amendments, by 184 votes to 175, except one, which enacted that all 'regicides', that is, the surviving members of the assembly that had condemned Louis XVI, were to be banished from France. That clause was carried by a majority that represented the real feeling in the Chamber—by 334 to 32.

Over education the Government went a long way to meet the royalists, though not all the measures passed were carried to their logical conclusion. Many of the professors and lecturers in the University were dismissed and their posts in most cases filled by clerics. The Polytechnic, where scientists and engineers were trained, had shown signs of Bonapartism and was dissolved. Provision was made for a very necessary increase in elementary schools, which were to be supervised by unpaid local committees presided over by the parish priest or, in Protestant districts, by the minister. All schoolmasters had to have two certificates—one from the parish priest and the local mayor testifying to their morals, and one from the University to prove they had passed their qualifying examinations. Poor children would be given free education in the primary schools; others paid fees. The power of the Church was slightly modified by a regulation that members of religious orders could act as teachers only if their methods were approved by a Commission of Public Instruction and their schools were open to inspection.

As the session went on, the fact that Richelieu's government was at loggerheads with the deputies could not be concealed. The Prime Minister wanted to resign; Artois was openly against him; Talleyrand seemed to be planning an alliance with the ultras and attacked the Government; the only support came from an unwelcome source —the foreign diplomats who protested against the royalists' policy.

The King was constantly using his prerogative to pardon men found guilty by the various courts set up under the new laws, or to reduce the penalties inflicted. The trial of Bruce and Wilson for helping in de Lavalette's escape was a great sensation; they could not be acquitted but were sentenced to a term of imprisonment so brief as to infuriate the ultras.

The royalists were now in a peculiar position. In theory they supported royal prerogative; in practice they were demanding that the ministers should be responsible not to the King but to the majority in the assembly. The right of the Chamber to amend bills, according to the Charter subject to the King's approval, was used so as, in effect, to introduce legislation. For example, in January 1816 the Cabinet introduced a humble little bill by which certain sums, put aside for the paying of pensions to the clergy, should become available when the beneficiaries died as an addition to the fund for paying small extra salaries to priests. This would help the poorer clergy without calling on extra money from the taxes. The bill was handed to the appropriate committee and lay with it until April; then the Reporter brought it forward amended out of all recognition. It was now proposed to set aside the interest on 40,000,000 francs in *rentes* for a general increase in clerical salaries.

This was going too far. De Serre made a powerful speech in defence of the King's prerogative, and said this introduction of new laws by pretence of amendment made the Chamber, not the King, sovereign. Violent debates led in the end to the original bill being passed, but with one important amendment—that confiscated Church lands still in the hands of the State should be used for the benefit of the Church. On this note of tension the session ended.

Louis was extremely angry with his matchless parliament. He consented to showing his indignation by dismissing de Vaublanc, the one minister really ultra in his views, and replacing him by Lainé as Minister of the Interior. Lainé was a man of forty-nine, a deputy from Bordeaux. A royalist called him 'a sort of Spartan, a severe and imperious doctrinaire, who saw despotism wherever there was a sceptre'.[1] He was an extremely honest man, and his excellent speeches in the deputies were a great additional strength for the Cabinet. Another change seemed of less importance; old Barbé-Marbois was allowed to resign and was replaced by Dambray. Actually, most of Marbois' work had been done by Guizot, a young man serving his political apprenticeship. It was he who had been mainly responsible for leaving nearly all the judges untouched in their posts.

Alongside their difficulties in legislation, Richelieu's cabinet had

[1] Frénilly, Baron de: *Recollections*. Trans. Lees. London, 1909, p. 280.

been having administrative troubles. The most sensational were those connected with Didier's conspiracy. Paul Didier was a peasant's son who had managed to qualify as a lawyer. He was a royalist and had left France, but returned when Napoleon came into power and had written a pamphlet in praise of the Concordat with Rome. His reward was to be appointed Professor of Law at Grenoble, but his ambition led him into speculation and he was ruined. At the restoration he, like so many others, did not receive the rewards he had hoped for, so he became a Bonapartist. Towards the end of 1815 he went about in the south of France saying that there was an organisation, backed by influential people like Talleyrand, which aimed at ejecting the Bourbons. Who was to replace them depended on the people to whom he was talking; to some he said Orleans, to others Napoleon's son.

In January 1816 he enrolled supporters in Lyons, and plotted to win over the garrison and the workers and seize the town. The plan was betrayed and the conspirators arrested, except Didier himself, who escaped. There were plenty of discontented people to listen to him, so he established himself in Grenoble, where he formed an organisation among the soldiers and the officers on half-pay. The poverty of his supporters was so great that they could not raise 1,000 francs, about £40, to pay for the printing of a proclamation.

The commander of the troops in the district was Lieutenant-General Donnadieu, an ambitious and unscrupulous man. The prefect was the Count de Montlivault, who had been trained under Napoleon but had been demonstrating his royalism by full use of his powers of arbitrary arrest. These two men intensely disliked each other. The police became aware that something was going on, and made some precautionary arrests of suspicious characters. The National Guard was used to support the police, and Donnadieu was very angry, for he said he ought to have been consulted, as the Guard was a quasi-military body.

In spite of the arrests, the rising took place on 5 May, 1816. Little groups of peasants assembled, were fired on by Donnadieu's men as they approached the town, scattered and fled. Six of them were killed and a number arrested. Out of this skirmish Donnadieu made a wonderful report which he sent to the War Office, saying that 'the King's troops had covered themselves with glory' and that the 'bodies of his enemies cover all the roads around Grenoble'. He also told the officers in command at Lyons and at Valence that a terrible battle had gone on for three hours.

When the first four arrested 'rebels' were brought before a court martial, one proved a complete alibi, two were found guilty, and as the evidence against the fourth was not convincing, he was recommended to mercy. This did not suit either Donnadieu or the prefect; the latter wrote to Decazes saying that the courts showed a dangerous leniency, the former went on sending more and more sensational accounts of a vast and dangerous conspiracy.

The Government was seriously alarmed. The reports came at a very unfortunate moment for Richelieu; he had just struck his first blow at the ultras by dismissing de Vaublanc, and now it looked as if they had been right in thinking severity was necessary to prevent revolution. Decazes wrote to all prefects ordering them to be ruthless in putting down disorder, and more troops were sent to the garrisons in the district.

On 9 May, 1816, thirty more of the men who had been arrested were brought up for trial. In spite of the violence of the president of the court martial, the evidence against nine of them was so weak that they were acquitted; five others were recommended to mercy, and the rest were condemned to death. Three of the prisoners were mere boys, the youngest only sixteen. When the condemned men were brought out for execution, two local worthies went to Donnadieu with proof of their innocence, and after investigation they were released. The others were killed. More trials were carried on in an equally haphazard way. Unfortunately, the Government in Paris was wholly deceived; it seemed as if local influence was interfering with the execution of justice, and orders were sent that all sentences of death should be promptly carried out. Donnadieu therefore executed all who were found guilty, even when the court had recommended mercy.

His reward came promptly. He was created a viscount and given 100,000 francs. The prefect was made a member of the Council of State. Then, gradually, the truth leaked out. The General and the prefect began their quarrels again and Donnadieu accused Montlivault of timidity and negligence. In self-defence, Montlivault said that quite unnecessary force was being used by the General.

Didier had escaped into Savoy, but was arrested by the Piedmontese Government and extradited to France. He was brought to Grenoble, and after a private interview with Donnadieu publicly tried on 8 June. At his trial he refused to give any information about his conspiracy, but after his execution Donnadieu declared that, in a last private interview, Didier had told him to warn the King to beware of both Orleans and Talleyrand.

The district had been placed in a 'state of siege', which meant complete military control. Before normal life was restored, twenty-six people had been executed. Gradually the excitement died down, and the Government decided to move Montlivault to another area. He was sent to Calvados on the English Channel, on the west side of the estuary of the Seine, well out of the way of Donnadieu. This department had been under Bertier, of the Knights of the Faith; he had done some good work in finding work for the unemployed as well as annoying many of the local people, and was not at all anxious to leave. Not only the King, but Artois, too, had to ask him to exchange provinces and go off to the poor mountainous region of Isère. He made Montlivault promise not to dismiss his officials, and made a similar promise with regard to the men in his new area.

He was greatly disturbed by the condition of the district. It had been occupied by Austrian and Sardinian troops, who had done much damage; the winter had been severe; more than half the peasants had bought confiscated lands and feared lest they should lose their property. Bertier realised that Donnadieu's policy of repression must lead to further trouble, so he persuaded him to recall the troops he had quartered on the villages. Food was scarce and dear, for speculators had forced prices up. The new prefect arranged for imports of corn at reasonable prices. He secured 300,000 francs from the Government and the King, which he doled out to local authorities for necessary improvements on condition that they themselves contributed equal sums from their own resources. His reports did much to counteract the stories sent by Donnadieu, and when, a year later, trouble broke out in Lyons, Isère remained quiet. But Decazes sent a special police official to the district, and Bertier resented this and quarrelled with him. He also, very improperly, sent copies of his official correspondence to the Duchess of Angoulême. This led to trouble between Decazes and his colleagues, and in 1817 Bertier resigned. It was yet another example of how inexperience and personal feeling prevented men like Bertier from doing lasting service to the King.

One reason why Decazes and other members of the Government had been so easily deceived by Donnadieu was that they had discovered a similar small-scale conspiracy in Paris. This was alarming, for on 17 June, 1816, de Berry, the hope of the Bourbon line, was married to Caroline, grand-daughter of the King of Naples, and Paris was full of visitors and festivities. The new princess was no beauty, but she was young and gay and fully shared her husband's love of parties. The immense cost of all the balls and ceremonies horrified a good many people, who were very much aware of the drain the peace treaty had made and was making on France's resources. The soldiers, too, were gratuitously offended when four new marshals were created as part of the official rejoicings; two of them were so old that they had fought in the war of 1756, one had seen no active service since 1792, and the fourth was Clarke, whose work had been wholly administrative. Experienced officers were being dismissed daily, and watched or even arrested on suspicion that they were plotting against the Government; there were marshals enough already, and these creations seemed to show contempt for the practical soldiers and made them listen to those who talked of revolution.

Richelieu was aware of the danger, and took advantage of the parliamentary recess to issue ordinances meant to check or prevent dangerous moves by the royalists. One abolished a committee which de Vaublanc had set up and empowered to deal with all matters connected with the Church, whether spiritual or temporal. The effect was to make it practically impossible for the ordinary departments of State to deal with any matter affecting the clergy. In future, according to the ordinance, the Grand Almoner, an ecclesiastic, was to deal with all questions of appointments, but financial matters were the province of the Minister of the Interior. Another regulation placed the National Guard under the control of local authorities. This greatly annoyed its Commander-in-Chief, Artois, who looked on it as, to some extent, his private army.

Two other ordinances prohibited the carrying of arms by civilians and the presentation by local bodies of gifts or testimonials to individuals. The aim of this last one was to stop the demonstrations which the royalists had got up in some places in honour of the deputies going home from their labours in the Matchless Parliament.

Such administrative action could do very little to improve the basic trouble: the Government's fear of the royalist majority and that majority's belief that true royalism was being thwarted by timid and disloyal ministers. Partial elections were due in the autumn; Decazes held that even if Government supporters gained many of the seats Richelieu could not hope for a working majority. As the summer went on, the Prime Minister sadly and reluctantly came to agree with him. The decision came from Louis himself; on 14 August he informed his Cabinet that for the safety of the country the parliament he had called 'Matchless' must be dissolved.

Chapter VIII

THE KING AND THE CHARTER

LOUIS' decision was not entirely due, as most people thought, to the influence of his beloved Élie Decazes. He had been deeply wounded by the attitude of the Chamber, which he thought was disrespectful to himself, and was alarmed at the way in which his brother was usurping his own position as the leader of the royalists. He wished to make it clear that he was the working as well as the nominal head of the State, and to indicate that the royalists must follow him if they really believed in monarchy.

A re-election on the lines of the 1815 arrangements would very probably not lead to a serious modification in the character of the assembly, so the Government decided to make full use of the political advantage they had from the vagueness of the Charter on the fundamental question of the method of election and the size of the House. Louis had increased the number of deputies in 1815; now it was decided to revert to the 1814 number of 258. The double method of election was maintained, but the additional nominated voters of 1815 were withdrawn from the electoral colleges. The age of deputies was again to be forty; the hot-headed younger men were to be left out. A royal ordinance announcing these changes was published on 5 September, 1816; the local colleges were to meet on 25 September and the departmental colleges to make the final choice of deputies on 4 October.

The interval between Louis' announcement to his ministers of his decision and the publication of what amounted to a *coup d'état* had been a very difficult one, and it is most creditable that none of the ministers, some of whom were very dubious about the whole scheme, let the secret out. Decazes had worked furiously, collecting information from the provinces about public opinion, and keeping Louis up to his decision. He was helped in this by a History of the Session of 1815–16 written by Fiévée, an extreme royalist, which applauded the conduct of the ultras, especially on those points which had most annoyed the King.

Artois was horrified and astounded at his brother's coup; he was only told of the dissolution late on 4 September; Richelieu, who had the thankless task of informing him, found that he had already retired to bed, and had great difficulty in preventing him

6   81

from rushing round to drag Louis out of his bed to hear his protests. The Duchess of Angoulême said nothing but looked volumes; her husband and de Berry were on the whole rather pleased. Public opinion outside Court circles seemed very favourable; in some of the provinces there were public demonstrations of joy. Representatives of the allied Powers expressed their satisfaction. Decazes was justifiably regarded as the originator of the plan and was praised or blamed accordingly.

Electioneering began at once with the greatest vigour. Some of the royalists went so far as to write to the prefects saying that the dissolution was due to foreign pressure, and that the King and his family would like the former deputies to be re-elected. Lainé intensely disliked using Government influence in elections, so Decazes secured the King's approval for a circular letter he sent to the prefects, asking them to get support for moderate men from all officials; no one who belonged to a secret society should be chosen, but only those who truly supported both the King and the Charter. A number of political prisoners were released, to show the Government's good intentions.

Two of the election manifestoes had more than temporary importance, Chateaubriand's 'Monarchy according to the Charter' and Guizot's 'On Representative Government'. From the modern point of view, the royalist seems to take the more liberal line, and the liberal the more royalist. Chateaubriand's main points were that the Cabinet, not the King, was responsible for policy and was, therefore, dependent on a majority in the Chamber. The King had a personal right of veto and of dissolution, but his name should not be used to win support for his advisers. He demanded freedom of the Press, the abolition of the issue of ordinances having the force of law, and the ending of a special ministry of police. On the other hand, he claimed great powers for a hereditary House of Peers, and he attacked the Government for depending on men who had served illegitimate rulers like the republicans and Napoleon. He realised that the material results of the Revolution could never be destroyed, the land sales for instance, but its morality was anti-Christian and must never be defended.

Guizot's was a hasty pamphlet rushed out in reply to Chateaubriand. He was already at work on a book on political liberty, in which he attacked courts martial and such things, but which he was never able to complete. His immediate duty was to defend the King, so he was forced to support the responsibility of the Cabinet to the King and its independence, and to urge that the duty of the Chamber was to co-operate and avoid factious opposition. He was on stronger ground in criticising some aspects of the ultras' policy.

Louis was extremely angry with Chateaubriand, and Decazes took the very unwise step of attempting to suppress his book. It appeared on 18 September, 1816, and on the excuse that some copies had been sold before it had been officially deposited with the authorities, the police seized the stocks in the printers' hands. Richelieu and the more conservative members of the Cabinet disapproved of Decazes' action, but the King, though agreeing that his Minister of Police had made a mistake, was so angry with Chateaubriand for indicating that he himself should have no control over policy, that he told his ministers that he would 'strike him from the list of Ministers of State as I struck out Fouché. We will see if he is flattered by the comparison.'[1]

To lose his honorary post, with its very useful annual income, was a tremendous blow for the author. It also indicated how wholeheartedly Louis was behind his Cabinet, and so probably had more effect on the voters than had Guizot's pamphlet. The election results were certainly as good as could have been hoped. Paris and the larger towns on the whole chose moderate middle-class men who would support Richelieu, and the eastern and central districts and part of the north had a majority of Government representatives. In the south and west the ultra-royalists predominated. On the whole, the Government could count on a majority of forty to fifty.

On 3 November, 1816, the new Chamber met. The King's Speech contained an adulation of the Charter. There was a good deal of bickering over the conduct of the elections, both sides with justification accusing each other of bringing improper pressure to bear on electors and officials. In this dispute Chateaubriand joined; in the House of Peers he introduced a motion to ask the King to investigate the conduct of the election. No representative Chamber would ever allow such a procedure to be initiated by the Peers; by such irresponsible behaviour Chateaubriand greatly lessened his chances of success as a politician.

Richelieu now devoted his time to negotiations with the allies; his main aim was to induce them to withdraw their armies and lessen the financial and the psychological burdens of France. Conduct of domestic business fell more and more into the hands of Decazes. Although his position in the Cabinet was a minor one, and he had no wide support in the Chamber, his close association with the King made him important, and he had a shrewd mind and great energy. He was convinced that the right direction for the Government was slightly to the Left; that is, it must try to win over the theoretical liberals of the new middle class, and remove the real grievances that lay behind the plots and conspiracies. Yet to abandon the restrictions

[1] Viel-Castel, op. cit., Vol. V, p. 251.

on the freedom of the Press and on political activity that had been made law by the Matchless Parliament would benefit the royalists rather than the constitutionalists. The Government's programme was, therefore, rather timid; it promised in the King's Speech a new electoral law, a new Press law, a modification of the laws with regard to individual liberty, and one new law, to be introduced first in the House of Peers, to permit ecclesiastical establishments to receive gifts of land under certain conditions.

There were a few changes in the administrative personnel, some ultra-royalist prefects being dismissed, but nothing like a wholesale purge. Though the ultra-royalists would be sure to remain implacable enemies of the ministry, there was a real hope of gaining the support of the more moderate and forming a solid centre party. The financial situation, complicated by a bad harvest, was difficult, and it was obviously sensible not to raise any controversial question that could be avoided.

The project of a new electoral law was, however, bound to cause opposition. The bill introduced on 28 November, 1816, had been drafted by Decazes, Guizot and two distinguished liberal theorists, Royer-Collard and Barante. The system of indirect election was not really appropriate for a House of 258 members, and had also led to a great deal of intrigue. It was, therefore, proposed that the department should elect its members directly, the number of seats to be filled depending on the number of voters in the constituency. The 300 francs tax qualification was retained; voters must be thirty years old. It was calculated that about 200,000 men would have the vote. All the electors were to meet in one electoral college in each department; its president would be nominated by the King.

A peculiar method of voting, which was frequently used later in France, was evolved, that known as the *scrutin de liste*. Each elector wrote out a list of the names of as many candidates as there were seats to be filled; these lists were checked and the votes given to each candidate added up by official scrutineers. Any candidate who received a number of votes equal to one more than a quarter of the electors present, and one more than a half of the total votes cast, was immediately declared elected, and the number of votes cast for each candidate announced. If, after the first vote had been taken, not enough of the candidates had received the necessary quota of votes to fill all the seats, then a second *tour de scrutin* was taken. This time, electors who saw that one of the men whose name they had put on their list had no chance at all, would leave him out in favour of a more hopeful candidate. A third vote could be taken in the same way if necessary; after that, a simple majority of votes cast was sufficient for election.

For example, say there were 5,000 voters present and voting in a college which had to elect four deputies, and there were ten candidates, Messrs A, B and C, royalists; D, E, F and G, centre party; H, J and K, Left-wing liberals. Of these only two got in at the first vote, A, a royalist, and E, a Government candidate. Two seats remained to be filled. A royalist voter who had originally put A, B, C and D (the most acceptable to him of the central group) on his list would study the results of the first vote. C had got so few votes that it was clear he had no chance; for the second vote, he would therefore write down B and D. To his disappointment, neither reached the quota, but H, a liberal, did. As D, the centre man, was much nearer the quota than B, the royalist, he might now decide to vote for D alone, lest J, who had secured quite a number of votes, should be successful.

Clearly a plan like this could lead to a far more correct representation of the wishes of the electors than if they had been divided into four single member constituencies, with a simple majority vote, as in England. On the other hand, it gave a great deal of room for intrigue; for promises to be made by candidates who were near the top in the first lists; for withdrawals by weaker ones in return for some favour, and so on.

Opposition to the bill came from both Right and Left. A valid criticism was that as the list of voters was drawn up by the prefect, and the president of the electoral college was a Government nominee, there was all too much opportunity for pressure by the Government. Fiévée wrote that the law could easily be shortened; it could read: 'In conformity with the constitution, the King nominates the presidents of the electoral colleges; the president nominates the officials; the officials nominate the deputies; the voters are witnesses.' The real objection of the royalists to the new law was that it placed far too much power in the hands of the middle classes. The moderates and many of the liberals believed in the system of double election, which they thought led to stability. In addition to serious criticism there was a flood of futile and irresponsible talk which actually helped Richelieu's government, and gave Lainé, the Minister of the Interior, an opportunity to score a great success in a really statesmanlike speech. Two amendments were made; one that the scrutineers and officials of the electoral colleges should be chosen by the electors, not nominated; the other that there should be no payment of deputies. The law was then carried on 8 January, 1817, by 132 to 100; some of those who usually supported the Government had abstained from voting.

Its passage through the Peers seemed doubtful. Louis forbade the members of his family to vote against it, and ordered his courtiers to support it. The ultra-royalists were rightly indignant at this kind of personal pressure, but as usual they, as nominal believers in the privileges of the monarch, were awkwardly placed. The law was carried by 95 to 70.

Richelieu's cabinet was strengthened by the resignation of Dambray, who had held two offices, that of Chancellor, which involved presiding over the House of Peers, and that of Minister of Justice. He had for a long time been unhappy about the trend of policy, for he was far more to the Right than his colleagues, and had also been quite incapable of carrying out his duties in a satisfactory way. He kept his position as Chancellor, for he was a success as President of the Peers, but his post as Minister of Justice was given to Pasquier on 19 January, 1817. Pasquier (1767–1862) had been elected Speaker of the Deputies; he was replaced in this position by de Serre. He was a clear and facile speaker, upright and sincere, not closely in touch with any political group but generally respected. He had been Minister of Justice in 1815 and had then employed Guizot as his assistant. He would have liked to do so again, but by now Guizot was thought to be too much of a liberal; his religion was also a disadvantage, for he was a Protestant and had been very active in the defence of his co-religionists against the ultras.

Pasquier was a useful man for a Government trying to work a constitution which two groups of opponents both wished to overturn. Had the attack come only from Artois and his friends, or only from the republicans and Bonapartists, life would have been much easier. Many of the moderate men, on whom the Cabinet had to rely, intensely disliked the powers of arbitrary arrest and summary trial given by the legislation of 1816, yet emergency powers were really felt to be necessary when at any moment either Left or Right might raise a riot or plot a rising. In February 1817 the Government carried a modification, not a repeal, of the 1816 laws, though both on the Right and on the Left there were demands for greater change. The new law made it possible for the power of arbitrary arrest to be used only in virtue of an order signed by both the Prime Minister and the Minister of Police. Wholesale arrests of suspects by excited local officials, therefore, came to an end.

Corvetto, the Chancellor of the Exchequer, had ever since the dissolution been studying France's economic position, with the help of a strong committee. His aim was to have a long-term financial plan and hope that subsequent governments would adhere to it; he wanted a substantial annual surplus to be used for the reduction of the mass of debt. There was a considerable 'floating' debt due to the failure of recent governments to pay their creditors; this he proposed to meet by giving them certificates of a permanent debt which they could, if they chose, sell for cash on the Stock Exchange. This would bring the interest due on the debt up to 151 million francs a year.

Taxes had to be increased; Corvetto raised the direct taxes sharply by adding 'centimes' to the standard rate, and he also put further duties on beer and wine. The King and his family again surrendered a portion of their incomes; the salaries of the highest-paid officials were cut. Even so, he feared there would be a deficit on the year, so he proposed to transfer to the managers of the Sinking Fund (*Caisse d'amortissement*), used to reduce the debt, about a quarter of the forest lands owned by the State, which they could sell if they thought right.

Corvetto pointed out that in a few years things would be much better; the foreign armies would have gone and gradually the immense sum paid in pensions to soldiers and officials would diminish. The report on the budget was on the whole favourable, though cuts were made in the sums voted for the army and navy. The cost of the bureaucracy was attacked in the debates, but it was clear that the real purpose of the speakers was not so much to reduce expenses as to lessen the power of the Government.

One major and contentious piece of legislation concerned the Press. Discussion of this is postponed to Chapter IX, p. 96, as it seems simpler to deal with all the laws and the nature of the newspaper Press in France together.

On the whole, things were going better for the Cabinet than the ultras had expected. The friends of Artois were alarmed at the extent of Decazes' influence over the King, and suspected him of being more radical in his views than he was. Various attempts were made to bring in a rival; Louis' old favourite, de Blacas, came to Paris from his embassy in Rome in April 1817, but the King ordered him to return. Direct action having failed, the ultras tried to exploit the disorders that occurred in the summer of 1817 when a shortage of corn led to bread riots in many places. The courts dealt with them severely, and imposed long sentences of imprisonment and even sometimes death.

The most sensational of the disturbances was in Lyons. It was, to some extent, a deliberate imitation of the events at Grenoble the year before. The commander of the garrison, General Canuel, was an ambitious man who had been a violent revolutionary, but in 1815 became an equally violent royalist. He had seen with envy the money and honours which Donnadieu had won and was waiting his chance to exploit any opportunity that might be offered by the local discontent. He used some of his subordinates to spy on the workers; that they acted as *agents provocateurs*, encouraging demonstrations, is not very likely, though it was believed at the time that they did, for there was plenty of inflammable material in Lyons. The silk trade had been badly hit by the general fall in demand for luxury goods, and bread was in short supply and dear.

After the great Corpus Christi processions on 8 June, 1817, the people remained in the streets, demanding food and work. One of Canuel's officers was thought to be spying on them; he was chased and killed by a pistol shot. Several of the men of the National Guard had arms, and the situation was really alarming, especially as many people had come in from the neighbouring villages. Canuel was doing his duty in quelling the riots, but went far beyond it in the days that followed. He reported a dangerous Bonapartist conspiracy; set up a court martial, refusing to allow the local police to take their proper share in the investigations, and for three whole months went on arresting people. In all 155 men were tried; 11 put to death, 26 deported, and others sentenced to forced labour or prison. Eventually the Government grew suspicious. Marmont, Napoleon's marshal, was sent to investigate early in September and promptly restored order. In his reports he indicated that the danger had been greatly exaggerated and that quite unnecessary severity had been used.

That was not the end of the Canuel affair. The Artois party was very anxious to defend him and to accuse the Government of being dangerously weak in dealing with revolutionaries. Books were written which blamed the royalists for working up a panic; Canuel replied and libelled one of Marmont's officers. While this Press campaign was going on, a year later, the Government was informed on 22 June, 1818, by a royalist officer, that Canuel, Donnadieu and others were plotting to kidnap the whole Cabinet. The story seemed fantastic, but on 25 June a similar report was made quite independently by another officer, who had been, so he said, asked to co-operate in the adventure.

Richelieu was greatly embarrassed. A major scandal would, he feared, cause the allies to draw back from the negotiations which he had nearly completed for the withdrawal of the occupying armies. His hand was forced by a publication of the story in English newspapers. On 3 July some of the people named by the informers were arrested, but Canuel fled. Everyone took this as a confession of guilt, so he decided to surrender to the police on 22 July, declaring that the accusations were the work of his personal enemies.

What Richelieu and Decazes most feared was that a thorough investigation of the charges would implicate close friends of Artois, possibly even Monsieur himself. That they would go to great lengths to get rid of the Government was shown in August 1818 by the famous Secret Note written by de Vitrolles and sent to the allied diplomats. It painted a black picture of revolutionary movements, encouraged by the feebleness of the Cabinet, and urged the allies to insist that the King should dismiss his ministers and replace them by royalists. Similar letters had been sent in 1816 and 1817, but this came when it seemed that the allies would withdraw unless they thought that it was unsafe to leave France open to a revolution.

Decazes acted promptly. He sent a copy of Vitrolles' Secret Note to the London *Times*, with which he was in touch. The publication shocked not only foreigners but Louis XVIII himself. It was a direct attack, he thought, on the very principles of kingship for subjects to try to get his chosen advisers dismissed through foreign influence. He dismissed de Vitrolles from his position as Minister of State. Richelieu's government was strengthened, not weakened, by this attempt to dislodge it, which met with condemnation from all moderate people.

The Canuel case dragged on; the preliminary investigations were not completed till early in October. Another royalist plot was reported; the ultras said this was an invention of Decazes, who had bribed one of Chateaubriand's servants to bring him the contents of the waste-paper baskets, and had misinterpreted a passage in a letter from Donnadieu. The police made enquiries and found out that Canuel, who was a free agent while enquiries were taking place, and Donnadieu had been meeting mysterious people on a terrace in the gardens of the Tuileries. Decazes arrested four people, who swore that all they had been discussing was a method of preparing charcoal; this nonsense strengthened his belief in the story which had reached him, that the two generals were planning to kidnap, not the Cabinet this time, but the King himself.

Richelieu strongly opposed a thorough investigation of what became known as the Tuileries Gardens Plot, and eventually Canuel was brought to trial and discharged for lack of evidence. At the time, and even by modern historians, two opposing views were taken of these peculiar incidents. One was that there were no real royalist plots at all; Decazes invented them to separate Louis from his brother and his associates. The other was that ambitious and irresponsible men were actually planning these childish schemes, and that it would have been better not to be so discreet but bring all the facts before the public, no matter who was implicated. It seems likely that there is something to be said for both views; in the state of nervous anxiety and irritation and personal antipathies that prevailed, Decazes probably did exaggerate reports which may not have been wholly true, and men like Canuel and Donnadieu may have discussed wild romantic schemes with no likelihood of really carrying them out. Whatever the truth, Richelieu's worries were greatly increased by all this mystification and gossip. He was a convinced royalist and very well aware that Monsieur might at any moment become King, for Louis' health was not at all good. To implicate him in public scandals was not possible; even if he were completely innocent, no one would believe it. For Decazes, too, one must feel sympathy; he was struggling to prevent disorder by conciliation and wanted to use his enemies' follies to discredit them, but perhaps it was not very wise or dignified to use foreign newspapers in his defence.

The divergence in the views of Richelieu and Decazes, shown over these incidents, was nothing new; it had been clearly emerging, almost from the beginning of their companionship. Changes in the Cabinet in 1817 had made their disharmony almost public. The inefficient old royalist, Dubouchage, had resigned from the Ministry of the Navy in June 1817. To everyone's surprise, Gouvion St. Cyr took his place, not Molé, an efficient administrator with liberal tendencies, who had hoped for the office. St. Cyr, though an aristo-crat by birth, had shown liberal tendencies and it was plain that Decazes wanted to have him as Minister of War to carry on the reforms he had begun as a member of the Talleyrand–Fouché ministry in 1815. Richelieu wanted to keep Clarke, the Duke of Feltre, at the War Office, not because he was efficient, but because he was one of the few men of the extreme Right in the Cabinet. He would have been wiser to give way at once, for Louis was backing Decazes, and in September Clarke was induced to resign and the re-shuffle took place. St. Cyr went to his natural place at the War Office, and Molé stepped into the Navy. The suggestion of intrigue which this sort of manipulation gave rise to led to endless gossip and exacerbated the divisions in the Government, preventing frank dis-cussion and leading to some important business being handled very clumsily.

One such matter of great complexity, but on which a wise settle-ment was vital for the peace of the country, was that of the relation of the Church in France to Rome. The ultra-royalists wished Napo-leon's Concordat repealed, but the Pope did not. Modifications in the Napoleonic arrangements were, however, necessary, and one of de Blacas' main duties as Ambassador in Rome was to discuss them with the Papacy. By June 1817 a plan was agreed on; the main practical point was that a number of new bishoprics were to be created, and therefore the boundaries of existing sees modified. The 1802 Concordat had fixed the number of dioceses at 50; the new plan was for 92.

The Pope selected 32 men to fill some of the new sees, many of them had been forced to emigrate during the Revolution. When the scheme, with which Louis was delighted, was brought to the Cabinet, Pasquier pointed out that relations between Church and State could not now be settled merely by the King and the Pope; the repeal of some of Napoleon's legislation was necessary to implement the scheme, and money must be voted for the bishops' stipends and expenses. Foreign newspapers got hold of the text of the agreement, and French constitutionalists were very angry at the King's independent action.

It is likely that the feeling caused over the Concordat partly accounted for the swing to the Left when one fifth of the deputies had to be elected in September 1817. In the department of the Seine Lafayette and other revolutionaries appeared as candidates, but clever intrigue led to the election of five supporters of the Government and three men who were of the Left but not extremists. In those departments which had to vote, the ultra-Right lost ten seats and the Left gained twelve or fifteen—three of the new members might support the Government, but twelve would certainly oppose it. So far as voting power went, Richelieu's cabinet had much the same strength in the Chamber, but Decazes' view that the middle class was moving to the Left and the Government should follow it seemed to be justified. When in November 1817 the Chamber met, the Right had about eighty members and the Left about twenty-five, but the centre was not a solid party, rather a collection of groups, so the Government could not wholly rely on its support.

When in the spring of 1818 the bills for modifying the Concordat with Rome came before the deputies, they were opposed both by the Ultramontane Catholics, who wished the Pope to have greater powers, and the Gallicans, who wished him to have less. The folly of Richelieu in allowing matters to go so far as they had in the summer was now very apparent, for there were thirty-two bishops in Paris waiting for their sees, and they were centres of agitation. A violent Press campaign and pamphlet warfare began; wrecking amendments to the Government's bills were proposed from the Right and from the Left. In despair, the Cabinet withdrew the measures in March. After much argument, some of the waiting bishops were appointed to sees that fell vacant; the rest were absorbed when thirty new bishoprics were authorised by a more ecclesiastically-minded Chamber in 1822.

The Government was more successful over the army. In November 1817 St. Cyr introduced his plan for the control and recruitment of the army. There were two new features. One was the reintroduction of conscription in a very much modified form. The bulk of the forces was to be of volunteers, but should recruitment prove inadequate men of twenty years old could be called up to a number not exceeding 40,000. Lots were to be drawn, and substitutes could be provided by the unlucky if they chose. The second point, which roused great opposition from the Right, was the regulation of the appointment and training of officers. An Officers' Training College was to be created, and no one could have a commission unless he had served in this college or as a non-commissioned officer in the army for two years. Promotion could only be attained by an officer after he had held his existing rank for at least four years; at least two thirds of all promotions were to be by seniority. These regulations hit hard at the young royalists, who had been given commissions without any training and promoted over the heads of professional soldiers. After a magnificent speech by St. Cyr, written for him by Guizot, the law was carried in February 1818 by the deputies. It was very doubtful if it would pass the Peers.

It was known that the allies disliked a bill which would lead to France having a much more efficient army. Artois was so angry about it that he wrote to his brother, asking him to dismiss Decazes, whom he blamed for St. Cyr's appointment. Louis very much resented his heir's intervention. He himself did not at all like St. Cyr's scheme, for it greatly diminished his own prerogative of appointing officers, but he determined to stand up for his Cabinet. Some of the peers most bitterly opposed to the bill held positions about the Court, and had to attend the King on the drive which he took every evening. Louis deliberately prolonged his drives to extend beyond the times of the Peers' debates; the courtiers had fast horses ready saddled so that they could gallop to the Chamber as soon as they were free. It was rather a silly business, but it served its purpose. Louis did not himself actually ask his courtiers to change their opinions or abstain from voting; he merely showed his own wishes by handicapping them. In the end the bill was carried in the Upper House on 9 March, 1818, and remained the basis of French army law for many years.

The National Guard, which was, as it were, halfway between a military and a police force, was also reorganised. Decazes got the King, by a royal ordinance issued in September 1818, to put the Guard under the control of the prefects, and confine membership to payers of direct taxes and their sons. Artois, as Commander-in-Chief, had recruited it largely from his own friends as officers and their dependants as ordinary members. It was certainly not right for a national force to be a sort of private army of a party, but Decazes' plan made the National Guard a purely middle-class institution. Angoulême persuaded his father not to make a public demonstration of his indignation, but Decazes had put an end to any hopes of reconciliation that Richelieu might still cherish.

Elaborate preparations were made for the partial elections of 1818. All Government officials were told to support candidates of the centre, and many men who had been exiled for their part in the Hundred Days were allowed to return. The extreme Left organised a regular electoral campaign, setting up committees and choosing candidates in the departments where elections were due. The Right started a new paper, the *Conservateur*, full of praise for the old France and attacks on the Revolution of 1789. Scores of pamphlets appeared.

The results were sensational. Of the fifty vacant seats, fifteen had been occupied by the ultras, and not one of them was held. Half of all the new deputies belonged to the Left, and Lafayette and Manuel (1755–1827), both of whom had played conspicuous parts in the Revolution, were elected.

Richelieu was horrified. He realised that the Government of which he was the nominal head had now slipped entirely beyond his control, and this greatly lessened his pride and happiness over the success of his long-drawn negotiations with the European Powers, which were just concluding. He had had two aims: first and foremost to relieve his country of the terrible burden of the occupation; secondly, to regain for France a position of equality with the other Powers. Under the Treaty of 1815, it was possible for the armies to be withdrawn in 1818, provided that all sums due for reparations and debts had been paid, and that the Powers were satisfied that France would remain a peaceful member of the European community.

The allies' own financial claims had been reasonable; the trouble had been over the clause which said that debts due to private persons must be discharged. From all over Europe claims had poured in. Quite reasonable demands, for goods requisitioned and damage done by Napoleon's armies, by themselves came to an enormous total, and were quite impossible to check. In addition, all sorts of fantastic bills were sent in for sums alleged to be owing by French governments as far back as the seventeenth century. With great skill and patience, Richelieu persuaded the allies to agree to the payment of a lump sum which they themselves would distribute to the creditors. The probability was that the distribution would be unjust, but there was no other workable plan.

The convention was signed in Paris on 25 April, 1818. The debts were to be discharged from a fund of 265 million francs, the equivalent of over £10,000,000. One hundred millions were to be covered by the transfer of French *rentes* at current market prices; this meant an annual payment of over six and a half million francs to the persons controlling the fund or to any people to whom they sold the shares.

The other 165 million was to be paid in cash in monthly instalments. This huge sum could only be raised with the help of international bankers; after trying a number of firms, Richelieu got the best offer from the firm of Hope and Baring. The terms were harsh, but the strongest bank would find difficulty in the regular provision of so large an amount of gold currency. Hope and Baring were to be given 5 per cent stock, but paid the Government only 67 francs for each 100-franc certificate, although at that time they were selling on the open market for over 75 francs. In addition they were to receive an annual payment for their services in transferring the money. The result was an addition of well over 600,000 francs a year to the interest on the national debt.

Napoleon's adventure of the Hundred Days had cost France very dear in cash as well as in political exacerbations. Before they left in November 1818 the armies of occupation had cost 633 million francs. The indemnities and other claims of the Powers amounted in all to over 1,200 millions. Over 1,800,000,000 francs had been added to the debt, and it seemed as if France would have to go on paying 5 per cent on this huge sum for ever; so much other debt had also to be repaid that it seemed unlikely that it could ever be extinguished.

Yet Richelieu had scored a real triumph. When the foreigners left, France was at last free; ordinary people could live without the constant reminder of defeat and the constant drain on provisions. The only grumblers were some of the French financiers, who were envious of the profits made by foreign bankers and who chose to ignore the simple fact that all their resources added together would not have been considered by the allies adequate security for regular payments. In their jealousy they started speculating during the summer of 1818, buying *rentes* till, at the end of August, the price stood at 80. Then many holders began to sell, and the price dropped to 71 within a month. It was an odd example of the extremely selfish and short-sighted attitude of many Frenchmen at this period.

Richelieu could be happy when the Duke of Angoulême made a very successful tour of the country when the foreign troops had gone. He could also register a diplomatic victory when France was admitted a member of the Congress of Europe, attending meetings on equal terms with the victors. As Foreign Minister he had earned the gratitude of the nation. As Prime Minister he was a deeply disappointed man. He disliked St. Cyr, the Minister for War; he felt that the whole trend of policy was wrong. When he returned to Paris on 28 November, 1818, he planned the reorganisation of his Cabinet.

Corvetto, the Finance Minister, was forced to retire by a Stock Exchange crisis caused by speculation. Baron Louis seemed the obvious successor, but Richelieu felt he was too closely linked with the Napoleonic system, and chose Roy (1764–1847), who had made a fortune in business and, as a deputy, had shown as Reporter on the budget a thorough understanding of finance. But no changes of one or two men could overcome the fundamental divergence in outlook between Richelieu and Decazes, who, owing to his friendship with the King and to Richelieu's absence, had really been responsible for policy. Throughout December the crisis dragged on. When one reads the memoirs of the men who took part in all the arguments, one feels that both Richelieu and Decazes behaved well; they were thinking of their duty, not of personal advantage. On 21 December, 1818, a series of resignations was laid before the King. Louis was distressed; he deeply loved Decazes, but he believed that Richelieu must continue in charge of foreign policy. Weeping, he agreed to send his Élie to St. Petersburg as ambassador. Four days later Richelieu reported that he had not been able to secure enough men whom he thought able and who would join him, and therefore could not form a government. With genuine reluctance, Louis accepted his resignation.

Decazes was most anxious not to appear as the supplanter of his Prime Minister, but Louis insisted that he should be a member of the new Cabinet. Dessoles, a man of moderate views and no remarkable ability, took Richelieu's double position as Prime Minister and Foreign Minister. Decazes at last secured the post he had long wanted, the Ministry of the Interior. St. Cyr remained at the War Office. Roy and Pasquier both refused to join, so Baron Louis went to the Exchequer and de Serre became Minister of Justice, clearly indicating that the new Cabinet would be based a little to the Left of the centre.

Chapter IX

THE SOFA PARTY AND THE PRESS

THE policy of the Cabinet that took office at the beginning of 1819 was very largely directed by a small group of men, known as the Doctrinaires or, more rudely, as the Sofa Party, for they were supposed all to be able to sit upon a single sofa. To stress their small number rather than their doctrines was really more apt, for though all members of the group were keen political theorists and had somewhat similar views and principles, they never held any very explicit political doctrines.

Royer-Collard was one of its principal figures. Born in 1763, the events of the Revolution had made him a firm believer in the monarchic principle, but he never joined any royalist plots. He confined himself to reading and thinking; his speeches were read and were more like a professor's lectures than a politician's arguments. He believed in a constitution with an elected parliament; he distrusted the power and traditions of an aristocracy. He was—and he knew it—wholly without capacity for practical politics, yet his absolute sincerity and his eloquence made him immensely influential.

De Serre, the new Minister of Justice, was thirteen years younger. He was more emotional and also more practical than Royer-Collard; he realised the inconvenience of much of the parliamentary procedure developed in 1814 and 1815 and as President of the Chamber of Deputies tried to get it modified so as to strengthen the Government's control over the process of legislation. His plan, which would have brought the French system nearer to the English, was rejected; De Broglie thought this was due to a 'spirit of routine', but it was more likely that the deputies were anxious rather to weaken the Cabinet than to strengthen it. De Serre was an eloquent and effective speaker, not reading from a script but improvising, which was very unusual and very much admired.

Camille Jordan, who died in 1821, was a very kind-hearted man and very popular, but quick-tempered and sarcastic—he was called 'the angry sheep'. The Duke de Broglie (1785–1870) was a good deal younger; he came from an old and famous family, and his father, though he had been very liberal in his views, had been guillotined in 1794. The boy escaped to Switzerland, but returned to France and

96

entered government service in 1809, though he disapproved of Napoleon's ambitious policy. He came into prominence by speaking in Ney's favour during his trial, and as he had married a daughter of the famous Madame de Staël, was hated by the royalists as a traitor to the aristocracy. He had had practical experience, yet seemed to be as abstract in his theorising as the others. Guizot (1787–1874) was a Protestant and had acted as a tutor in a German family. He was genuinely interested in history and became a professor; Royer-Collard was professor of history at the Sorbonne and Guizot was much influenced by him. He got his first lessons in politics under Pasquier in the 1814 government, but was still predominantly a theorist. He was not exactly a member of the Sofa Party, but was closely in touch with it.

Charles de Rémusat, the clever son of a lady famous for her writing and her literary influence, wrote some verses to describe the feelings of a young man listening to one of the Doctrinaires. Here is a very rough and inelegant translation of part of the poem.

The Doctrinaire.   '. . . In following our flag,
          Speak that the whole world may hear;
      Speak loud, and long, and spread the light,
          But take great care it's not too clear.

      Study metaphysics well
          Without failing, every morn;
      But all year long, refrain from deed;
          Practice is a thing we scorn.

      Criticise all theories
          That you may live long and free;
      Of our abstract brotherhood
          These are the commandments three. . . .'

The follower.   '. . . Sir, when can we hope to see,
      Do you think, our reign begin?'
Doctrinaire.   'Sir, we rule the future, we!'
The follower.   'But there are no signs as yet.'
Doctrinaire.   'The time's not ripe, so just endure.
      'Twill come.' 'But when?' 'I do not know,
          And that is why I am so sure.'

One of the urgent tasks for the new Cabinet was to deal with the newspaper Press, and it was in this field that the Sofa Party left its lasting mark on French law. Since the first years of the Revolution, France had been subjected to a series of restrictions, of greater or less severity, on newspapers and also on pamphlets, books, and at times even medals, pictures and statuettes; the Charter had promised

7

freedom of the expression of opinion, but at first sight it seems that a
narrow-minded and tyrannical government was breaking its pledge.

There were, however, three main difficulties to be overcome
before France could have a free and yet a responsible Press.[1] A
major one was the French legal system and tradition. There was no
effective machinery for the development of the law of libel, and no
recognised tradition of what was and what was not reasonable comment on moral or political issues. Secondly, the newspaper Press
was, during the period 1814–48, largely owned and written by
irresponsible people who attacked the Government's policy but had
no constructive ideas. Thirdly, France's position in Europe,
especially before 1818 and round about 1830, was dangerously weak,
and the disorder that might be worked up by newspaper campaigns
might have serious consequences.

The daily newspaper was a novelty; even less frequent periodicals
were not common before 1789. The first years of the Revolution had
led to a spate of violent journalism, and papers were looked on as a
vehicle for disseminating propaganda, not news of events. Only one
paper founded.in 1789 survived; it did not come to an end until
1869. This was the *Moniteur*, which became an official organ for the
Government and printed laws, regulations, appointments and, after
1814, a summary of debates in the Chamber of Deputies. It had no
rival in endurance; all the other newspapers were ephemeral, lasting
often for a few weeks or months, rarely for years. They consisted, as
a rule, of a single sheet, badly printed on a hand press; only one
Paris newspaper in 1823 had the use of one of the new steam presses.
They were circulated by post to subscribers, not sold in shops. In
the provinces there were a few local papers, mainly concerned with
market reports and so forth, but the political Press centred on Paris.

Newspapers were expensive. A stamp duty was charged, as it was
in England, and postage costs had to be included in the subscription
rates. Only the well-to-do bought newspapers, though in the
eighteen-twenties some cafés and inns began to take in journals for
their customers and a few reading-rooms were opened. Their circulation was therefore limited, and their finances correspondingly
shaky. The *Moniteur* itself had only 4,000 subscribers in 1816, and
it was taken by all the upper ranks of government officials; three
years later it had lost a quarter of its purchasers. The most famous of
the royalist papers, the *Conservateur*, to which Chateaubriand and
other well-known writers contributed, claimed to have 25,000 subscribers, but recent research has shown that its real maximum was
8,500 and its life was not long; it was founded in 1818 and died in

[1] I am indebted to Mrs. Irene Collins for permission to consult her work,
mainly unpublished, on the French Press.

1821. The liberal journal, the *Constitutionnel*, did much better; it was founded in 1821 with a capital of 75,000 francs in fifteen shares of 500 francs each. It enrolled 20,000 subscribers, and in 1824 one of the original shareholders was able to sell half of his share for 50,000 francs.[1] In 1826 the dividends paid came to 25,000 francs for each of the fifteen shares, or fifty times the original investment. Both papers were lively and well written; the difference in their success came from the general move towards the Left in the politics of the wealthy middle classes, especially the business men.

The general tone of the newspapers was that of attack, often scurrilous, on institutions and policies and people. This made it hard for a government based on moderation to compete; its papers were on the defensive and, therefore, not at all as amusing as those of the opposition. Every grievance against the Government, genuine or exaggerated, was publicised by the opposition papers of the Right or of the Left, and sometimes this did lead to useful reform. Young writers and politicians, such as Adolphe Thiers, who left a mark on French history, had a chance to make not only their reputations but also a fair amount of money.

To found a new paper was not difficult. A group of wealthy men put up some money and secured the help of authors. They then made a contract with one of the Paris printers, all of whom had to have a government licence, and enrolled as many subscribers for as many months as they could. Their aim was not, as a rule, to secure converts to their political views, but rather to heighten the emotions and increase the activity of their sympathisers. The failure of a paper was generally due to its inability to retain the interest of its readers, but sometimes it was the result of legal action taken against the authors, publishers, printers or proprietors.

A Press can only be free when it is conducted with a sense of responsibility, and the early papers of the restored monarchy showed a terrifying lack of conscience. False rumours were spread, unjust attacks made on individuals, violence incited. Only the law can enforce responsibility, and the succeeding cabinets tried different methods. Direct censorship was imposed in 1814, dropped in 1815 and then re-enforced temporarily. In 1817 each paper was supposed to have its own private censor, but this plan was a failure. Official censorship was reintroduced in 1820 and spasmodically up to 1827, but it was very difficult to find intelligent and willing censors. The papers, too, were ingenious in covering comment by disguising it as a romance or a historical essay, or when a phrase or item was struck out by the censors, printing lines of dots which made readers guess what was missing. At one time this was prohibited, and papers had

[1] Aubert, J.: *De Quoi Vivait Thiers?* Paris, 1952, p. 30.

to keep on hand a number of innocuous paragraphs of varying lengths which could be inserted to fill gaps.

Both personal and seditious libel were illegal, but the guilt or innocence of the accused journalist was decided by a court, and the judges or, when they were used, the juries were apt to be prejudiced, usually in favour of the defendant. In 1817 the Government had a law passed that no new paper could be founded without its authorisation, but that proved inadequate as a check, for no continuity of policy could be guaranteed. Then in 1819 the help of the Doctrinaires was invoked by Decazes. The Press Laws of 1819 were largely the work of de Broglie, who took great pride in his work.

Three distinct laws were passed, so that one or another could be amended, yet leave the rest intact. One attempted to define offences which might be committed by writers in the Press, and imposed minimum and maximum penalties. Publishing anything likely to encourage people to break the law was one category; this would include sedition as well as incitement to violence. If no actual breach of the law could be attributed to the writing, the penalties were less. Personal libels on the King, his family and his servants and also on all ordinary citizens were actionable; defamation, even if there were no direct accusation of crime, was a punishable offence.

The second law aimed at preventing the appearance of ephemeral papers with no real support behind them; in effect, it meant confining the ownership of the Press to the wealthy middle class. Caution money had to be deposited with the Government by the proprietors of every newspaper. A considerable sum in cash or in government stock had to be handed over as a security for the payment of any fines that might be incurred, and also to add to the difficulty of raising capital for a new paper.

The third law imitated the fairly recent English plan for the trial of Press offences; a jury was to decide whether or not a libel or incitement to violence was contained in the writing which had led to prosecution. Here again the middle classes alone were considered trustworthy; all jurors had to be payers of direct taxes.

These laws underwent many minor modifications. In 1821, after a series of acquittals by juries, the decision in Press cases was left to judges. A new offence was added to the list; a paper could be prosecuted for 'tendency'. Often it was difficult to say that any one article was an incitement to breach of the law, but the cumulative effect of successive articles might be dangerous to public order. Journalists intensely disliked this new weapon in the hands of the Government, but, as often happens, Press trials tended rather to advertise than to suppress the views of which the Government complained, and the continued acquittal of journalists of the opposition even by the magistrates indicated that the prosecuting ministers did not represent public opinion.

The Government's own lack of support in the popular Press continued; a wild scheme of a hot-headed royalist for buying up papers and changing their tendency only led to a great waste of money and to making a laughing-stock of the party. News was the last thing expected from the papers; foreign correspondents did not exist and such items as appeared of foreign news were very belated extracts from the Press of other countries. Provincial papers copied from the Paris ones, so that what news they did publish, beyond local items, was always four days late. The most serious defect of the French Press was that, apart from the factual, official and, therefore, dull *Moniteur*, it stimulated ideas and emotions but gave the reason very little hard fact on which to work.

In 1824 the smaller papers were hit by a rise in postage rates, and two years later by a rise in the stamp tax; they had paid at a lower rate than the larger ones. These two regulations involved an extra cost of nearly a halfpenny on the very smallest papers. They had the interesting indirect result of leading them to increase their size and use the additional space for advertisements. Income from this source was a most useful addition to that from subscriptions, and also tended to increase the connection between Paris business houses and the provinces.

A further check on the Press by regulation was that in 1826 all printers and publishers had to hand in their old licences and get new ones; a certificate from the police of his good conduct had to be submitted by every applicant. These rules were very unevenly enforced; as in so many other aspects of life in France, all depended on the character and views of the local prefects. Another regulation made it necessary for the printer's name, as is the law in England, to appear on everything that issued from his presses, whether papers, books or anything else.

In 1826 a far more serious attack on the Press was planned, but so many politicians both of the Right and the Left had connections with the Press that, though the bill, called the 'Law of Justice and Love' from a phrase used by a supporter, was passed by the deputies, the Government met such an opposition that it was withdrawn before it could be thrown out by the Peers.

More lasting influence was exercised by writers through their books than through the journals, though the two were closely interconnected—a successful journalist won a wider public for his books and vice versa. Not only well-known men like Chateaubriand could get large sums for their books; a comparatively unknown man like Thiers made 50,000 francs out of his *History of the Revolution*. By the eighteen-twenties a new generation was growing up keenly interested in the events of 1789, and the survivors, too, were glad to read an account of the years through which they had lived. The tone of histories by Thiers and by Mignet and others did a good deal to counteract the anti-revolutionary tone of the royalist authors. A purely Bonapartist work, Las Cases' *Memorial of St. Helena*, had, as might have been expected, an immense success when it was published in 1823. Not only recent history, but that of earlier times could serve to propagate political doctrines; Guizot's lectures on the history of the Stuarts in England led inevitably to parallels being drawn and the fall of the Bourbons being predicted.

The passing of the new Press laws led, naturally, to a great increase in the number of papers, books and pamphlets in 1819. It was not long before Decazes began to find himself in much the same position as Richelieu had been. Although he was not officially Prime Minister, he was the real head of the Cabinet, and it seemed to be moving further to the Left than he wished. The first open clash came over his proposal to give Richelieu a substantial reward as a proof of the nation's gratitude for his successful foreign policy. Decazes proposed that he should be given a portion of the lands still held by the State, sufficient to bring in a good income, for Richelieu was a poor man and had refused Louis' offers of money. The Left-wing deputies opposed the plan; they disliked hereditary landed estates and took the chance of speaking with violence against all aristocrats, past and present. They were joined by some of the ultra-right, who still regarded these lands as the property of the Church or of their former owners, and chose to word their objections in a way that hurt Richelieu's sensitive feelings very deeply. In the end the grant was approved, but only on condition that the lands should revert to the State on Richelieu's death unless he had a son to inherit them. It was well known that the Duke had agreed to the plan largely because he wanted to assure the future of his nephew, for he had no son. Richelieu acted with great dignity and restraint. He accepted the gift, but transferred the whole of the income to charity. The King then made him Grand Huntsman, an office which bore a large salary, but strictly on the condition that he made no attempt to interfere in the actual organisation of the royal hunts.

Once again factious opposition from both Left and Right made effective action by the Dessoles–Decazes cabinet difficult. Some of the ultra-royalist prefects and other officials and some of the inexperienced generals were dismissed and replaced by trained men, many of whom had served Napoleon during the Hundred Days. Such changes seemed necessary if the Government's policy were to be effectively carried out, but the constant shuffle in the upper ranks

of the Civil Service was a most unfortunate result of the bitter party
feeling of the times. The one section of government service that on
the whole escaped this sort of 'spoils system' was the foreign service;
although many of the ambassadors were politicians whose appointment was mainly due to a desire to get them out of France, they and
their staffs were often kept on through many Cabinet changes.

The universities, too, were a hotbed of political intrigue, and their
policy often determined by non-educational considerations. Decazes
ordered them to grant the University teacher's diploma to every
member of the Christian Brothers—a teaching order—who chose to
enrol, without his attending courses or passing any examination.
This was intended to win support from the Church, but was not as
absurd as it seems, for they were experienced men and on the whole
the standard of their schools was higher than that of the State.
Official direction in the schools and colleges of the University was
often in the hands of men of the Right, but the students were, on the
whole, radical. Every act of indiscipline on the part of undergraduates immediately took on a political character; for instance, in
1819 there was a revolt in the College of Louis le Grand against harsh
regulations, and the medical students in Montpellier rioted because
their privilege of cheap tickets at the theatre was withdrawn. Both
demonstrations assumed a strong anti-royalist character.

It was the Peers' opposition that was the greatest handicap to the
Dessoles–Decazes cabinet's legislative programme. After throwing
out Government bills, the Upper House demanded changes in the
law for the election of deputies. Decazes felt that this was un-
constitutional and a good excuse for strong action. Some of his
Cabinet would have preferred to dissolve the Lower House before
dealing with the Peers, but Decazes was afraid that the Left would
gain more heavily than he wished in a general election. He persuaded a very reluctant Louis to create sixty new peers on 6 March,
1819; they were to take their seats at once even if they had not got—
and few of them had—the entailed estates demanded by the law;
unless at their death they had such estates, their heirs could not
succeed them. In effect, therefore, Decazes was creating life peers.
Sixteen of the new lords were men who had been removed from the
House after the Hundred Days, and several others had served
Napoleon then; the rest were wealthy men who supported the
Government or were personal friends of Decazes. The Royal
Family was extremely angry at this degradation of the aristocratic
principle, and the European Powers not at all pleased at an action
that smacked of the *coup d'état*.

With this support in the Upper House the Government got some
bills passed; one a useful little measure which allowed offices to

be opened in the provinces for the registration and sale of shares in the national debt, so widening the basis for Government borrowing. The budget was passed, after the allocation for the army had been reduced; a small surplus was estimated and a lot of parliamentary time spent in arguing about how it should be used. A law was passed restricting the importation of very cheap corn so as to protect the farmers. But a bill for the sale of some State lands, not valuable as forest land, and using the money for the reduction of the debt, was rejected by a combination of the Right and the Left. All through the session the Government was harried from both sides, and in the country there was a spate of propaganda, of vulgar anti-clerical and Bonapartist cartoons, and endless rumours of plots. The session closed on 17 July, 1819, in an atmosphere of strain.

It was quite clear that either the Right or the Left had to be won over. Decazes, reversing his position in Richelieu's cabinet, wanted to move to the right; Dessoles and St. Cyr favoured the Left. It was impossible for the ministers to agree on schemes for reform needed in a variety of directions; local government; the jury system; and, above all, the electoral law, which they believed must be modified again. St. Cyr was in bad health, and the King had some severe attacks of gout. Curiously enough, the King's illness stimulated the trend to the Left; many people felt that as much reform as possible should be carried out before Artois became king.

When the election of one fifth of the deputies took place in the autumn, the Government had to fight against both wings. The Right made the triumph of their real enemies, the extreme Left, almost certain by refusing to support any Government candidate and wasting votes on men who had no chance whatever of success. When the results came out, the ultras were taken aback at the result of their policy. The outgoing deputies' party grouping had been 23 ultra-Right, 20 Government-centre, and 12 Left. The newly-elected included only 2 ultras, 5 centre, and 35 of the Left. Twenty of the new deputies were 'men of the Hundred Days'; one was an ex-priest, Grégoire (1750–1831) who had been prominent in the establishment of the State Church during the Revolution and had demanded the trial of Louis XVI, though he had not actually voted for his death. His election for the department of Isère, where there had been trouble in Grenoble, caused a great sensation. He was not allowed to take his seat; when the Chambers met, after violent debates it was agreed that to fulfil the law he ought to have resided in the department and did not, so his election was invalid.

By now it was clear that the system of partial elections every year made any kind of stable government impossible, and kept party propaganda always at election heat. It might have been expected that an electorate of comparatively few wealthy men would have been less fickle. That they changed their opinions so rapidly was due to their peculiar position; as rich men they were naturally conservative, but as newly-rich men they greatly disliked the extreme royalists, who snubbed them socially and felt that they owed their wealth and position to the downfall of the monarchy and aristocracy.

Before the new parliamentary session, plans for modifying the electoral law were discussed. The Cabinet was so sharply divided that the cracks could no longer be papered over, and on 17 November the Left-wing ministers, Dessoles, St. Cyr and Baron Louis, resigned. Decazes did his best to persuade Richelieu to come back, but he refused. Pasquier was, therefore, given the Foreign Office, Decazes became officially Prime Minister, and another of Napoleon's old generals, La Tour Maubourg (1757–1831), then ambassador in London, took the War Office. These changes did little to meet the Government's need of parliamentary support. The Left had lost their share of Cabinet offices in spite of their greatly increased support from the voters; the Right continued to hate Decazes. The newly-created peers were of the Left, so there would be opposition in the Upper House as well.

The session began very badly. Decazes fell ill with inflammation of the lungs soon after it began, and de Serre, whose oratory was of the greatest value to the Government, was ordered by his doctor to go to Nice, as he was in very poor health. Every proposal made in Parliament by the Government was opposed; there was a spate of petitions—there were 139 by 8 January, 1820—all critical of the Cabinet. Attempts to curb violent attacks in the Press were in vain; the juries impartially acquitted the journalists of both Right and Left. Decazes in despair thought of resigning; de Villèle was approached to see on what terms his followers would give their support. Then, on 13 February, 1820, the assassination of the Duke de Berry shocked Europe and for a time reversed the political tendencies in France.

De Berry had been attending a gala performance at the opera, with his wife. She became tired, and he took her down to her carriage at eleven o'clock. As he turned to go back to the theatre, a man named Louvel pushed his way through the onlookers and stabbed the prince. Louvel was chased and seized; de Berry was carried, bleeding profusely, into the theatre, followed by Caroline, his wife. Doctors were summoned who, using the peculiar medical technique of the time, put leeches on a man who had already lost much blood, to relieve him. Monsieur, his father, came to his improvised bed, as did Decazes; for once the future Charles X behaved kindly, and spoke in a friendly way to the distracted politician, who knew that he was sure to be blamed. The Royal Family crowded round; de Berry even sent for his baby daughter, aged five months, that he might bless her before he died. Priests came, and the poor old King, who had been told by Decazes. Soon after Louis' arrival, the prince died, at about 6.30 a.m.

Decazes was right in thinking that the murder of de Berry would have a bad effect on his own position. Though Artois himself took no part in the attacks on his brother's favourite, the whole of his party blamed the Government for failing to protect the Royal Family. Élie himself was openly accused of complicity with Louvel because he had spoken a few words to him in private; he had been asking if the dagger were poisoned. Some of the more hot-headed ultras once again thought of kidnapping the Prime Minister, but were persuaded to use political manœuvres instead. Louis was extremely angry at the absurd and unjust accusations, and showed no sign of parting with his dear friend.

When the Parliament met, Right and Left politicians joined to throw out a bill for modifying the electoral system and also one to give the Government extra powers for security. That he must resign was obvious to Decazes, and he approached Richelieu, asking him to resume office. The Duke was genuinely unwilling; he had been sickened by his experience of political intrigue. All sorts of combinations were being discussed; Talleyrand even approached de Villèle, the most influential man among the less extreme royalists, and suggested that they should co-operate; this was a remarkable example of the lack of real principle in politics. Monsieur then took a hand; on 18 February he asked his brother to dismiss Decazes. He then saw Richelieu and promised him his full personal support if he would form a Cabinet. Richelieu was a genuine royalist and a very conscientious man, so, greatly against his inclinations, he accepted. Louis yielded to his own favourite's urgent demands to be released, and on 20 February, 1820, a public announcement was made that Decazes had resigned for reasons of health and that Richelieu was once more President of the Council.

The new Prime Minister, in his turn, was anxious to demonstrate that there was no personal ill-feeling between him and Decazes. He persuaded the King, who was most willing, to make him a Duke and give him the important post of Ambassador to England, which was fortunately vacant. He asked all the other ministers to remain in office. Decazes' post of Minister of the Interior was given to Siméon, a lawyer, who had been trained under the Empire. He himself took no office.

So, with colleagues who had shared in the unpopularity of their leader, the King's favourite, and whose views were on the whole more radical than his own, Richelieu entered upon his second ministry. He realised that the Centre party had more or less crumbled, so his aim was to get solid support from the more moderate royalists. Their leaders in the deputies, de Villèle and Corbière, promised support. If the ultras were really ordered by their leader, Artois, to keep quiet, there seemed to be some hope of a genuine two-party system, with a united royalist yet reasonable party in opposition to the Left, and some stability in politics.

Chapter X

PLOTS AND POLITICIANS

RICHELIEU soon found that it was still as difficult to maintain a steady march down the middle of the road as it had been in his first ministry. De Berry's assassination had strengthened the royalists in their belief that a very firm hand was needed to suppress the enemies of the Bourbons. Louvel's trial dragged on for five months, keeping feelings which might have died down very much alive, because no one would believe him when he declared that he had acted entirely alone, after brooding for years on the best way of destroying Bourbon rule. There were, in fact, a number of vague plots being discussed by the considerable number of discontented people in Paris and some provincial towns, but Louvel had had no connection with them. He was questioned again and again to discover the names of his fellow conspirators, and it was not till 6 June that he was finally condemned, and he was executed the next day.

Paris was restless in the summer of 1820. On 2 June students demonstrated outside the Palais Bourbon, where the deputies sat, shouting ' *Vive la Charte!* ' Young men of the Royal Guard countered with ' *Vive le Roi!* ' and free fights went on all over the square. They were renewed next day; the irrepressible Lafayette began to have hopes of a revolution. Swiss Guards were sent to clear the crowds away, and a university student was shot. Then the Government acted; the Royal Guard was confined to barracks and the students told that if they were arrested during demonstrations they would be expelled from the University. The ordinary troops replaced the unpopular Swiss and order was restored.

Religious intolerance again raised its head in public to worry Richelieu. A petition from a lawyer in Nîmes to the deputies asked for protection of the Protestants against an 'invisible government' which threatened them. A circular letter was quoted which the extreme Right-wing Catholics had sent to their friends; this was almost certainly the work of the Knights of the Faith. Debates on this petition were extremely stormy.

The Government had secured the passage of laws which gave it temporary powers of arbitrary arrest and reintroduced censorship of the Press. Purely administrative measures could not give real security; only a government with full parliamentary support and a coherent programme, no matter on what lines, could do that, for one or other of the two extremes must be convinced that there was no chance of its being overthrown. The electoral system made this impossible; incessant electioneering kept opposition alive and made long-distance planning impractical. Richelieu wished to renew the system of double election, and the Cabinet as a whole to end the annual partial elections. Their bills were heavily amended by the deputies and, as finally passed on 28 June, 1820, introduced one of the oddest of the French experiments in representative government.

Once again the number of deputies was increased, by 172, and a kind of double election introduced; 258 *arrondissement* colleges were each to elect one deputy directly, and departmental colleges were also created from one quarter of the electors, those who paid most in taxes, and they were to elect the extra 172 members. The annual partial renewal of the Chamber was to remain. The effect was a queer sort of oligarchy, for the wealthiest people had double representation. The bill having been passed, and the budget been approved, the parliamentary session ended on 22 July, 1820.

Freed from endless debating, the Cabinet hoped for some peace. Pressure for a wholesale purge of officials was resisted, though some prefects and others were dismissed and men of more Right-wing views replaced them. More of Bonaparte's officers were placed on the retired list. Lafayette and others of the old revolutionaries were organising a new underground movement, in touch with the Carbonari of Italy. The Government knew some plotting was going on, for the old soldiers' fears and hopes kept them restless, and in August the most sensational of their attempts was made, that known as the Bazar Français conspiracy.

A number of old soldiers had opened a shop in Paris, and it served as a centre for former officers and N.C.Os. who dreamed of a restoration of Napoleon or his son, and other discontented men who wanted a republic or Orleans as king, they were not quite sure which. The belief grew up that if the fort of Vincennes, close to Paris, could be seized, revolution would break out in the city and support would come from the provincial garrisons. Slowly, small sums of money were collected to buy arms; it was calculated that the conspirators had about £4,000 in all.

As happened again and again in these rather pathetic conspiracies, the plan for a simultaneous rising on 10 August, 1820, was postponed, as some areas were not ready. The attempt on the fort of Vincennes was fixed for the night of 19 August. By the 15th the police were suspicious, but what utterly destroyed the plan was a pure accident; some fireworks exploded and did some damage in the fort, and extra troops were sent there. Many of those involved in the plot panicked and went to the police. Some of the leaders escaped, but others were arrested at nine o'clock on the evening of 19 August as they were making their final arrangements.

Immense excitement was caused. The provincial risings were feeble and easily dealt with, but the notion of a nation-wide military conspiracy was really alarming. To show how gravely they took the matter, the Cabinet decided that the leaders should be accused of treachery, and this meant a trial before the House of Peers.

The duty laid on the Peers by the Charter to judge cases of treason was one which they very much disliked. The case of a Ney was bad enough, but to have to disentangle the intrigues of a number of obscure old soldiers was not the sort of task that a political chamber could reasonably be asked to perform. The Peers had only just reached their homes after a long parliamentary session, and were very annoyed at being summoned to meet as a court on 26 August. Investigations were difficult and lengthy; procedure was awkward when so large a body of men was acting as both judge and jury. Moreover, several Peers were themselves old soldiers, and though they by no means condoned conspiracy, they felt a good deal of sympathy for the dreams of men who had served the Empire.

All through the autumn of 1820 inquiries dragged on. On 4 January, 1821, the Peers dismissed ten of the accused for lack of evidence, and refused to continue the trial of those against whom the sole evidence was that they had been named as accomplices by others. The ultras were furious at what they considered dangerous clemency; the Peers themselves for once agreed whole-heartedly with Talleyrand when he said that, if the Peers were to act as a law court, it should only be when one of themselves was charged, or someone really important like a cabinet minister or a general.

The trial proper only began on 7 May, 1821, by which time only twenty-nine accused were left, and five others who had escaped arrest in the previous August; 182 witnesses had to be heard; famous lawyers defended the accused. The defence took the line that the aim of the conspiracy was to ensure the terms of the Charter being observed, not to overthrow the constitution. The hearing ended on 8 June; then judgement had to be delivered. The Peers decided to vote on each case separately, and that a majority of five to three was necessary not only for acquittal or condemnation, but for the sentence to be imposed; this procedure took a great deal of time. On the whole the discussions were judicial in tone, but the irritation felt by the Peers at having to do such work probably weighed on the side of mercy. When, on 16 July, judgement was delivered only three men were sentenced to death, and none of them could be executed, for they were among the five not in custody. Six men were given prison sentences and fined; the rest were acquitted.

No one except the prisoners was pleased by this result of eleven months' activity. The Left-wing politicians said that it proved there never had been any dangerous conspiracy. The Court party said the Government had suppressed evidence, and that Lafayette and every other known Bonapartist or republican must have been involved. Ordinary people were afraid that discontented men would be encouraged to rebel by this proof that there was a reasonable chance of escape even if they were caught. Everybody agreed that some regulation must be made if the Peers were to act as a law court; both the type of case they should try and their procedure must be defined. But, though there were long discussions, no acceptable scheme was evolved.

Long before the Bazar Français case ended, though soon after it had begun, on 29 September, 1820, the Government and probably a majority of the people of France rejoiced at the birth of a son to de Berry's widow. De Berry had not been unpopular, and everyone had felt sorry for his wife. For the royalists the birth of a boy to continue the Bourbon line was so welcome that they called the child 'miraculous'. All over the country fireworks and festivities provided grand free entertainment for the common people.

Inevitably, the Government thought what political use should be made of this happy event. Richelieu, still hoping for a reconciliation with the 'new' France, persuaded a reluctant Louis to give honours and posts at Court to some of the wealthy middle class. It may be doubted if this really helped; the men themselves were pleased, but the old nobility were very angry, and they had a good deal more influence on Parliament. Some of the Cabinet thought that the chance should be taken for a complete dissolution, especially in view of the new electoral law. It seems to later observers that they were right; at any rate it would have clarified the situation.

Richelieu decided against it. He was afraid that a dissolution would be looked on as yielding to the Left, which had been demanding one, so a most peculiar election took place in November 1820. One fifth of the existing Chamber retired, and in addition 172 new deputies were chosen by the departmental colleges; in all 220 new members. The results were a triumph for the Right. The Left secured only about 34 seats; the ultra-Right 75, men who had sat in the Matchless Parliament; 44 were men who had been put forward by the Government; the rest were not committed but expected to be of the Centre or even the extreme-Right. Louis was worried by the royalists' victory; he still held Decazes' view that the real danger to the monarchy came not from the liberals but from the ultras.

The Prime Minister saw that he must come to terms with the majority in the Lower House. He discussed matters with Chateaubriand, whose influence was supposed—especially by himself—to be very great. He suggested that de Villèle should be given Cabinet office, and that he himself would not object to being an ambassador —preferably at Constantinople.

Once again the long-drawn-out negotiations with groups, which were becoming a feature of French political life, began. De Villèle found that his party were thinking in terms of 1815, of wholesale reaction. A suggestion that he and Corbière should become ministers without portfolio was rejected by their supporters. The session opened on 19 December, 1820, with a King's Speech which showed by its vagueness that the Cabinet was without a programme. By the 22nd more negotiations led to Richelieu's plan being accepted; Villèle and Corbière became members of the Cabinet without portfolio, and Chateaubriand was made Ambassador to Berlin. There are conflicting accounts of these manœuvres, but the upshot was clear, no matter who should be praised or blamed for a plan which was fundamentally unsound.

To be in the Cabinet but have no departmental responsibility put the two new ministers in a position of either great strength or great weakness. They could use the votes they commanded in the Chamber to influence general policy, and yet hold themselves aloof from criticism as they had no administrative duties. On the other hand, they were but two; should the other ministers be united they could do nothing, yet they were morally bound to give at least tacit support to the bills introduced by the Cabinet.

The year 1821 opened with more and very peculiar plots. An explosion of a sort of bomb on 27 January shook the palace of the Tuileries, and a few days later there were two further explosions of gunpowder set off by a slow match. These 'infernal machines' seemed to have been placed where it was highly unlikely that they would do any serious damage. Then threatening letters were found by the Duchess de Berry on her dressing-table. That an enemy should be able to get into her private room seemed at first sight most alarming, but police investigation proved that the culprit was a member of her own household. The incident confirmed the general belief that the royalists were busy, trying to discredit both the police and the opposition groups. Artois had to ask for the whole affair to be hushed up, so no one was brought to trial, which did not prevent gossip but rather encouraged it.

It was not these childishly romantic actions which worried the Prime Minister, but the revelation they gave of the dislike felt for him and his Government, and the irresponsibility of the courtiers who surrounded the heir to the throne. Camille Jordan, who was very ill, made a moving speech when the Chamber was discussing the Tuileries explosion, urging the royalists not to bring baseless charges against the King's ministers and so bring themselves and France into disrepute. But it was in vain. As the extremists of the Left had wrecked Richelieu's first ministry, those of the Right wrecked the second.

Debates in the Chamber on every issue continued to be mere wrangles. The Left demanded that help should be sent to the Neapolitans and Spaniards who had revolted against their monarchs, and Manuel, in a speech on 21 February, 1821, seemed to threaten to appeal to the army to act independently. Pasquier, the Minister for Foreign Affairs, declared that foreign policy was a royal prerogative, not to be debated by the deputies. This made it hard for the ultras to demand support for monarchs, for in theory they respected royal rights. To placate Villèle's friends, more posts were given to royalists and more power to the Church; the bishops were given the right to inspect all schools in their sees. Only the King himself seemed loyal to his ministers; he wrote letters daily to his beloved Élie Decazes, but would not see him when his wife's illness brought him to Paris.

The revolutionaries in Italy were crushed by Austria, who was practically policing the peninsula. This disheartened the French revolutionaries, who were linked with the Italian through the Carbonari, and some by-elections in March 1821 added to the strength of the Right. Meantime, the new electoral divisions created by the bill of 1820 were being drawn up. By ingenious divisions of industrial areas the new *arrondissements* would, it was expected, secure the preponderance of the landowners. The Peers amended some of the more peculiar arrangements, and the Cabinet accepted their changes and passed the bill, in spite of the anger of some of the ultras.

One useful piece of business was put through during the session of 1820–21. De Serre persuaded the House of Deputies to strengthen the hands of its President and introduce some discipline into the debates. After long and stormy discussion, in March 1821 the standing orders were amended to allow the President to have the same right as his counterpart, the English Speaker, of calling a member to order. The deputy would be allowed to defend himself, but no one else could speak either for or against him. If a man were twice called to order, the Chamber should vote, without any debate, as to whether the offender should be prohibited from speaking on that particular subject for the rest of the session.

Though debates were a little more orderly after this, the Government still found it hard to get business through. A mild proposal to raise the salaries of curates, who were absurdly badly paid, to pro-

8

vide priests for 350 villages where there were none, and to create
twelve new bishoprics, led to clamorous demands from the ultras
for the Church to have all the bishops it liked, without State leave
A compromise was made; the twelve new sees were created at once
and eighteen more promised for the near future. On the other hand
great difficulty was found in passing a bill to give a moderate compensation to those of Napoleon's officers and ministers who had been
granted lands outside France and had lost them as part of the
terms of the peace treaty. The ultras took the chance of pouring
insults on Napoleon and his men. In both cases Richelieu had to ask
de Villèle to induce his party to be reasonable, and compromises
were arranged.

The ultra-Right had a majority on nearly every committee for
the examination of a proposed measure, and in nearly every case
reported unfavourably. Every concession led to further demands. In
July the ultras demanded that the post of Minister of the Interior
should be given to one of their group. As all prefects and officials
held office at the pleasure of the minister, this involved a transfer of
the main administrative power of the Cabinet, and Richelieu refused
firmly. Villèle and Corbière then resigned their position as ministers
without portfolio, though they promised their continued support to
the Government, and Chateaubriand in sympathy resigned his
embassy. Thus, in an atmosphere of strain, the session ended on
31 July, 1821. Except for the budget, few laws of any serious importance had been passed, and hour upon hour had been wasted in
acrimonious debate.

Richelieu's hopes for a moderate royalist government had again
proved vain. There had been no move towards unity of the Right;
instead intrigues had multiplied. Yet he still felt convinced that
his right course was to go on steadily, and that common sense must
in the end prevail. This was probably why he once again allowed
partial elections to take place in the autumn, instead of asking for a
dissolution of the whole Chamber.

In May 1821 an item of news had greatly relieved not only the
French Government but the whole of Europe; Napoleon was dead
It was hoped that this would end Bonapartism as a political factor
His son, the Duke of Reichstadt, was safely in Austrian hands. His
widow, Marie Louise, now Duchess of Parma, mourned her great
husband officially for one month and then married the Austrian
Count of Neipperg, who had been assisting her in the administration
of her duchy. This duty seems to have consisted mainly in raising all
the money possible from the inhabitants, building a palace with some
of it, and safely investing the rest with the Rothschilds.

A flood of pamphlets appeared; Las Cases' *Memorial of St*

Helena; poems from the rising romantics, Lamartine, Béranger and the rest, celebrating the melancholy end of a great hero. Napoleon had made a will, leaving large sums to a variety of people, but the actual funds in his estate came to surprisingly little. The legend began to take shape, but the effects of all the emotion were not to have any practical significance for a long time. The immediate result was the fusing of the Bonapartists with the old republicans headed by Lafayette, and to some extent with the newer liberal groups. An organisation known as the Knights of Liberty had been formed in and around Saumur, a garrison town on the Loire, in 1820. This now merged into the Carbonari, a very well organised middle-class revolutionary society that had arisen in Italy as a result of the restoration of the old régime after the Treaty of Vienna.

The anti-clerical feeling that was strong in the middle classes was sharpened by the constant threat to all officials from the Knights of the Faith, seeking posts for their own adherents, and by the folly of the Catholic clergy who associated religion with politics. An opportunity for the expression of their views was given when a great public subscription was opened for the purchase of the Chambord estate as a gift to de Berry's posthumous son. The costs of the Court were openly criticised, and a contrast drawn between the future planned for this child and the way in which the Duke of Orleans was bringing up his large family, sending his sons to the ordinary schools, not keeping them in magnificent seclusion.

Richelieu was sadly aware of this opposition to the monarchy, in which he sincerely believed. He was deeply engaged in foreign affairs throughout the summer of 1821; at one time it looked as if France might get embroiled in a war with Turkey in aid of the Greeks, with Russia as an ally. Such a war would have been generally popular: with the Right as a crusade against the infidel, with the Left as a war of liberation. The Prime Minister knew that France was quite unprepared for any serious campaign, and that war would check the steady improvement in her economic situation. Fortunately for him, pacific counsels prevailed, but everyone blamed Richelieu for being timid and for yielding to pressure from England, who was opposed to the war.

In Spain, all too close at hand, there was trouble of two kinds. The King, Ferdinand VII, had been forced to grant a constitution in 1820, and the Cortes, the Spanish parliament, was in power and taking an anti-clerical attitude that in some cases amounted to religious persecution. Then in the summer of 1821 an appalling outbreak of yellow fever spread infection from Barcelona into the surrounding country. Some nuns of a nursing order and four doctors went from France to Barcelona and did heroic work. In August the

French Government proclaimed a closure of the frontier, and sent troops to guard the routes from Spain from the coast to the Central Pyrenees. The 'sanitary cordon' was effective; the scourge did not cross the frontier. For once Richelieu's action met with general approval, and the ultras, who had been thinking of intervening to help Ferdinand, postponed their plans to healthier times.

Early in October the partial elections took place in an atmosphere of unusual calm. The control of the electoral colleges was largely in the hands of royalists, and the results were what might have been expected. Only 15 members of the Left were successful, and only 20 of the centre-Right, Richelieu's supporters. Of the 50 ultra-Right deputies, 20 were of the most extreme views. The Prime Minister's position was badly weakened; he would need to the full the support which Monsieur had promised. The King, too, was no longer wholly to be counted on, for he had a new favourite who was replacing Decazes in his affections.

The Countess du Cayla was a young and charming woman who, in the last months of 1820, was engaged in a lawsuit with her husband, who wanted to take her children away. She was on intimate terms with the Duke of Doudeauville and his son, Sosthènes de la Roche-foucauld, who suggested that she should be introduced to Louis personally, as she believed he was prejudiced against her. When she was moving towards the seat she was to take, in her shyness and embarrassment she stumbled against a little table and knocked down some papers. She picked them up and tried to sort them, reading a few words from each. Louis was greatly taken with her voice, and said: 'Continue, Madame, the charm of your voice will add to that of your appearance.' He asked her to come and read aloud to him, and soon was seeing her every day—at fixed hours, according to his orderly plan of life.[1]

Soon she was recognised as the King's confidante. Louis had begun building a grand new house in the park of St.-Ouen, which everyone thought was intended for the Duchess of Angoulême. He presented this to Madame du Cayla. She was closely in touch with Artois and his circle, and though she tried to be honest and loyal it was inevitable that her influence would weigh with the susceptible elderly monarch.

The victorious Right was divided as to how its power should be used. Should the aim be to get rid of Richelieu? He was very unco-operative over the demands made for offices and posts. Yet it might not be easy to persuade Louis to dismiss him; though he was not a close personal friend, the King seemed to trust him and he had a high reputation as Foreign Minister.

1 Neuville, Baron Hyde de: *Mémoires*. 3 vols. Paris, 1888–92. Vol. III, p. 5

When the session began in November 1821 de Villèle, who was recognised as the leader of the Right in the Deputies, renewed the promises of support he had given to Richelieu. All the official positions in the Chamber were filled by ultras. The Cabinet had to produce yet another very non-committal King's Speech in the hopes of soothing the majority. Some of the ultras were not at all placated; they approached the liberals and suggested joint action to turn the Government out. Royer-Collard, rather surprisingly, seemed to welcome the idea; he had quarrelled with de Serre, and he also objected to the censorship of the Press. Direct attack was agreed on, so, in the formal Reply, foreign policy, Richelieu's own responsibility, was criticised. This time de Serre's declarations that foreign affairs were a royal prerogative were ignored, and the adverse Reply was carried by 176 to 98 votes.

Richelieu was aghast at this open coalition of his enemies. Louis was extremely angry, and approved a very strong response to the Reply. Though he realised this meant that he would not dismiss Richelieu, he indicated that he himself took responsibility for his Government's policy. This startled the moderate Right and especially de Villèle, who had not at all liked the idea of intriguing with the Left. But he had no power over the extremists, and Donnadieu in particular made bitter personal attacks on the Prime Minister.

Richelieu now called on Artois and reminded him of his promises. Monsieur hedged, saying that circumstances had changed. That a prince should break his word deeply distressed the Prime Minister, and on 12 December, 1821, he told Louis about his interview. The King asked him what else he had expected. 'He conspired against Louis XVI, he has conspired against me, he will conspire against himself.' But he made it clear that he felt he had already done his duty to Richelieu and was not inclined to go on struggling; he asked him to suggest names for a new Cabinet.

De Villèle was the obvious man to approach, so Richelieu saw him and arranged for him to meet Louis. On 15 December the expected notice appeared in the *Moniteur*; the Cabinet had resigned and a new one was appointed. Once again there was no Prime Minister. Villèle took over finance; Corbière got what he had long wanted, the Ministry of the Interior. The Ministry of Justice went to de Peyronnet, a lawyer who had helped Madame du Cayla in her case against her husband. Montmorency at the Foreign Office owed his post more to his distinguished ancestry and his connection with the Congregation than to any noticeable suitability for the work. The Duke de Bellune went to the War Office; he was a man of fifty-five and a marshal; his title came from Belluno in Venetia, where the

Austrians had been defeated in 1797. He was now a convinced royalist. Clermont-Tonnerre (1780–1865) was an aristocrat; he had charge of the navy. In the words of a royalist, Hyde de Neuville, 'Louis had accepted M. de Villèle from the hands of his brother.'

Whether the new Cabinet would be a success depended, indeed, largely on de Villèle. De Neuville's summary of the man's character seems to be fairly accurate. 'The conceptions of a man of genius who can save his country, like Mazarin, were too vast to inspire a mind far more preoccupied with getting good laws passed than with defending a monarchy which was being attacked at its very base. In a normal state, M. de Villèle could have been a Colbert.'[1] The English parallel would perhaps be Walpole; de Villèle might have done for the Bourbons what Walpole did for the Hanoverians had he had a parliament as experienced as the English to support him. As it was, de Villèle won the nation's confidence by his sound finance, but was not strong enough to resist the pressure of the extremists of his own party, or to dominate the assembly by the force of his personality. His error had been, considering his own moderate views, not to support Richelieu more strongly, but the Doctrinaire element in the Cabinet had been in theory and in practice unacceptable to him as well as to his followers.

As in all the royalist ministries, the inexperience of the members laid an unfair burden on the leader, who was also embarrassed by demands from the Knights of the Faith and others for posts for which they were clearly unfit. Chateaubriand was pacified by the London embassy; Decazes had resigned on Richelieu's fall. De Serre, to the annoyance of Montmorency, the Minister for Foreign Affairs, was given the Naples embassy as de Villèle appreciated the valuable work he had done in spite of his political views. Donnadieu, in spite of all the criticism of his actions in Grenoble, was replaced on the active list. Twenty prefects were dismissed to make room for some of the *pointus*, the 'shrill people', as the clamouring ultras were now nicknamed.

The new Government had some excuse for once again changing the responsible officials in the departments. The whole of Alsace was restless; even fairly large-scale business men were associated with the plotting that was going on near the garrison town of Belfort. Saumur, on the Loire, and Marseilles were known to be full of conspiracy. Once again the revolutionaries made the mistake of planning for a simultaneous rising, in theory excellent, in practice difficult to organise and conceal. The scheme was for Saumur to rise at the end of the year on the same day as towns in Alsace. The night of 28 December was agreed on; the garrisons were to mutiny, and the

---

[1] Neuville, Baron Hyde de, op. cit., Vol. II, p. 133.

townsfolk, it was hoped, would support them. Lafayette, properly dressed in general's uniform, was to head the movement.

Accident, as so often happened, played into the Government's hands. On Christmas Eve a house caught fire in Saumur and some of the conspirators who were helping to put it out were killed; on their bodies were papers which betrayed their plans. Between thirty and forty non-commissioned officers were arrested. In Alsace there were delays; one of the leaders did not turn up when he was expected on the 28th. Lafayette was hastily summoned, but he was at Meaux, attending a family reunion, and on the 31st, when the rising was to take place, only his uniform had arrived. At Belfort the authorities had no suspicions, so well had the secret been kept; but the very secrecy led to an accidental betrayal. A sergeant who had been away on Christmas leave reported that his men were ready for action on the night of 31 December to an officer; he did not know that this particular man was not in the conspiracy. When the leaders of the revolt heard of the accidental betrayal they lost courage and fled; they got word in time to Lafayette, who turned aside on his journey.

Even if this plot had succeeded, and the troops had seized Belfort in the name of liberty, it is perfectly clear that no large-scale rising against the Bourbons would have followed. The effect of this endless series of futile conspiracies was to show how widespread was the opposition to the Bourbons in the army, and to strengthen Artois' party in its distrust of all who had served Napoleon, while at the same time frightening middle-class voters and weakening the constitutional liberals. There was another pathetic failure of a revolt near Saumur in February 1822; there were demonstrations against the Missions preached during Lent, and in theatres where plays were thought to have a political significance. All through the winter there were riots, especially in Paris; the Paris University Schools of Medicine and Law were closed for six months after demonstrations by the students, which had met with obvious sympathy though not active support from the ordinary people on the streets.

Much parliamentary time in January 1822 was taken up by the proposed Press bill. Small though their numbers were, the liberals fought it clause by clause and excellent speeches were made, notably by Royer-Collard and by de Martignac (1778–1832), a lawyer who was one of the few moderates successful in the 1821 elections. Again, when the budget came up in March, Manuel took the chance to make a violent attack on the Government. He was loathed by the royalists; the Baron de Frénilly called him 'a little Marseilles advocate', 'a tiger with the face of a cat', with 'the soul of a hyena'.[1] De Broglie thought him 'rather nice-looking; he is very

[1] Frénilly, Baron de: *Recollections*. Trans. Lees. London, 1909, p. 297.

fair and at ordinary times rather insignificant' though 'like all demagogues, his dignity is mingled with vulgarity'.[1] Manuel's interposition in the debate led to such storms that the new rules of procedure were applied for the first time; after he had been twice warned by the Speaker, he was forbidden to speak again on foreign policy, the main theme of his attack, for the rest of the session. It took five weeks for the debate on the budget to be completed in the Deputies; once again a small surplus was anticipated.

De Villèle's orderly mind was distressed by the peculiar system by which the taxes for the current year were often not made law until the middle of the summer, while at the same time the accounts for previous years were often not finally approved till after two years' delay. For instance, the 1820 accounts were formally closed in this summer session of 1822. He also disliked the method by which the Government was given provisional power to levy taxes for six months before the Chamber had passed them. He therefore proposed that there should be two parliamentary sessions each year, in autumn and in spring; the budget could be introduced in the autumn and passed before 1 January.

The session was, therefore, closed on 1 May, and once again little had been accomplished. Twice laws had to be dropped because both the extreme-Right and the liberal deputies absented themselves, and the violence of the debates had been disgraceful. The partial elections took place in May. Villèle sent out a circular which practically threatened all officials with dismissal if they did not support Government candidates. During the election there were anti-royalist and anti-clerical demonstrations at Lyons, but the result as a whole was 'no change'; the Left lost some seats but gained three more than it lost.

During the summer the Duke de Richelieu died. He was barely fifty-five, but had been exhausted by the worries and disappointments of his political career. Several people now realised that he had done a great deal for France and been treated with ingratitude. Among them was Villèle, for he now faced Richelieu's problem of trying to keep the ebullient royalists in hand, and was finding it very hard. For instance, the clerical party forced him to choose a priest as Grand Master of the University. Though he chose an able and moderate man, the Abbé Frayssinous, to make a cleric head of the whole educational system of the country was asking for trouble not only for the Government but for the Church. This appointment was partly responsible for renewed demonstrations by the Paris students before the second session of the Chambers opened on 3 June, 1822.

[1] Broglie, Duke de: *Personal Recollections*. Trans. Beaufort. London, 1887, Vol. II, p. 69.

The chief measures laid before Parliament were of economic rather than political importance. France was, on the whole, prosperous, but afraid of competition; protective duties were, therefore, imposed on iron, sugar and livestock. Germany and Switzerland, both of whom exported cattle to France, promptly retaliated by prohibiting the import of French wine and brandy. More constructive was a plan for building canals. For a long time the Chambers had been discussing schemes to improve communications by extending inland waterways. Opposition had come from the Right, because Laffitte and other liberal bankers were known to be anxious to profit by the great demand for capital which works on this scale would create; and also from some theorists of the Left, because the government's proposals were for a mixture of State and private enterprise and they thought this was a mistake.

De Villèle now proposed, as Richelieu's government had done in previous years, that companies should be formed to build four major canals. They would be promised interest of 5 to 6 per cent, with an additional 2 per cent for twenty years as repayment of part of the capital, and a share in the profits from the canals after that date. In the earlier plan, no interest would be paid till the work was completed; now it was proposed that payments should be made as soon as the undertakings began, for few French financiers had enough funds to tie them up without an immediate return. De Villèle's law was carried. The terms were certainly very favourable to the investors, but France was short of capital, and the canals proved immensely useful.

More army plots were revealed during the summer, at Saumur again, and at La Rochelle, where four sergeants were the ringleaders. The plotters talked too much and were betrayed; in the questioning of suspects the existence of the central organisation of the Carbonari in Paris was discovered. The four sergeants were executed and made into heroes by their sympathisers. Very many death sentences were passed on those found guilty of the large number of small conspiracies which were hatched during the summer of 1822; several of them had been betrayed by Government spies who did not find it too difficult to join a revolutionary group. Lafayette was very fortunate; again and again it seemed as if his complicity in the general plans for revolution would be proved, but he was never betrayed.

Guizot published a pamphlet arguing against the death penalty for this kind of treachery, and a great many people felt unhappy not only at the severity of the sentences but also about the use of spies, who could only too easily become instigators of plots. In one trial a Government prosecutor spoke as if Lafayette and others were definitely involved in a conspiracy; this led to a quarrel between the

Peers, who said he should be called to the Bar of their House to answer for his improper accusation of a peer, and the Deputies, who defeated the Peers' motion. Whether it was the fear of being suspected of opposition, or whether it was the fear of revolution that was responsible, the partial elections in the autumn showed a change in the minds of electors. Of the outgoing deputies 37 were Left wing, and only 7 were returned. In the departmental colleges the Left secured only a little more than a quarter of the votes. It is true that official pressure was very strong, but it seems clear that the middle classes felt it was prudent to vote for the Right.

De Villèle probably also gained support from the financial situation. In his autumn budget, to fix the taxes for 1823, he planned for a considerable surplus, in part due to his thorough reorganisation of the financial system which made the Treasury very much more efficient and a good deal less expensive. But to secure the full fruits of his policy of winning over France by giving it prosperity, peace was essential. Events in Spain made this very difficult to secure.

Chapter XI

WAR IN SPAIN

THE domestic history of France was strongly influenced by what was happening across the Pyrenees, for two main reasons. The peculiar nature of the mountain boundary made surreptitious crossing of the frontier fairly easy. On the west the line runs across fairly flat country where the River Bidassoa winds down to the sea, but almost all the rest of the frontier is dominated by the great mountain mass of the Pyrenees. There are few natural passes and they are not much lower than the surrounding peaks so, as Napoleon had found, it is hard to transport a great force from France to Spain. Though even to-day there are few roads crossing the ranges, the number of mule paths is very great, and quite recently smuggling was the local industry of the shepherds, foresters, mule and cattle breeders, who live in the remote villages on both sides of the border.

The other, and immediate reason, was the sort of parallel that existed between the two governments. The Spanish monarchy had been overthrown by Napoleon, and the French occupation had developed two divergent parties among the Spaniards. One, based on the middle classes, had admired the French Revolution. It was strongly anti-clerical and in 1812 produced an extremely democratic constitution in which the Cortes, the old national assembly, was modernised and given great power. The other group was supported by the bishops and the nobility, and was very conservative and royalist. When Spain regained her freedom it was hoped that Ferdinand VII, a Bourbon, would accept this constitution, but instead he carried through a sort of White Terror and governed despotically. In 1820 a revolution forced him to accept the constitution of 1812.

The French royalists had envied their Spanish counterparts and were regretful that Louis had not overthrown the Charter as Ferdinand had got rid of that of Spain. Similar events in Portugal, where John VI had accepted a new constitution in 1821, now made the whole peninsula subordinate to the comparatively small and new middle class, who were, in fact, not strong enough, in a land of poor peasants and undeveloped industries, to obtain wide support. The nominal acceptance of their diminished powers by both the kings made intervention difficult, but the ultras in France were longing to help to restore despotism in Spain as Austria was helping the princes of Italy.

As the Church supported the King, the Spanish Government became violently anti-clerical, and a reaction set in. In Seo de Urgel, a little grey town in the heart of the central Pyrenees, a so-called Regency was set up to restore Ferdinand to full power, and counter-revolutionary risings sprang up in different places. Spain was to be placed on the agenda of the Congress to be held in the autumn of 1822 at Verona, and the French royalists were very anxious to play the part of restorers of a Bourbon monarchy which had been over-thrown by Napoleon and replaced by English armies defeating Frenchmen. Moreover, it was felt that France ought to be playing an active rôle in Europe, not merely sending representatives to Con-gresses dominated by Metternich, who seemed supreme in the Holy Alliance. On this point a good many people who were by no means ultras shared their feelings.

De Villèle was very much against intervention in Spain. He knew that many Frenchmen would look on a war against the Spanish constitutionalists as the first step in a campaign to rid France of the Charter. He felt doubtful about the loyalty of the troops; there had been plenty of proof of their discontent. Above all, a war would certainly cost a great deal of money, and he was anxious to diminish, not to increase, the burden of the debt.

Whatever its policy, the French Government had to be repre-sented at the Congress. De Villèle himself could hardly be spared, considering the weakness of his colleagues, nor had he any diplomatic experience. Chateaubriand was openly convinced that he was the man. He believed he was doing marvels as Ambassador in London, and wrote to de Villèle: 'When I have carried on negotiations with kings, I shall have no rival.'[1] He tried to win Madame du Cayla's support but, characteristically, gave no hint of what policy he wished should be pursued. Montmorency, the Minister for Foreign Affairs, was not at all in favour of this idea; he was jealous, and thought that he himself would be France's best representative. Both de Villèle and the King doubted it; Montmorency had shown plenty of proof of religious fervour but none of political capacity. Still he certainly had a right to be heard on a matter so important in the foreign policy of France.

De Villèle, as was too often his way, tried to escape by a compro-mise. Chateaubriand was appointed as one of France's delegates to the Congress, but was joined by the ambassadors at Vienna and St. Petersburg. Montmorency himself went to Vienna, where pre-

[1] Quoted Viel-Castel, op. cit., Vol. XI, p. 426.

liminary discussions were being held. To strengthen his own position, de Villèle early in September 1822 took the title of President of
the Council, thus becoming officially Prime Minister. This wounded
his Foreign Minister's feelings; he thought it very improper that a
commoner should take precedence over a peer.

How little control de Villèle really had was soon shown. Instructions were given to all the French representatives that they should not
take the lead at Verona on the Spanish question and above all avoid
the appearance of being anxious to make war on Spain. Montmorency
soon made his passionate interest perfectly clear, and took the excuse
that Wellington was attending the Verona Congress to follow him
there. An absurd rivalry between him and Chateaubriand amused
the other diplomats, but made the carrying out of de Villèle's instructions even less likely. Chateaubriand was now clearly for war;
Montmorency began to draw back; the four representatives of
France did not even meet for a formal discussion of the attitude they
were to take until 8 November.

On 19 November, 1822, the Congress passed a series of resolu-
tions. These took the line that unfriendly relations between France
and Spain were improbable unless Spain herself declared war, or
provoked France to do so by open incitement to revolution in
France, or deposed Ferdinand, or altered the normal succession to
the Spanish throne. The English would not admit that either of the
last two actions would justify a war. The other Powers agreed that, if
such circumstances arose, their ambassadors in Paris would consult
with the French Government. This seemed to be a tacit approval of
French intervention.

Another odd event at Verona was the appearance of a financier
called Ouvrard. He was a man of fifty-two who had made and lost
fortunes by speculation during the revolutionary and Napoleonic
wars. At the moment he was a bankrupt, but this was thought to be
due to misfortune; Napoleon had let him down badly over some
contracts. He advocated the floating of an international loan for the
benefit of the Regency at Urgel. De Villèle thought this not a bad
idea; it might allow the Spanish royalists to manage without French
help. Unfortunately, the Spanish Government drove the Regency out
of Urgel; its members took refuge in France, and the international
bankers showed little sign of confidence in their prospective debtors.
Nor were the English at all likely to be helpful; the Portuguese
Government was already asking for an English guarantee of aid
should France invade Spain and then turn on Portugal.

For some time after the French delegation returned to Paris
discussion went on. Should France show her disapproval of the
Spaniards by withdrawing her ambassador from Madrid? It was

expected that if she did, Austria, Russia and Prussia would follow suit. When the King joined in the discussions he showed his poor opinion of Montmorency so very clearly that the Duke resigned on Christmas Day 1822. Chateaubriand's appointment as his successor was generally expected, but there were obstacles. The King disliked him; Montmorency's friends, very influential in ultra-royalist circles, thought it would be treachery for him to join de Villèle; the moderate-Right admired him but distrusted his ebullience. Yet so strong was his personality, and so weak his rivals, that after some hectic negotiations he got the post of Foreign Minister, which he had long desired.

De Villèle had hoped that Montmorency's dismissal would mean peace, but though he tried to pacify the ultras by giving them more administrative posts, their pressure was too strong for him. On 18 January, 1823, the French Ambassador was recalled from Madrid. On the 27th Ouvrard and another financier publicly appealed for subscriptions to a loan for the Urgel Regency; the Spanish Government tried to bring an action against them, but was told that the French courts did not recognise its right to speak for Spain.

When the parliamentary session opened on 28 January, 1823, the King's Speech included a phrase that 'Ferdinand must be free to grant his people institutions' and expressed hopes that war might be avoided. The *rentes* immediately fell; Canning in London remonstrated with the French Ambassador; angry speeches were made in the English parliament. But though England had lately made a commercial treaty with the Spanish Government, it was not likely she would go to war with France in its support.

Both Houses in France greeted with approval the possibility of war, though de Villèle's own speech, far below his usual level, showed clearly that he still wanted peace. General Foy (1775–1825) made a powerful attack on the Government. He knew well what fighting in Spain might mean; he had covered the retreat of the French troops before Wellington's army in 1813–14. He asked why Montmorency had resigned, if war were decided on; why there should be intervention now when there had been no change in the Spanish system; the people, he said, could not possibly want such a war, and he practically accused Artois and his friends of forcing on a dangerous and unnecessary crisis. Chateaubriand replied to him in a speech whose emotional and brilliant phrases successfully concealed the absence of any real answer to Foy's points.

Manuel spoke, and this gave rise to a tremendous storm in the Deputies' chamber. He was trying to point out how dangerous to a monarchy was foreign intervention, and to draw a lesson from the invasion of France and the execution of Louis XVI. As soon as he mentioned the king's name the royalists began shouting; he was not allowed to finish even the sentence, which had been misunderstood, and the sitting had to be suspended.

Next day, 27 February, 1823, de la Bourdonnaye demanded that Manuel be expelled from the House. Whether the deputies had this right was doubtful, so a committee was appointed to consider the matter. Most improperly, de la Bourdonnaye himself was chosen to report its conclusions. This led to further agitation on 1 March, and again the sitting was suspended.

On 3 March, when the debate resumed, a great crowd assembled outside the Chamber. The ultras, of whom de la Bourdonnaye was one of the most violent, wanted Manuel declared to be no longer a deputy, but de Villèle knew that this would mean a by-election in which Manuel would probably be successful. It was decided, therefore, simply to suspend him for the rest of the session; when the crowd heard this they demonstrated in his favour. Next day Manuel took his seat, declaring that his suspension was illegal. The National Guard was sent for to remove him, but the sergeant in charge refused to obey orders and use force. This man at once became a popular hero; a subscription was opened to give him a testimonial. The gendarmes, the armed police, then seized Manuel and took him away. All the Left-wing deputies followed him. They decided as a protest to absent themselves from debates, hoping that some of the centre-Right would support them. In this they were mistaken; though many of the moderates thought the expulsion of Manuel unwise and a dangerous precedent, they also hesitated to weaken the Government.

War was now inevitable. A special credit was approved; the Duke of Angoulême was nominated as Commander-in-Chief; army reservists were called to the colours. When the generals and responsible officers were being selected, the prince took a firm stand. He would not have the aristocrats and the politicians, such as Donnadieu and Canuel, who were chosen by his father's party; he said he must have experienced soldiers, no matter what their politics might be. He insisted on Oudinot and also on General Guilleminot, who had actually fought under Napoleon at Waterloo, but was known to be extremely able. Only those of Napoleon's marshals and generals who had actually spoken against the invasion of Spain in the Parliament were excluded.

Bellune, as Minister for War, had the difficult task of arranging for the provisions, munitions and transport for an expeditionary force of 90,000 men who were assembled near Bayonne ready to cross the frontier into Spain. Ouvrard, the irrepressible financier, offered to arrange everything for him, but Bellune refused, not unnaturally. Instead he appointed his own friends and political supporters as contractors to the army, with quite inadequate enquiry into their resources and experience.

The Spanish Government began its preparations. The ministers were well aware that its armed forces were inadequate and that, particularly in the northern provinces, it was not very popular. On 2 March, 1823, the Cortes decided that the Government must leave Madrid, and told the King he should go to a safer place. Ferdinand, very reluctantly, chose Seville, and after delaying his departure as long as he could, reached it on 20 March. The removal of the King from the capital seems to have been a real blunder by the Spanish liberals; it strengthened the case for intervention by making it clear that he was not a free agent, and stimulated the royalists in Spain. Moreover, as the Cabinet accompanied him, the direction of the war was much more difficult.

In France the opponents of the Bourbons seemed to have a wonderful opportunity in the assembly of a large army containing a considerable number of Napoleon's men. That the revolutionary plans which were prepared came to nothing was largely due to the good sense of Angoulême. When he reached Toulouse on 20 March he found the royalists talking of the holy mission of the army to defend the Church and the monarchy of Spain, while Napoleon's veterans were grumbling at having to fight for the monks and against freedom. Guilleminot's presence as the prince's chief of staff had an excellent effect; and the satisfaction that many men felt at resuming their uniform and re-entering Spain to wipe out the memory of their retreat over-rode their political opposition.

The royalists in Paris did not at all realise the situation; they were intensely suspicious of Guilleminot, and the Minister for War appointed himself Major-General of the Army of the Pyrenees without consulting Angoulême, the Commander-in-Chief. One of Guilleminot's aides-de-camp was arrested on suspicion of being implicated in a plot to raise a rebellion among the troops. The quick-tempered prince, who took his duties very seriously, was furious. By the time the Duke of Bellune joined him, he was at Bayonne. He told the Duke that unless his appointment were cancelled he would himself resign as a public protest; he had complete confidence in the chief of staff whom he himself had chosen. Bellune was forced to report to de Villèle that Guilleminot had done his work very well; he also reported, without adequate investigation, that all the arrangements for provisioning and transporting the troops were excellent.

It was impossible for the King and Artois to allow the prince to resign, so Guilleminot was confirmed in his office. The unhappy

Minister for War was now in an intolerable position. He tried to save his face by holding reviews and so forth; he would have been wiser to return to Paris and resign. As soon as the army began to move it was evident that though the stocks of munitions and food were adequate, the transport was not. Once again Angoulême had been given just cause for anger with the War Office.

The ingenious speculator Ouvrard had hoped for just such a situation. He himself was still bankrupt and could not enter into a legal contract, but he produced a nephew and induced the un-business-like prince to enter into a formal engagement with him. The contractor was to be allowed to draw on Government stores and also to make local purchases with Government funds while the necessary animals and carts were being bought and assembled. Of these arrangements Bellune had no official knowledge; he refused to enter into the negotiations, saying he was ill. He wrote a formal letter to Guilleminot saying that no contract would be legal without his approval as Minister of War, and that all draft contracts should be sent to him in Paris. As he stayed near Bayonne, this seemed to amount to a tacit approval of the arrangements already started. Bellune was forced to admit that he had been badly let down by the men whom he had entrusted with the transport, and wrote to the Prime Minister saying that they ought to be prosecuted, but he had neither the force of character nor the business experience to repair the damage himself.

Meantime, the army lingered near the frontier. Another of Angoulême's difficulties was to find an authority in Spain with whom to negotiate. He sent de Martignac to co-ordinate plans with the Spanish royalists, but he found a number of rival cliques who refused to co-operate. So, early in April, the impatient prince set up a new junta of men whom he himself nominated to represent Ferdinand's party, and published a proclamation saying that he was entering Spain not to impose laws or occupy the country, but to free the King, the Church and the people from an illegal government.

When the French troops reached the River Bidassoa there were no bridges, and a bridge of boats had to be constructed. The last test of the men's loyalty had come when some Frenchmen on the Spanish side of the river waved a tricolour standard and urged their comrades to refuse to obey orders; the French artillery scattered them with a few rounds. There was no opposition from the Spaniards; the town of Irun was evacuated by the Government's forces, and the unwieldy procession of French soldiers and guns solemnly began their mission of liberation.

There was little feeling of triumph in Paris, however. De Villèle's government was in a most awkward position. Each day the de-

9

ficiencies of Bellune's organisation of the commissariat became more
apparent. The Duke was so popular with the royalist politicians that
de Villèle did not dare to dismiss him, yet he was sure that Ouvrard,
of whom he had well-founded suspicions, was making a fortune out
of improvising schemes for feeding the army and that Bellune could
not or would not interfere. Nor could the advance be called a
glorious victory which would bring popularity to the Government.
The Spanish Government had hoped for the sort of guerilla attacks
which had proved effective against Napoleon; it had overestimated
its popular support, and the peasants, instead of fighting the French,
were rushing to them to sell their food and animals at immense
profit. Angoulême's worries were not those of a campaigner, except
for the constant trouble about supplies; they were concerned with
the Spanish royalists who were taking brutal vengeance on their
enemies as the French advanced, and shocking and horrifying their
liberators.

The pattern of the manœuvres, which could hardly be called a
war, remained much the same. One Spanish army was defeated and
surrendered on 26 July; the other conducted guerilla operations in
Catalonia. Madrid had been reached in May, and a Regency was set
up to act in the name of Ferdinand. The French were most popular,
but the Spanish royalists continued to alienate the people by their
'White Terror', and Angoulême was much distressed. He had made
up his mind that Spain should be given a workable constitution and a
complete amnesty be granted to all political offenders. The Spanish
royalists were wholly opposed to his plans; they were united only
in their desire for revenge, and quarrelled so violently among themselves that rival juntas were set up. The restoration of all Church
lands that had been confiscated and sold to the peasants was ordered
without any compensation being given. Tithes and other burdens
that had been abolished were restored, and these steps were taken by
a nominal government wholly dependent on France for its very
expenses, for de Villèle was, with the greatest reluctance, allowing it
two million francs a month.

The international repercussions of the Spanish War were also
rather disturbing. England was angry and suspicious, especially after
a counter-revolution in Portugal had restored King John VI in June
1823 and the liberal leaders had fled to England. Austria, Prussia and
Russia recognised the Madrid Regency as a legitimate government,
pending the liberation of Ferdinand, so Angoulême was unable to
destroy his own creation. His anxiety was to set the King free, but
when the French advanced on Seville the liberals removed him to
Cadiz. The local resistance they had failed to rouse was now being
achieved by the royalists. The Regency was raising an army with no

means of enforcing discipline; the result was anarchy. The middle classes were alienated by a decree that every Spaniard who had served in the constitutional national guard or militia would lose any rights he had to either pay or pension. Arbitrary arrests were countered by murders of royalists and by much stiffer resistance to the French. There was real fighting in July before Corunna was taken, and Barcelona held out for a long time.

The only people who might have approved Angoulême's plans for Spain, if they could have been enforced, were the ordinary peasants and the middle classes of Spain. Neither the French royalists nor the Congress powers approved them. Prussia, Austria and Russia had no desire to encourage the setting up of constitutions; they shared his own father's dislike of charters that tied a monarch's hands. The prince was sadly disillusioned; he had thought of himself as leading a crusade of liberation and reconciliation, instead he was constantly harried by criticisms of the arrangements he had made to repair the defective organisation of his army, and distressed by the stupidity and injustice of the Regency he had created. On 8 August he issued an ordinance directing his troops to free political prisoners, especially the militia men who had surrendered to the French and been sent home, only to be arrested by the royalists. This action horrified the French Government; de Villèle wrote saying the ordinance must be withdrawn, for it was an interference in the internal government of Spain. Angoulême had with great reluctance to modify his orders, but he wrote bitterly and frequently to Paris complaining of the Spaniards.

The last stage in the liberation of Ferdinand proved rather a long one. Cadiz was a strong place to defend and a difficult one to capture; unless the peninsula on which it stood could be attacked by sea as well as by land, and the French naval forces were inadequate, it could only be taken by the reduction of a series of outer defences. Angoulême was constantly asking for the dismissal of Bellune and receiving in return letters from de Villèle urging Angoulême himself to direct the operations against Cadiz and hurry on the capture of the city; in reply, Angoulême pointed out the remarkable incapacity of the French naval command. The English were worrying him too; they asked for assurances that when Ferdinand was freed the French should ensure that he granted a constitution; the prince knew only too well that no such assurance could be given.

The Cortes, besieged in Cadiz with the King, decided by the end of September that there was no hope of improving their position by further resistance. On the 28th they decided to set the King free. The soldiers refused to surrender unless they were given solid guarantees of their personal safety; they had heard of the fate of many of their comrades at the hands of the royalists. On 30 September, 1823, Ferdinand signed a document in which he pledged his word that a complete amnesty should be granted to all his opponents; that the debts incurred and the appointments made by the Cortes should be recognised as valid; and that he would adhere to a Constitutional Charter. On these terms he was released and received in triumph by the French.

What faith could be put in the word of a Bourbon king was soon made clear. Before he entered Madrid, Ferdinand ordered that every man who had been a member of the Cortes, an official of high rank under the Government, or an officer in the militia, should be removed to a distance of fifteen leagues (about 65 miles) from Madrid or any other royal residence. It was not merely the serious distress caused to hundreds of families by such an order that shocked the French; it was the realisation that as soon as they withdrew, Spain would be at the mercy of an unscrupulous man. Rather than witness Ferdinand's entry into his capital, Angoulême left for France.

One valuable result for France of this peculiar expedition was that it brought about a reconciliation between the Bourbons and the army. No longer did officers have to be on their guard lest their men should be plotting revolution. There was also a general feeling that Napoleon's failure in Spain had to some extent been expunged; the indignation of the English over the expedition was in a way a triumph for France. Certainly her status as a European power had improved.

On the other hand, it was questioned whether the enormous expense had been justified when the aim of the expedition—to restore peace and good order across the Pyrenees—had so lamentably failed of success. While the royalists in France rejoiced, ordinary citizens, hearing the stories of the returning soldiers, feared more than ever a triumph of despotism. The inefficiency of the Government had been demonstrated; even allowing for all that Angoulême could and did blame the Minister of War for, he himself had not been a great success as a general. Considering the lack of opposition, the campaign had been very long drawn out, and too often he had acted irresponsibly, without adequate consultation with his staff or with the Government in France. The Prime Minister's weak position when faced by Court intrigue was shown by his unwillingness to dismiss the Duke of Bellune; it was not only that Artois befriended him —he might have given way to his son's demands—but that it was generally known that Madame du Cayla was involved. She was trying to persuade Louis to appoint the Duke of Doudeauville, the father of her great friend Sosthènes de la Rochefoucauld, to some important office. Any Cabinet change meant all sorts of intrigue and intervention, so de Villèle feared to act. Angoulême was also pressing for a reward for Guilleminot; this was easier as he was not a politician. He was made Ambassador at Constantinople, according to the plan so often adopted when embassies were used as prizes for success or consolations for failure.

Madame du Cayla persuaded Lauriston, who held the important Court position of Minister of the King's Household, to resign and de Villèle could not resist Louis' choice of Doudeauville for the office. On 11 October the King told Villèle that Bellune must be dismissed. The Cabinet persuaded him to resign and become Ambassador at Vienna; but the Austrians would not recognise his title, as it was taken from a city in Venetia now under Austrian control, and he was too proud to abandon it. Lauriston was Madame du Cayla's candidate for the War Office, in exchange for his making way for Doudeauville, and she was also clamouring for the navy for another friend. De Villèle and the Cabinet resisted and Louis gave way, though he was deeply distressed and, indeed, made ill by the scenes the lady made. De Damas, who had been a mere child when his family emigrated, and had served in the Russian army, was made Minister of War; he was not in the least clever, but neither was he an extreme royalist.

All through the summer de Villèle had been under constant pressure from the ultras to provide posts for their supporters. Many minor officials were dismissed to create vacancies; everyone in a government position who subscribed to one of the liberal newspapers was in danger of losing his appointment. The Prime Minister had little help from his colleagues; Chateaubriand in particular was constantly attempting to take the leading place in the Cabinet.

The Foreign Minister suggested that general rather than partial elections would allow the Cabinet to profit from the satisfaction felt over the ending of the Spanish War; this de Villèle might have considered more favourably had Chateaubriand not also demanded that Donnadieu, Canuel and Vitrolles should be made peers. This de Villèle wholly refused; the first two had created such scandal over the plots of 1816 that to reward them at this stage would have looked like a surrender to the wildest elements in the *pointus* group. Instead, when on 23 December, 1823, the names of 27 new peers were announced, they were men of the moderate-Right, including Lainé. This angered Chateaubriand, while de Villèle in his turn was very much annoyed by a silly squabble over decorations. Alexander of Russia presented both Chateaubriand and Montmorency with an Order, ignoring the Prime Minister. Louis was very angry and promptly gave de Villèle a decoration; then Chateaubriand wanted to have that too. It all seemed quite childish to many observers, but beneath the Court intrigues there was a real problem. Could de

Villèle, whose sole strong point was his financial ability, succeed in keeping office long enough to deal with the pressing questions of the expenses of the war and the old debt? Was there a sufficient support for him among the moderates or would the country be governed by the caprices of a Court party?

Chateaubriand had no doubts about the situation. He was convinced, with some justification, that de Villèle was too immersed in finance, and was missing great opportunities for bringing France forward in European politics. His friends—and some later writers have agreed with them—thought that if he were Prime Minister he could have lifted politics out of the sordid atmosphere of intrigue. One may seriously doubt if there were any likelihood of such a success. He was as unpopular with the Court as was de Villèle; the King disliked him intensely. He was brilliant, but he lacked the steady wisdom of a great leader.

For example, he, like all European statesmen, was interested in the Spanish colonies in South America, which had revolted and declared themselves independent. Chateaubriand produced a plan for making them into kingdoms, each ruled by a member of the Bourbon family. In theory, there was a lot to be said for the idea; hereditary monarchs could have given stability to states long ruled despotically, and the subsequent history of the colonies showed how inappropriate republican government was for people of such diverse social and cultural standards and with so little political experience. As a practical plan, it was impossible; the revolt had been against the Bourbons, and that family, though fairly prolific, had few, if any, members suitable for the difficult part they would be asked to play. Moreover, though Austria would have approved such a scheme, England emphatically would not. English traders had been waiting for a very long time for unrestricted access to the great markets of South America, and English politicians had a great suspicion of French plans. The Spaniards themselves would not admit that their control had gone for ever, and the way in which the French diplomat seemed to ignore both legitimate historic rights and the wishes of the people concerned alienated both royalists and liberals. French agents in Spain were having a very difficult time trying to restrain Ferdinand, and being blamed for intervention in Spanish affairs by the English and for restoring a tyrannical government by the French liberals. If a neighbouring state could not be taught good sense, what hope was there for influence being exercised across miles of ocean in South America?

Chateaubriand did persuade de Villèle to have a dissolution in the spring of 1824 instead of the usual partial elections. Had de Villèle been a wiser man, this election might greatly have strengthened his position, for it is quite likely that many of the centre-Right and few of the Left-wing liberals would have been elected. But he was in such a panic that Government pressure on electors exceeded that at any previous election. Bishops wrote propaganda; every official was threatened; people's names were left out of lists of voters and men without qualification allowed to vote. The result was the practical elimination of the liberals; in Paris they had held six of the eight seats, now they had three. In the rest of the country they secured only thirty-three representatives. It was really dangerous for the Prime Minister to have an overwhelming royalist Chamber; the *pointus* could attack him safely if there were no fear of the liberals.

De Villèle and Chateaubriand were now agreed that the system of partial renewal of the deputies must end and general elections be held at stated intervals. Chateaubriand wanted a five-year term, de Villèle preferred seven, and he had his way. A law for septennial elections was introduced and, after much debate, passed in the summer of 1824; members took the chance to speak freely about the lack of real freedom of election.

Chapter XII

ROYALISM TRIUMPHANT

THE Prime Minister had been anxious for a long pause before new elections had to be fought, for he was planning a great financial scheme for which stability in and outside Parliament was essential.

He had two ends in view. One was to reduce the drain of the annual interest on the debt; the other to remove a persistent cause of political friction by giving official compensation to the people whose property had been confiscated during the Revolution. The two distinct aims were linked in practice, for he felt that to add seriously to the taxes in order to give money to the royalists who had emigrated would destroy any hope that remained of making the restored monarchy acceptable to the middle classes.

The time seemed propitious. Government credit was good; in February 1824 the 5 per cent *rentes* were selling for over their face value. Over 140 millions of this stock was privately owned; another 57 millions was held in trust for certain payments by the Government itself. If holders of the stock could be induced to accept a lower rate of interest, the annual saving would cover the expense of the proposed compensation.

During January and February 1824 de Villèle was absorbed in negotiations with financiers. His plan was discussed in the Cabinet and approved; Chateaubriand in his memoirs says that he opposed it, but de Villèle, in his contemporary letters as well as his recollections, contradicts him. Probably the opposition was tacit, for finance did not interest the Minister for Foreign Affairs. The chief point was that the Government must have a large sum in cash available so that holders of the 5 per cent stock could be offered the alternative of repayment of their capital in cash or a lower annual income. De Villèle decided that as there was already in existence a mass of 3 per cent *rentes* issued in connection with the payments under the treaty of 1815, the 5 per cent stock holders should be offered 3 per cent *rentes* but that their capital holding should be increased; the new issue would be valued at 75 francs for each certificate of 100 francs debt. This would mean that a man who owned, say, 7,500 francs in 5 per cent *rentes* from which he got an income of 375 francs a year would be offered in exchange 10,000 francs in 3 per cent stock bringing in only 300 francs per annum. Should the general level of interest fall, he could hope to sell his new stock above the price of 75 francs and so make a profit. At any rate, he would not have the trouble of reinvesting the 7,500 francs he would receive if he refused to convert his holding, and the probability was that he would not get a greater income with equal security if he did seek another investment.

Such conversion schemes had been carried out in England; by Walpole in 1721 and Pelham in 1751 for example. For their success two things were necessary; that there was an ample fund for the government to repay stockholders and that the banks and financiers had plenty of money available for lending so that the market rate of interest was not likely to be higher than that offered by the conversion scheme. Earlier conversions, though, had been purely financial transactions and had led to a substantial lowering of government expenditure. De Villèle's scheme was intended to raise money for a particular purpose, the payment of large sums to those whom the royalists felt had a moral claim on the State.

Four large banking firms were asked to participate in the scheme. As in the loan arranged by Richelieu (see p. 93) they were to place the 3 per cent stock on the market at the price of 75 francs for each 100 franc certificate and take in exchange the 5 per cent stock which was surrendered by its owners or offered for sale. For all the 5 per cent *rentes* they were to continue to receive full interest until 1826, so their profit was assured. One of the four firms, a purely French one, withdrew from the plan leaving three banks, Baring's, Rothschild's and Laffitte's, to carry it out in co-operation. All three had strong international connections and had hopes of additional profits when, as they expected, the value of the 3 per cent loan rose above its issue price. The terms of this contract were kept secret.

When the parliamentary session opened on 23 March, 1824, the Lower House was crowded with triumphant royalists. The appearance of the King was pathetic, and threw a shadow over their rejoicings. He was clearly very ill; his speech had been written out for him in enormous letters, but even so he had difficulty in finishing it. It announced the two major bills proposed by de Villèle: the Conversion scheme, and the Septennial Act.

De Villèle introduced his financial plan in a long and careful speech. Opposition was immediately forthcoming; some of it reasonable, some ignorant, some prejudiced. The Prime Minister very much needed support, but especially on such a technical matter his Cabinet was very inadequate. Had he chosen, Chateaubriand, the major orator of the ministry, could have lifted the affair into a wonderful scheme of justice and wisdom, but he took the line that it was a sordid sort of stock exchange transaction which he did not understand and in which he took no interest whatever. De Villèle took enormous pains; when the committee was chosen to examine the bill he saw its members privately, and coached them in what they were to think and say. Debates were long; many amendments were introduced and defeated; but the law was finally carried by 238 to 145 by the exhausted deputies.

On 4 May, 1824, the Prime Minister introduced his bill to the Peers. Had he not had the right to speak in both Houses, there would have been no one capable of explaining it. In the Upper House opposition was even stronger; many of the Peers had large holdings of 5 per cent *rentes* and stood to lose by the conversion. On 27 May de Villèle had an interview with Chateaubriand and accused him of opposing a government measure, but thought it beneath his dignity formally to demand that the Foreign Minister should speak in its favour. Louis allowed it to be known that he strongly favoured the scheme; Artois did not openly oppose it but neither would he approve. In despair de Villèle thought of giving a place in the Cabinet to some outstanding royalist; he was apt to try to bribe people by giving them offices, a measure of his weakness. His struggles were in vain; the Peers threw out the bill by 128 to 94 in an unusually full House.

The poor, sick King was greatly upset. He implored de Villèle not to resign; 'Do not abandon me to these brigands'. It was perfectly clear that one of the two leaders, de Villèle or Chateaubriand, must resign. On 6 June Louis insisted on the immediate dismissal of the Foreign Minister, and the Cabinet agreed. Even if Villèle had been more tactful, and not so clearly shown his distrust of the romantic diplomat, the connection could never have lasted for long. Chateaubriand had demonstrated that whatever his constitutional theories might be, he had not grasped the need of loyalty to the decisions of a cabinet.

The outcry in the Press when it was announced that Chateaubriand had resigned and that de Villèle had taken over his duties was very loud indeed. Chateaubriand himself attacked the Government of which he had just been a member; though he did not sign his articles, everyone knew their author. The King's health made it almost impossible for de Villèle himself to resign, which would have been dignified and probably wise; the personal tie between the monarch and his advisers was very close, and Louis fully believed in his constitutional right to choose his own ministers.

The session of Parliament went on. A law was passed modifying St. Cyr's Army Act by making recruits liable to eight years' service instead of six, but repealing their obligation to be six years in the reserve, liable to be called up in an emergency. During the debates, the extreme Right showed its strong desire to alter the law with regard to the promotion of officers by seniority. The budget gave rise to storms over the contracts which Angoulême had made with Ouvrard. In spite of the royalists' respect for their prince, they ordered the printing in full of a speech by Foy attacking the terms made; as Foy was one of the few members of the Left this caused a sensation. The budget showed an expenditure of nearly 1,145 million francs as compared to 909 million the previous year, and by no means all the costs of the Spanish expedition had been included. The Duke of Bellune wrote a pamphlet defending himself, but it had little success. In the end the budget was carried, but a committee was appointed to investigate Ouvrard's accounts.

Another subject debated had been the Church; as the costs of the upkeep of the Church formed a regular item of State expenditure, there was every year a chance for criticism. This debate was memorable for a phrase used by Bourdeau who attacked the clerical party for demanding all sorts of additional privileges for the Church. 'All they want can be reduced to two phrases: the old régime with the Jesuits added and the liberties of the Gallican Church subtracted.' This became current all over the country.

As the parliamentary session neared its end de Villèle could look forward to relief from his constant attendance in the Lower House, but he could not face the future with confidence. He had been forced to follow rather than lead; he must get more solid support. Could he use the vacant Foreign Office to win over a fair-sized group of royalists? The trouble was that such a group hardly existed; there were many leaders but none of them could count on steady and loyal support from many of his friends. Madame du Cayla could not be ignored. She even persuaded Louis to sign a decree dismissing Corbière, one of the few able men in the Cabinet, and appointing her friend, Sosthènes de la Rochefoucauld, to his post as Minister of the Interior. Artois intervened, and the plan was dropped.

De Villèle decided on a compromise, not at all a satisfactory one. On 4 August, 1824, the day the session ended, a reshuffle rather than a renewal of the Cabinet was announced. The Foreign Office was given to de Damas, a most surprising choice. He was loyal, but that was about all that could be said for him; he had been able to follow the routine of the War Ministry, but had no qualifications whatever for conducting negotiations with foreign Powers. Once again de Villèle had shown his lack of appreciation of the importance of any but purely domestic concerns. The War Office went to Clermont-Tonnerre, who as Minister for the Navy had been justly blamed for the weakness of the naval side of the Spanish expedition. The navy was taken over by a new man, Chabrol de Creuzol, who had at any rate some administrative experience, but no definite parliamentary influence.

Madame du Cayla was partly pacified by the creation of a new post for her friend Sosthènes, that of Director of Public Exhibitions of Art and Manufactures. Lauriston, who had retired to allow Sosthènes' father, Doudeauville, to take charge of the King's Household, was at last rewarded with the sinecure post of Grand Huntsman, once held by Richelieu. Some of the deputies were given minor posts, and, in an attempt to please the clericals, de Villèle set up by decree on 24 August a new Department of Catholic Religion and Public Instruction; the first minister in charge was the Abbé Frayssinous, the Grand Master of the University. But in a reorganisation of the Council of State, Bertier, the head of the Knights of the Faith, and other extremists lost their posts, as a hint to the *pointus* that opposition did not pay.

Louis gave his formal consent to these measures, but he was visibly weakening. The Press was full of comment and anticipation, and de Villèle seized on the excuse to reimpose the censorship and stifle criticism of his policy. Artois, waiting for his own accession to the throne and anxious for tranquillity, saw how foolish was so very unpopular an action, and how much a proof of weakness. The King went on with his routine as best he could, showing himself to the people in his evening drives, sitting 'working' at his desk even when he had not the strength to hold up his head, which drooped down till it lay upon the desk and Villèle gently slipped a cushion beneath it.

By 9 September, 1824, Louis was breathing with difficulty, and two days later Madame du Cayla persuaded him to send for his confessor. The last sacraments were administered on the 13th and he died on 16 September early in the morning. His body was embalmed and lay in state till it was buried with most elaborate ceremony on 25 October.

Though his last years were shadowed by the influence of his favourite Madame du Cayla, Louis had proved himself to be, if not an able man, at least one very genuinely anxious for his country's welfare. His hopes for a reconciliation between the old monarchy and the new France had not been fulfilled, but so far as he could he had laid the foundations. It was not the King but those who professed to love and support monarchy who were responsible for the doubts so widely felt whether constitutional monarchy would survive his death.

Louis, who at his coming had been mocked, was at his death

sincerely mourned. Silent crowds gathered round the palace; all theatres closed spontaneously; even the shops put their shutters up. The people filed past his body and lined the streets for his funeral; so many obsequies had been used as a chance for political demonstrations, but the King's were symbolic of genuine emotion. No one now had any grudge against him; the eulogies in the papers were sincere.

His death was, so to speak, better timed than his first entry had been. It was most fortunate that the victory of the royalists had preceded it, and that Villèle was already in power. Charles had, through de Villèle's constant communication with him, a far better idea of the practical difficulties of ruling than he had had a few years before. The change of monarch did not involve a change in policy. Charles as king seemed to be a different man from Monsieur, who had caused so much trouble to his brother and his cabinets. He spoke favourably of the Charter; he even went so far as to make approaches to the Duke of Orleans, who had been cold-shouldered for so long. He was given the title of Royal Highness, which Louis had refused him; and next year Charles' ministers introduced and passed a law which restored to him and his heirs male lands which had been confiscated in 1791 and which had been returned to him in 1814 but with a very dubious title. This was the more remarkable because strong personal opposition to the son of 'Égalité' was openly expressed by many royalists even in the debates in Parliament.

Immediately popular was Charles' order to raise the censorship. He had advised de Villèle against its imposition and felt with justification that to alienate the journalists was very unwise. The Government had the security of the seven-years' term; there was no need to anticipate malicious opposition. The reception given to the new king as he made his first formal procession through Paris was very warm and cordial.

The royalists at once began their campaign to get rid of de Villèle who was, they felt, a barrier to the attainment of their full programme. Charles was convinced that he was essential, especially as the funds for compensation for the émigrés were not yet available. But the Prime Minister was forced to give way on several points. Angoulême, now the Dauphin and heir apparent, had a keen interest in the army. He thought with much justification that the army as a career was not offering enough scope to the younger men; too many of the senior posts were still held by Napoleon's officers and by men of even greater age who had been appointed as a reward for their royalism not for their military efficiency. On 1 December the Cabinet issued an ordinance by which 167 senior officers were placed on the retired list. The conditions for retirement had been so ingeniously drafted that they affected only the soldiers of the Imperial armies; the royalists, many of them very much older, kept their posts. Many of the men retired were comparatively young, in the forties and fifties. Once again the Bourbons seemed to be going out of their way to antagonise the troops.

On 22 December, 1824, Parliament assembled. The drafting of the King's Speech had taken a lot of the Cabinet's time, because Charles was deeply interested in the plans for his coronation and spent so long discussing details of ceremonies that serious planning of a political programme was almost impossible in his presence. De Villèle had asked for new peers to be created, to offset the liberals who had thrown out his conversion bill, but partly owing to the Dauphin's opposition the King refused. The balance of power in the Chambers was, therefore, unchanged when he made his first speech.

The terms of the speech seriously checked the hopes of the liberals that there had been a real modification of Charles' views. He did not refer to the Charter, but to 'institutions granted by my brother'. He spoke of his Government's plans for improving the position of the Church and for providing compensation for the victims of the Revolution. In the Reply the Left-wing deputies wanted a reference to the Charter by name; the symbolic word indicated that the basis of the monarchy was a contract, not a grant. They were defeated and a formal approval and congratulation was submitted to the King.

On 3 January, 1825, the discussion of the new laws began. The Civil List had to be fixed; the Government asked for an annual income of 25 million francs a year for the King and 7 million for his family, with an additional 6 million for the costs of the funeral of Louis and the coronation of Charles. The size of the grants disturbed many people; the total income of all members of the Royal Family, Louis, Artois and both Artois' sons, had been 33 million francs in 1816; now 32 million were asked when both Louis and de Berry were dead. The expenditure on ceremonies also annoyed people who knew that it was being proposed to cut down the revenues of holders of the 5 per cent national debt.

The law for giving compensation to the victims of the Revolution was, oddly enough, introduced by Martignac, who was not a minister. Though the men who had emigrated and their families formed the great majority of those who would receive grants, other non-royalists who had had their lands confiscated were included. The proposal was to issue 6 millions in 3 per cent *rentes* each year for five years, and distribute them to the survivors of the landowners or their direct heirs. Martignac's speech was excellent; he pointed out that so long as the feeling of injustice remained, no purchaser of confiscated land would feel completely safe, and that to right a great wrong was prudent as well as just.

The opposition, when discussion began on 17 February, 1825, had a number of criticisms to make. One speaker pointed out that there were no less than 320 deputies, of whom 266 held Government posts, who would be included in the compensation and held it improper for them to vote money to themselves. Others attacked the émigrés for having taken up arms against their own country; while it was also remarked that a considerable number had already been given compensation in the form of gifts and well-paid offices. On the other side, royalist speakers denied that the present holders of lands had any claim to them in justice; this led Foy to say that if the royalists were not satisfied by the proposals, he failed to see why the State should burden itself for them; and Benjamin Constant to protest against the insult offered to landowners by denying their moral right to their property.

When the law was finally carried, by 259 to 154, the size of the minority showed how many royalists were still not satisfied, and the attacks they had made on de Villèle in the debates seemed to show a great lack of gratitude to the man who was giving them so handsome a present. Public opinion, noting this, took a step towards the Left. In the Peers, Chateaubriand attempted with great ingenuity to defend both the émigrés and the present owners of their lands. Amendments were carried in the Upper House which gave additional security to existing landowners; the deputies agreed to these and the law was finally passed in April.

The distribution of the payments with strict justice was an almost impossible task. Proof of title to their former lands was often difficult for poorer men, when so many records had been destroyed, and it was the great nobles who got the lion's share of the fund. The closing of a chapter of revolutionary history had good results, however; for many owners of disputed property had been unable to sell it save at a price well below its market value. Now there was no differentiation between the various estates; and many property owners who were not royalists were relieved at the righting of what they felt had been an injustice.

The counterpart to compensation was conversion of the debt. A report on the operation of the Sinking Fund indicated how far the value of the debt on the market had risen during nine years; stock bought for 573 million francs was now worth 715 million. De Villèle's law, rejected in 1824, was reintroduced with an amendment which gave the holders of 5 per cent stock the right to refuse conversion, though they were threatened with forced conversion on worse terms in the future. Discussion on the bill began on 17 March, 1825;

opposition, based mainly on fear that speculators would gain from the operation, was still expressed, but the law was passed by both Houses. In the Peers Chateaubriand came out openly against the plan; in his view, the right rate of interest for a Christian state was 5 per cent.

The Ouvrard contracts still troubled Villèle; when the accounts of 1823 came up for final closure in the summer, they included payments for the Spanish expenses. The reckless and extravagant nature of the arrangements made was now clearly exposed, but a disturbing feature of the discussions was that blame was laid not on Angoulême, now the Dauphin, which was understandable, nor on Bellune, to whose inefficiency the trouble was due, but on Villèle, who had from the beginning protested. His budget, too, which showed a satisfactory surplus in spite of extraordinary expenditure, did not bring him the congratulations he had earned for economies in administration. Instead, he was attacked on all sides: by the royalists for the over-centralisation of the administration, by the liberals for his foreign policy and for the unfair way in which high-ranking officers had been withdrawn from the active list. The budget was carried, but the re-appearance of a sharp double opposition from Right and from Left was alarming to the Prime Minister.

Much of the Cabinet's time during the spring was taken up by arrangements for Charles' coronation. He was persuaded to accept a modification of the traditional oath by the insertion of a reference to the Charter, and to agree that the deputies should send all the officials of the House and 100 of their members to take part in the ceremonies. It was decided, to the disappointment of many, that no new peers should be created. Five of Napoleon's followers were included with sixteen of the old nobility in a distribution of the Order of the Holy Spirit; the wrangles over this were long and bitter. In return for these concessions, the King insisted that the Coronation should be held at Rheims and that every possible traditional ceremony should be discovered and included.

On 29 May the magnificent pageantry of the rite delighted the immense majority of those who were able to see it. There was some jesting over the quaintness of some of the antique costumes and ceremonies, and more over the King's solemn 'touching for the King's Evil' two days later; the old belief in the healing power of the hands of the Lord's Anointed was dead and could not be revived. Criticism was limited to a very few, however; the ordinary folk of all classes greatly enjoyed the festivities which followed Charles' return to Paris on 6 June and endured for a fortnight, and the corresponding bonfires and shows which took place all over the country.

De Villèle got little help from these rejoicings. Any credit went to the King, not to the ministers. He badly needed help in the summer of 1825, for events which he could scarcely be blamed for not fore-seeing were seriously upsetting his great financial operation. The new 3 per cent *rentes* had been issued in considerable quantities during the summer, both in exchange for the old 5 per cent stock and as payments to those who had claims for compensation. Not surprisingly, their market price fell a little below the issue price of 75 francs for each 100-franc certificate. Some of the bankers who had not participated in the plan were also deliberately selling them to keep the price low. A syndicate was formed to counteract this move by buying the stock; Chateaubriand seemed to be justified in his view that the plan would lead to stock exchange manœuvres. By the end of July most of those who had accepted conversion were foreigners; only 9 millions of French-held *rentes* were converted, out of a total of 30 millions, when the period for accepting the offer ended on 5 August. Then a commercial crisis in London affected the French financiers. They sold *rentes* to have funds to use in London, and by the end of the month the 3 per cent issue stood at 71. This was a very small fall; worse was to come. English consols fell in value during the autumn as bankers sold them to get ready money; by November they stood at 81 compared to their midsummer figure of 95. The French stock went down to 60 from its issue price of 75, and de Villèle alone was blamed. Then, just as prospects were looking better and prices of stocks were rising, on 17 December the Prime Minister heard of the death of Alexander of Russia. This news was bound to cause uncertainty about the international situation, and it led to a renewed fall on the Stock Exchanges of London and Paris.

All through the autumn de Villèle had been aware of the steady weakening of his position. The extreme Right had clamoured for and to some extent secured legislation which they believed would benefit their Church; they were asking for laws to ensure landed estates being entailed; they wanted modification of the Press laws to check the growing influence of the liberals. Charles might have meant to be a constitutional monarch, but nothing could prevent him from discussing Cabinet business with his courtiers, and the hothead Sosthènes de la Rochefoucauld, having failed to buy up all the liberal papers, was now suggesting control of the theatres. One can only imagine that it was his anxiety to watch over his financial plans that prevented de Villèle from resigning in December, before the next session of Parliament. Instead, he clung uneasily to office.

The more active were the royalists, the greater the opportunities for the liberals. In October Lafayette, who had been making a tour in the United States, returned in an American warship to Havre.

10

Here and at Rouen acclaiming crowds surrounded him; in Rouen the demonstrators were dispersed by force, but a cavalcade accompanied the revolutionary hero on his road to Paris. In September General Foy, who had been visiting a spa in the Pyrenees in the hope of some improvement in the heart disease from which he had long suffered, was crowned with laurels by the business men of Bordeaux. Scenes of great enthusiasm showed the popularity of a man who, by his honesty, sincerity and eloquence, had gained a very genuine respect.

Foy's illness was too deep-seated for cure; on 28 November the news of his death shocked and grieved not only the Left-wing extremists but many of the moderate royalists. His funeral was arranged for 29 November and enormous crowds gathered to do him homage. It was calculated that about ten thousand people walked in the procession to the grave; peers, generals, undergraduates, literary men all joined in; the Duke of Orleans sent his carriage as a mark of respect. Most of the shops on the way to the cemetery were hung with black; in spite of a cold rain 30,000 people were gathered in the cemetery when the coffin reached it at six in the evening. It was said that no such demonstration had occurred since Mirabeau's funeral

Practical proof of sympathy was given by the opening of a public subscription for his family, whom he left badly off, and the erection of a monument. Within six months nearly a million francs was subscribed, an immense sum for France in those days. Laffitte, the banker, had given 50,000 francs, and the Duke of Orleans 10,000 rich men and the middle classes all combined to show their sympathy and their homage. Foy had sincerely accepted the new constitution, but had been hated by the royalists as a man who had fought for the Revolution and been a defender of Napoleon's policy in Spain. Politically, it can be said that Foy's death gave an opportunity for French liberalism, which had seemed to be on the decline, to show that it was very much alive and had a far wider support than the recent election results had indicated.

Chapter XIII

CHURCH AND STATE

THE reign of Charles X was overshadowed by the spirit of intolerance. Not only did the clerical party attempt by every means to increase the wealth and power of the official Church, ignoring the rights of unbelievers; the liberals themselves denied their own principles by attempts to restrict the freedom of the Catholics and by ill-founded and sometimes deliberately false accusations. Men whose religion was based on love and justice showed themselves greedy and unscrupulous intriguers; their critics, who proclaimed individual freedom of thought and action as a means of reaching the truth, constantly distorted facts and met exaggerated claims with factious opposition.

The international affiliations of the Church in France combined with the strong 'Gallican' tradition of maintaining as much independence as was compatible with union with Rome to make the situation even more complex. Sometimes the intervention of the Papacy helped to calm down violent agitation; sometimes papal pronouncements applicable to the whole Catholic world were used in France as a weapon in a political struggle. Many of the extremists in the Church retained the pre-Revolution attitude of resentment at papal interference; this partly accounts for the rise in France of a non-royalist Catholic group that was 'ultramontane', looking to the Church in Rome for guidance and help. It was difficult, under Charles X, for a convinced Catholic to combine his religious convictions with opposition to a government that was constantly proclaiming its support of his Church while carrying out a policy which he thought radically unsound.

As in most European countries at some time or other since their foundation, the Jesuits by their very existence complicated the issue of the relations between Church and State. Since they had been temporarily disbanded, they had been legally excluded from France. Actually, individuals had always remained, and after the Restoration their numbers increased. The suspicion, often amounting to hatred, which they aroused was probably partly due to their past history, when so often they had acted as confessors to monarchs and been accused of exercising political influence, partly to the aftermath of the great seventeenth-century controversy in France partly to their efficiency as an organisation. Their schools were probably the best in France in the standard of education reached by the pupils.

The educational system in France in the eighteen-twenties was still very imperfect. Although the University was under a clerical head and many of the professors were in orders, the general tone of the students was anything but pious. In a students' debate in 1826 the motion that God existed was carried by only one vote. The secondary schools supported by the State were often inefficient as a result parents often chose to send their sons to schools which like the Jesuits', were really illegal or to the seminaries, which were preliminary training schools for boys aiming at the priesthood. There were no less than 126 of these 'little seminaries' recognised by law and about 53 without official status. The majority of the pupils had no intention whatever of entering holy orders.

For girls, the State's provision was hopelessly inadequate; their secondary education was carried out by governesses or in convent schools. New teaching orders of nuns had sprung up and were very popular. The primary schools suffered from the parsimony of the Government; a system invented in England, which two men, Lancaster and Bell, both claimed as their idea, was adopted because of its cheapness. One master only was engaged for a school; he taught the larger boys and they in their turn taught the smaller. Such instruction could only be of the parrot type and was most superficial at the best. The schools run by religious orders were far more thorough, for the Fathers and Brothers needed only enough in the way of fees to support them in a frugal way and could afford to have several teachers for the salary of one schoolmaster who had a wife and family. One of the weak points in the widespread opposition to the Church schools was that by any standard they were generally far more efficient than the undenominational State schools.

In January 1825, when Parliament began its session, two bills were introduced which at once roused sectarian passions. The first was an apparently modest little bill. A number of young women had been joining both the older and the newer religious orders in France, and additional establishments were badly needed. It was proposed to allow congregations of nuns to be founded by royal ordinance if their bishop approved, and to allow nuns to bequeath not more than a quarter of their property to the community which was supporting them. In debate, de Villèle told the Peers that there were 1,800 communities of women in France of which only fifty belonged to the contemplative orders whose contribution to the State was their prayer. The others were teaching 120,000 children nd nursing 14,000 sick people in hospitals. Surely such women vere no danger to the State? Pasquier, however, got an amendment arried that a law, not an ordinance, would be required for each 1ew foundation, a process so uncertain and expensive as to be a erious barrier. Part of the liberal opposition is to be explained by he demands of the clerical party that no authority whatever should be required from the State and that nuns should have complete reedom to dispose of their property.

Another law introduced into the Peers was of a different character. Wise churchmen, including some of the bishops, did not like it at all; it was due to the excessive fervour of the Knights of the Faith and their like. It proposed the imposition of the death penalty for the commission of sacrilege by profanation of the consecrated Host. As a oken of impartiality, sacrilege included similar profanation in churches of all denominations, which very much annoyed the ultra-clerical party. As, however, the whole point of the law was to express the Roman Catholic doctrine of the Real Presence of the Saviour in the consecrated wafers, the inclusion of the Protestant Churches had little meaning. Opposition to the law was vigorous; even Chateau-briand, the defender of Christianity, spoke against it. It involved the creation of a new crime which differed from the normal offences against property because it was based on a religious dogma not universally accepted. No enemy of the Church had, in fact, been committing such an offence; indeed, many Catholics were afraid lest the law itself should suggest to some fanatic that he should break it as a demonstration. The sole point seemed to be that belief in the sacrament of the altar should be written into the penal code.

The law, fortunately, remained uninvoked and therefore com-pletely unnecessary. All it did was to rouse justified suspicion with regard to the Government's submission to the demands of a minority of churchmen. Foolish ecclesiastics seemed to be doing their best to exacerbate opposition; for instance, the Archbishop of Rouen suggested in a Pastoral Letter that the names of all persons who did not attend mass or who were married only by civil law should be posted on church doors for public reprobation. This led, naturally, to demonstrations against the Church in Rouen. Similar follies by other clerics gave the *Constitutionnel* newspaper and the rest of the liberal Press a magnificent opportunity. The *Constitutionnel* began to publish a regular Church gazette in which it listed acts of in-tolerance by priests and bishops. Many of the items were incorrect or even invented; for instance, persecution of Protestants at Nérac was described. The Protestants themselves wrote to say that there was no such thing; they were on the best of terms with their neigh-bours. But the *Constitutionnel* did not publish the letter.

The cumulative effect of such attacks was very great. One comprehensible policy of the clergy caused great outcry: the refusal to bury in consecrated ground with religious rites persons who in their life had not in practice been members of the Church. Sometimes, however, they showed great lack of charity, as in the case of a judge who died away from his home without having summoned the local priest to his death-bed. In spite of appeals from his colleagues, he was refused Church burial, though it had been customary in such cases to take the view that the deceased should have, so to speak, the benefit of the doubt.

The preachers of missions continued to annoy the public; in one extreme case at Besançon, an old walled town, the gates were closed and the old drawbridges raised for eight hours, during which a procession of rather a military type, with gunfire and trumpets and numbers of soldiers, accompanied the missionaries in their last ceremonies and the planting of a cross. Pious hymns were sung to the tune of the 'Marseillaise'. Hypocrisy, especially in the army, was encouraged and a sort of unofficial police censorship on books attempted to suppress the works of the eighteenth-century philosophers and the Bonapartists. The moderate and prudent clergy and their followers found themselves much embarrassed.

In November 1825 the *Constitutionnel* and another paper, the *Courrier*, were prosecuted for libel. The prosecution showed clearly how many of their statements were false, but as generally happens the trial gave a chance for the editors to claim that their attacks were on the policy of the Government and especially its toleration of the illegal Jesuits. The case was heard before a bench of 27 judges, some of them known to be practising Catholics, yet the result was a mere warning to the papers to be more discreet. The Government was aghast at this result, and the crowds cheered wildly.

The idea of modifying the laws concerning the Press naturally was taken up by the King's circle of advisers, and an encyclical letter by Pope Leo XII in February 1826 encouraged them. The encyclical proclaimed the keeping of a Jubilee, a special period of prayer, the precise dates of which were fixed by each country to suit local conditions; it also contained severe criticism of the licence and impiety of the Press. The French clergy fixed the dates for the Jubilee as 15 February to 3 May, 1826; thus immediately they gave a local political emphasis to a world-wide act of piety, for 3 May was celebrated by the royalists as the anniversary of Louis XVIII's return to Paris. The plan of altering the Press laws, which Polignac, Ambassador in London, was urging on Charles, was resisted by de Villèle and by the Dauphin, and no law was proposed. The deputies in their Reply to the Address asked for such a law, but the Prime

Minister persuaded the King that they had no right to do so, and in his response Charles gave no suggestion of legislation.

This disappointment may have encouraged the royalists in the Lower House. to undertake a most foolish attack on a newspaper. In February 1826 it was proposed to cite at the Bar of the House the *Journal of Commerce* for having pointed out, three months earlier, what a large number of deputies were officials and émigrés. In spite of a strong protest from Royer-Collard, the House decided to call the editor to appear on 1 March to answer charges of breach of parliamentary privilege. The ministers markedly refrained from taking part in the proceedings; the crowd outside the Palais Bourbon, where the deputies sat, was so large that troops were called out to prevent disorder.

The editor's lawyer took the line that all the facts given in the *Journal of Commerce* were correct, and that the comment on them was much milder than remarks which had actually been made in the Chamber itself. This was perfectly true, yet the deputies voted by 213 to 129 that the paper had been guilty of an attack on their House. The punishment was then fixed; by 188 to 151 a fine of 100 francs and a month's imprisonment was imposed. This was absurd; a quite exceptional procedure suitable for a really important political case had ended in a punishment which could have been imposed by a police court, in a magnificent advertisement for the paper, and a justification for its criticism of the royalists.

Meanwhile, a bitter controversy was going on between an émigré, Montlosier, who in spite of his royalism was attacking the Jesuits, and Lamennais, a priest who had written for Chateaubriand's *Conservateur* and other royalist papers, and was a fanatical defender of the Church. Montlosier published a book dealing with what he called 'a religious system tending towards the destruction of both religion and the throne', in which he declared that the policy of the Congregation and the Jesuits would lead to a disaster such as had overtaken King James II of England. It had a great success, several reprints being demanded. Lamennais published on the very same day a book called *Religion Considered in Its Relations with Political and Civil Order*. It was a wild attack on the Government, which he declared was revolutionary, on members of both Houses, even on some of the bishops. All political liberty was denounced as leading to atheism; the Pope was declared to be the sole legitimate ruler, with the right to call upon Christians to overturn any government. The defenders of Gallicanism in particular were fiercely attacked. So wild were the claims and so exalted the language of the book that the priest's friends were afraid he was losing his reason, but the young priests in many places were excited by it; the idea of looking to

Rome to set right the complications of the Church in France stirred their imaginations.

De Villèle felt that his Government could not ignore these two publications. Against Charles' advice, he decided to punish Mont-losier by withdrawing a pension he had enjoyed ever since he had returned to France under the Empire, and to prosecute Lamennais. Before the trial, he got several bishops to sign a document in which they repudiated Lamennais' views on the total subjection of the State to the Church. When the priest appeared before the court on 20 April, 1826, he was defended by Berryer, a brilliant lawyer. Once again the judgement was peculiar; he was in effect acquitted of attacking the rights of the King, but was fined the ludicrous sum of 30 francs for the quasi-theological offence of teaching false ideas. It seemed as if the judges were determined to permit the greatest possible freedom to all propagators of political ideas.

Inevitably the whole subject was taken up in Parliament. On 15 May, when the budget was being debated, a chance was given by a proposal to raise slightly the income of parish priests. Agier, a member of the centre-Right group, which was apt to co-operate with the liberals, criticised the whole of the Government's policy and then laid the blame on the Congregation. He showed clearly that it was not the religious work of the Church that he attacked; he spoke warmly of the devotion of many of the clergy to their duty. It was the political activity of a part of the clergy and their supporters that he denounced as an 'occult power'. He, too, referred to the fall of the Stuarts and urged the Government to learn from the history of the English restoration.

Other speakers criticised the Government with regard to the army, to foreign policy and so forth, and urged the rejection of the budget as a means of ensuring a change in the Cabinet. No one defended the ministry till de Villèle himself, skating lightly over the Church and its problems, assured the Chamber with a good deal of truth that France was enjoying greater liberty than she had ever had, but hinted that some censorship of the Press might be necessary.

When the clauses of the budget specifically dealing with the pay-ments to the Church came up, the clerical party demanded once again a permanent arrangement which would prevent religion being mixed up with ordinary financial questions. At such a juncture, the proposal was unwise. Bishop Frayssinous, who was Minister for Ecclesiastical Affairs, had to reply to the very varied attacks that were being made. He tried hard to be firm and yet moderate. He pointed out that the Jesuits controlled only seven schools, all 'little seminaries'; he traced the history of the Congregation and denied that it exercised any political influence; he pointed out that the missions, so much criticised, were necessary because of the inadequate number of parish priests.

The Bishop had not submitted a draft of his speech to the Cabinet; it was in effect quite honest and straightforward. But he had been too honest; he had admitted that he knew perfectly well that Jesuits were in France and were teaching young men. This was seized upon; in the Peers it was pointed out that though there were only seven schools run by Jesuits, they were so popular that they had more pupils than all the 38 State secondary schools in the provinces.

Montlosier returned to the attack and laid a formal accusation against the Jesuits before the Royal Court, which said it was not competent to act merely on information that an order existed in France without legal permission. The Knights of the Faith, meantime, had realised that their organisation, which could not be defended in public, was deeply embarrassing the cause it aimed at supporting, and it was dissolved. The members were not released from their oath of secrecy, and of course continued as private persons the friendships they had formed, so the unfortunate Congregation was not at all helped by the winding up of the association.

In January 1827 Montlosier continued his attempt to get the Jesuits turned out of the country; he sent a formal petition to the House of Peers. Frayssinous again tried what a very moderate support for them could do; a Cardinal pointed out that genuine religious freedom should include the right of men to join any order they liked. Lainé said that this order was definitely excluded by a law, and that open breaches of the law were dangerous. In the end, the Peers sent a petition to the Cabinet, asking for the enforcement of the existing law. This led to great rejoicing among the liberals and to consternation in Charles and his Cabinet, but to no immediate result.

The quarrels over Church and State went very deep and had a permanent effect on the history of France; the division between clerical and liberal views can be traced far back, but the fierce controversy of the eighteen-twenties made the gulf impassable. A man like de Villèle, who had no very strong views on the subject, found himself dealing with a sort of hydra-headed monster; it turned up incessantly and in unexpected places, and he could see no way for arriving at his usual solution for a problem, a compromise. Nor was he in a strong enough position to impose one. He had not succeeded in winning over any of his royalist opponents among the *pointus*, and he was uneasily conscious that the obvious decline in the popularity of the Government was laid by the King on his shoulders.

Every move he made was treated by the liberals with suspicion; even a proposal to reduce taxes was thought to be a subtle means of reducing the number of voters. A bill to set up local institutions for the training of public health officers and midwives was so heavily amended that de Villèle dropped it. Early in 1827 he introduced a bill to amend procedure with regard to the selection of jurymen. Juries were drawn from direct taxpayers and in effect the prefects were hand-picking juries for trials. The proposal now made was that complete lists of all men eligible for jury service should be printed, that the prefects should select a panel of 200, from which names should be drawn by lot whenever a jury was needed. The liberal Press burst out in factious opposition, calling the proposed reforms insulting and intended as an instrument of tyranny, which was ridiculous, for though they were very limited they did mean an improvement. In the Peers the bill was immensely widened in scope and effect. Amendments were carried for professional men to be added to the list even if they had not the parliamentary vote, for the prefect's list to include one third of the eligible persons, up to a maximum of 500 (1,500 in Paris), and that no one should be placed on this list for more than two years running. The bill thus amended was accepted by the deputies with slight modifications on 17 April, 1827.

This law was of the very greatest constitutional importance. The permanent lists of jurymen involved also permanent lists of voters, and made election scandals of arbitrary omission or addition of voters impossible. It prevented prejudiced juries being selected for political trials. Such machinery, once established, could not be destroyed without great publicity. Politically, too, it showed the weakness of de Villèle's cabinet. He had tried to win popularity by a minor reform; the liberals in the Upper House had turned his bill into a major one, for which they, not he, got the credit.

Even worse was the defeat over the bill which proposed seriously to alter the law with regard to the Press. It had been demanded by a section of the clerical royalists, but was opposed on all hands. Chateaubriand wrote against it; Peyronnet, replying in another article defending the bill, called it a 'law of justice and love'; this phrase was seized on and the bill usually referred to ironically by that title. Debates in the Lower House were long and confused and showed very plainly that the weakness of the Government had allowed a considerable revival of liberalism. It was carried by 233 to 134 votes, but the Peers introduced and passed such wrecking amendments that de Villèle withdrew the bill on 17 April. By-elections during the spring had gone against the Government, which lost six seats.

Charles did not make matters better. He actually agreed to pay some deputies 500 francs a month; he was constantly being asked for money and found it hard to refuse when he thought he could buy political support. Even Talleyrand was a suitor, not to speak of men like Donnadieu who lived from hand to mouth and promised to reveal plots in exchange for cash down. Madame du Cayla came forward, threatening to print some of Louis XVIII's letters in which he criticised his brother, but in this case de Villèle persuaded Charles not to give in to blackmail, and she had enough good feeling not to carry out her threat.

Without consulting his Prime Minister, the King agreed to hold a review of the National Guard of Paris on 29 April, 1827. It went off not too badly; there were some shouts of opposition but no demonstrations while the King was present. After he left, a crowd went to de Villèle's house shouting threats and demands for his dismissal. The minister lost his common sense entirely; he went to the King and demanded that the National Guard of Paris should be dissolved, as many of its members had taken part in the agitation. Next day, an ordinance to this effect appeared in the *Moniteur*.

This drastic and unnecessary action was a bad mistake. The Guard was not really a popular force, but its very name was symbolic and it had its uses as a supplement to the police when force was needed to break up crowds. When, for instance, in May the students from the law and medical schools of the University demonstrated against the appointment of a professor, they had to be dispersed by the armed police.

During the remainder of the parliamentary session de Villèle struggled on. Doudeauville resigned from the cabinet, in which he sat as Minister in charge of the Royal Household, and was not replaced. A bill for army reform was thrown out by the Peers; the budget gave the normal opportunity for attack on all aspects of the policy of the Government, but was only very slightly amended before it was passed. There was a dangerous tendency for the opposition of the Left to be supported by dissident royalists. The session ended on 22 June, 1827; de Villèle, worn out and irritable, immediately took a most unwise and dangerous step—he imposed a complete censorship on the Press.

He had difficulty in obtaining censors and as a result those whom he appointed were not only harsh but unintelligent in their policy. The word 'Jesuit' was not to be used; an article praising small farms as compared to large was excised as it was thought to be a veiled attack on the monarchy; a comment in a report on the wholesale sugar market 'Bourbons declined' was deleted. Chateaubriand wrote a pamphlet of protest which was distributed free of charge and so escaped the censors.

Manuel, the radical, died in August and his funeral was used by

Laffitte and Lafayette as an opportunity for speechmaking. The author of a pamphlet describing the scene was accused of seditious libel and acquitted by the court. Charles tried to counteract the growing liberal movement by making tours through the country and visiting exhibitions and so forth. One tour in September was particularly successful; he visited the industrial areas round Lille and the weather was exceptionally fine. In his company was Polignac; this was a bad omen for de Villèle, for Charles had already suggested to his Prime Minister that this fervent Catholic and ardent royalist might be given the position of Foreign Minister.

Throughout the summer rumours of some kind of *coup d'état* were constant. Charles went so far as to consult with the Duke of Orleans; the creation of new Peers was discussed, but once again the Dauphin was opposed to this method of diminishing the opposition in the Upper House. Finally, after long hesitation and discussion, on 22 October it was decided to dissolve the deputies and create some new Peers; the announcement was made by ordinances issued on 6 November. There was to be a new election on 17–24 November; the censorship of the Press was lifted, as the law demanded; 77 new Peers were nominated, 5 bishops, 3 generals, 35 deputies, some gentlemen from the country districts. Except for Marshal Soult, there was no outstanding person in the list.

For the elections, the two oppositions openly collaborated in order to prevent the Government candidates gaining from three-cornered contests, as it were. As soon as results began to come in the leaders of the Right began to regret this policy, for it was the liberals, not the ultra-Royalists, who were defeating de Villèle's candidates. In Paris, where election riots had led to the troops firing on the crowds, eight liberals were successful; and Peyronnet of the 'law of justice and love' was defeated in two constituencies in which he had been nominated. The final results showed that the liberals held about 170–180 seats, roughly equal to those in which the Government candidates had succeeded. The royalist opposition held only between 70 and 80.

De Villèle still hesitated about resigning. Charles consulted everyone he could think of; he suggested that de Villèle should reconstitute his Cabinet, but when Chateaubriand was proposed as a member the King refused to accept him. At length on 3 January, 1828, the King sent for de Villèle and told him he must go, 'You have become too unpopular.' 'God grant, Sire, that it is only I,' replied the politician.[1]

[1] Villèle, Comte de: *Mémoires et correspondance*. Paris, 1889–90, Vol. V, p. 311.

Chapter XIV

THE ROYAL REVOLUTION

MANY people anticipated that the fall of de Villèle would be followed by the appointment of a ministry of men known to be personal friends of the King. They were surprised when on 5 January, 1828, the names of the new ministers appeared. The Minister of the Interior, usually the most important member of the Cabinet, was the Viscount de Martignac (1776–1834). During the Spanish expedition he had been with Angoulême and had done his best to bring some sort of order and good sense into the Spanish administration. As a deputy he had been a success; a royalist said of him that: 'He loved pleasing people, almost seducing them. His appearance was elegant, his voice penetrating, his eloquence facile.' So effective was his personality, that a deputy cried out once: 'Be quiet, you siren!'[1] as he felt Martignac's speech influence him. Under normal circumstances, his would have been a personality invaluable to a party, for he had the good sense and the charm to reconcile rather than to exacerbate personal differences. He had no party, however, of which he was recognised as leader; he had helped de Villèle and, like him, belonged to the rather amorphous collection of men who formed the centre-Right.

As colleagues, he had at the Foreign Office de la Ferronays, an able man but not well known; as Keeper of the Seals, Portalis, who had proved to be one of those capable politicians who can follow loyally but cannot lead; Roy, at the Exchequer, was also a good practical man rather than a politician. At the War Office was Decaux, another capable administrator, but behind him was the Dauphin, who took over all appointments and promotions. Chabrol at the Navy, and Frayssinous in charge of Church affairs, had been in former cabinets. The sensible step was taken of removing the recent subjection of the Department of Education from the control of that of Church affairs; it was offered to Chateaubriand, who refused to take any office but that of Foreign Affairs, and on 20 January Vatismesnil was appointed. He had been a passionate royalist, but when in office proved to be far more liberal in his views than anyone expected. A new Ministry of Commerce was created; St. Cricq was placed in charge.

[1] Neuville, Baron Hyde de: *Mémoires*. Paris, 1888–92, Vol. III, p. 372.

Charles' reasons for selecting a government of this character, no more assured than had been de Villèle's of a parliamentary majority, were freely discussed at the time and later on. His was an impulsive not a reasoning character, and it is likely that he acted on two misconceptions—one that he himself was popular, and that any trouble there had been was due to de Villèle; the other that, as he himself wrote to his ex-Prime Minister, the new Cabinet 'will easily yield to my will'. Probably he realised that the royalists were still far too divided among themselves to form a strong government, and he hoped that by putting a man like Martignac forward some reconciliation might be achieved.

That his hopes were not fulfilled was largely due to himself. He never gave the new Cabinet his full-hearted support. It was in any case impossible that any policy acceptable to the middle-class electors would also satisfy the religious enthusiasts who surrounded the King. When Parliament assembled on 5 February, 1828, Charles' speech relieved many by referring to the Charter 'which I have sworn to maintain' but gave little indication of the policy which the new Government would follow. It was predominantly occupied with foreign policy. France had been, with Russia and England, engaged in attempting a reasonable settlement of the Greek problem. On the point that France should assist the Greeks, both Left and Right were for once agreed; the Left because they were a people striving for freedom and independence, the Right because they were Christians, though not Catholics, seeking liberation from the Moslem. De Villèle's lack of interest in any but domestic matters had led to a good deal of disappointment; France seemed to be playing only a minor part in the eastern problem in its current phase. A squadron of warships under Admiral de Rigny had been co-operating with a British fleet which on 10 October, 1827, had destroyed the Egyptian fleet, which was supporting the Sultan, in the Bay of Navarino. The victory was most welcome to Charles, and he referred to it in glowing terms in his speech.

He was also able to describe other naval achievements. For a long time Mediterranean shipping had been pestered by quasi-pirates from North Africa, and a French squadron was now blockading the port of Algiers in the hope of getting recompense from the Dey for damage done to French ships and of preventing his being a nuisance in the future. While many people were glad that some action was being taken, others felt a little doubtful about the success of such an expedition. With regard to Spain, Charles could only say that he hoped the French troops would come back home very soon.

The Cabinet, with no official Prime Minister, soon had to meet a vigorous and embarrassing attack on the late government. A storm of criticism of de Villèle, much of it unjustified, made it almost impossible for the two ministers who had been in his cabinet to remain in office, so Chabrol and Frayssinous resigned. Charles wanted his hot-headed friend de la Bourdonnaye to take Chabrol's place at the Navy Department, but the other ministers firmly refused. Chateaubriand was approached, but rejected the offer, and Hyde de Neuville was appointed. He was an able but rather irresponsible man, royalist by birth and tradition, but whose experiences in Spain had greatly sobered his enthusiasm for unchecked royal power. He was a pleasant rather than a very useful colleague, a great admirer of Chateaubriand and anxious to use what influence he could exert to bring him back into power.

The charge of ecclesiastical affairs was given to Bishop Feutrier of Beauvais, a strong Gallican but a man of liberal sympathies. These appointments were announced on 4 March, 1828, along with a few changes in minor posts. Martignac had wished to remove some prefects who had been over-active in the last election, but Charles resisted and only four were actually dismissed.

The formal Reply to the King's Speech was not passed until 9 March. It had been hotly debated, and included a severe criticism of de Villèle. Charles, in spite of the fulsome praise of himself included in the Reply, was extremely annoyed. At first he thought of a public demonstration of his displeasure, but in the end was contented with dignified hints rather than outright expostulation.

The early months of the new Government indicated a liberal tendency in its policy. A law was introduced to limit the possibility of the prefects' intervention in elections; the famous Black Cabinet in the Post Office, where letters were opened, was officially suppressed; and on 14 April, 1828, a new law repealed much of the recent Press legislation. The censorship, prosecutions for 'tendency' and the need for newspapers to have preliminary authorisation before appearing were all repealed; in return, additional caution money was required and all papers appearing more than once a week had to deposit it, and stiffer regulations were made to ensure that the men designated as responsible editors were not, in fact, men of straw. De Broglie was consulted over this measure, but was offended because he was not invited to expound the plan to the King. He himself in later years recognised how foolish and petty this was, for he put personal feelings before political duty and did not give the support to the Cabinet which it badly needed.

During the spring, by-elections took place as a result of irregularities in the 1827 general election. The Left gained considerably, and it seemed as if the Cabinet were moving in the same direction as the electors. Over the parliamentary scene a shadow of coming

events was hanging; the report of the committee set up to examine
the question of the existence and activities of Jesuits in France was
anxiously awaited. It was known that there was sharp division of
opinion among the members, who included such very different
people as de la Bourdonnaye and Lainé, the fierce royalist and the
philosophic liberal.

The report bore the date of 28 May, 1828, and was not at once
published, though, inevitably, its contents soon became known. On
the fundamental question as to the legal position of the Jesuits, the
committee was divided. One problem was, did the Society of Jesus
constitute a religious order? As its members were not bound to live
in community, but often worked independently, some held that they
did not come under the ban of the law. In this case they enjoyed the
religious freedom guaranteed by the Charter, and if bishops chose
to employ them as teachers they had a right to do so. Five of the
committee took this view; the other four held they were an order and
as such illegal. With regard to the 'little seminaries', the committee
agreed that they were quite irregular; either they must come under
the University's control, or they must be limited strictly to their
nominal duty of training boys for the priesthood. Pupils should wear
ecclesiastical dress, and not be entered for the usual State
examinations.

The Cabinet expected trouble from the King over the action
which the issue of this report would force them to take, but the
Provincial of the Jesuits strongly advised Charles not to provoke a
resignation of his ministers over the position of his Society. On
17 June, therefore, to the great indignation of the Ultramontane
group in the Church, ordinances appeared by which the Jesuit
schools were placed under the University, and the 'little seminaries'
restored, on the terms suggested by the committee, to their original
purpose.

The enforcement of the regulations was not always easy. Feutrier,
the Bishop of Beauvais, secured papal support in dealing with the
more intransigent of the bishops; but even so, when he sent a circular
letter to all bishops asking for information with regard to their
seminaries, he met with some resistance. On 8 October, 1828, for
instance, the Cardinal de Clermont-Tonnerre sent him this reply:

'Monseigneur, The motto of my family, given to it by Callix-
tus II in 1120, is *Etiamsi omnes, ego non.*' ('Even if all do so, I will
not'.) 'This is also the guide of my conscience. I have the honour
to be, with the respectful consideration which I owe to a minister
of the King, A.F., Cardinal-Archbishop of Toulouse.'[1]

[1] Debidour: *Histoire des Rapports de l'Église et l'État en France,* 1789–1870.
Paris, 1898, p. 407, footnote.

This letter, which was printed in the newspapers, made Charles very angry, which rather helped the Bishop in the enforcement of his duty. Lamennais, however, and all the extremists in the Church turned on the unhappy Feutrier with every sort of accusation.

During the summer the discussion of the budget had allowed the normal criticisms of the Government. As usual, the Government had with difficulty to defend the immense expenses of the Court; they also had to promise to overhaul the cost of collecting taxes, which was said to be over 50 per cent higher in France than in England. On the whole they came fairly well out of the ordeal; they were helped by the prosperity of the country, which was shown when the floating of a loan for the costs of the war in Greece did not lead to a fall in the market price of earlier loans. The Cabinet also succeeded in preventing a formal accusation of de Villèle on a series of thirteen charges drawn up by his opponents. One section of the opposition was kept quiet by the appointment of Chateaubriand as Ambassador to Rome.

During the summer Charles was sent on an official progress through Metz, Strasbourg and the surrounding district. Martignac arranged this hoping to please him, but the effect was not to make the King like his ministers any better but to convince him that he was very popular. In the autumn Charles was told that some of his ultra-royalist friends in official posts must be dismissed, as they were not loyally supporting the Cabinet. He hesitated and thought of having another election to see if the Right wing in the deputies could be strengthened, but was persuaded that the opposite would be a more probable result. On 14 November, 1828, the dismissal of nine prefects and some changes in the Council of State were announced; the unusual course was taken of publishing a manifesto from the Government expressing its regret at having to make alterations in the Civil Service.

During the autumn the remaining French troops were withdrawn from Spain, to everyone's satisfaction. The Cabinet was finding it hard to make plans for the approaching session. The amount of gossip going on about a possible rupture between Charles and the Cabinet made planning very difficult; the greater part of the royalist Press was freely criticising the ministers, while some more by-elections showed that the leftward swing of the electors was continuing. It was perfectly clear that Charles had miscalculated. So far from disarming the liberals, the appointment of another Cabinet based on the centre had encouraged them.

At the New Year, 1829, a minor crisis showed how awkward was the situation. Ferronays, the Minister for Foreign Affairs, was seriously ill. He wanted to resign, but Charles immediately wanted

11

to appoint his friend Jules Polignac in his place, or at any rate to juggle offices round so as to insert him in the Cabinet. This was resisted by all the others; the claims of Chateaubriand to the office were equally strongly resisted by the King and not at all warmly pressed by the Cabinet. Polignac came to Paris and tried to collect a possible ministry, but failed to get support and rather ignominiously returned to his embassy in London. The immediate problem was solved by Portalis taking over the Foreign Office while de la Ferronays was given leave of absence.

Martignac and his colleagues had won but a barren victory, and faced the session of 1829 with little confidence. The Right was now openly aiming at their fall; the Left was anxious to push them into reforms which would serve as some sort of bulwark against any plan of Charles to modify the constitution. Together, the Left and the Left Centre had a small majority over the Right Centre and Right. Martignac's only hope was to introduce measures just liberal enough to secure the Left without wholly antagonising the more friendly elements in the Right Centre.

Such a policy was bound to fail. Bills to reform local government by setting up elected councils in the departments and the towns were prepared by the Government and had a very half-hearted reception. The Right objected to a diminution of the King's powers; the Left wanted a wider electorate than the Government suggested. All through February and March the Government struggled. The result of a by-election in March was embarrassing; the new deputy was Clauzel, who had been sentenced to death in 1816 for opposing the Duchess of Angoulême at Bordeaux during the Hundred Days, but had escaped and returned to France later. Twice the Cabinet was defeated; once on the order in which the two bills for local government should be taken, once on an amendment. In both cases the Right wing refrained from voting, leaving the way open for the Left to attempt to force a more radical plan on the Cabinet.

After an interview with the King, Martignac withdrew his bills on 8 April, 1829. It has often been said that from this day the fall of the Bourbons was inevitable. This is the kind of judgement that is easy after the event; what is certain is that later on the doctrinaires and leaders of the liberals deeply regretted their action. It was due to their suspicion that Charles was playing some deep and subtle game; that now was their only chance to get a quasi-democratic system of local government founded that would make the tyranny of the prefects impossible. What they did not fully see was that Charles' peculiar plan of appointing a moderate cabinet after de Villèle's fall had served as a very useful brake on the ultra-royalists, and that to defeat it was giving him a valid excuse for swinging over to the extreme Right.

Throughout the summer intrigues and disappointments were the fate of the Cabinet. Chateaubriand believed, with no justification, that he had been very influential in the papal election that had taken place in February. He came to Paris in May still hoping that he might be offered the Foreign Office, but when he called on the King he was merely asked when he was returning to Rome. In the Chambers one bill after another failed to pass; several useful minor measures were passed by the Peers, but had to be dropped because there was no time to push them through the deputies. The Lower House had been too busy bringing accusations of theft against Peyronnet, the former Minister of Justice, whose department had overspent its allocation, and suggesting that other members of de Villèle's cabinet ought to be prosecuted for spending Government money on pamphlets for the 1827 election.

The Left demanded a reduction in the cost of the Church, and pointed out that while in 1818 the cost to the State had been 18 million francs, it was now over 49 millions. This was, of course, due in large part to the creation of additional bishoprics with all their attendant expenses. Laffitte, the banker, bemoaned the increased indebtedness of the nation, and blamed the compensation of the émigrés and the costs of the Spanish War. Charles' plan of paying a regular income to some deputies was also brought to light; Martignac had to say that, as the King could spend his income as he chose, he could not intervene. Every clause in the accounts of 1827 and the current budget gave rise to disputes and wrangles, though the reduction in allocations for the current year was very small when it was finally passed.

During the five-weeks' debate on the budget, Charles and the Dauphin had been getting more and more angry with the Parliament. They considered that they had been personally insulted by the deputy who pointed out that while the King and his sons had between them 62 aides-de-camp, costing nearly half a million francs a year, the Emperor of Austria had only two and the King of England one. That the ministry would last no one believed; Benjamin Constant on 9 July, 1829, openly referred to what was being thought.

'When we have granted you funds, will you still be there?' he said, and 'It is not so much against' the present ministry 'as against its presumptive or possible successors that I speak.'[1] Martignac replied by saying gravely that he trusted the Chambers would give any future government 'justice, confidence and good will. Believe

[1] Viel-Castel, op. cit., Vol. XIX, p. 501.

me, gentlemen, that is necessary for the interests of the country.'[1] Again in the Peers on 28 July he made a dignified complaint. 'We have encountered all around us difficulties and obstacles, we have had to keep up a constant war against contrary passions and parties.'[2] How many modern Prime Ministers of France have said much the same? 'Moderation,' he claimed, 'is not weakness.'

Charles was annoyed by this speech, and Martignac well knew that it would not be long before he was forced to resign. He knew that on 26 July the King had seen Polignac, though Charles pooh-poohed the rumours by saying: 'Poor Jules, he is so incapable.' When the session ended on 30 July everybody was aware that, had he chosen, the King could have kept his ministers in power by ordering members of the Right to give active support. On 5 August the Cabinet called on Charles, who informed them that he had plans for another ministry. So fell the last of the governments based on the moderate groups forming the centre.

Already Polignac had been discussing plans with the King and his friends. His was a peculiar position. He was by nature a conciliatory man who genuinely believed in a constitutional monarchy he was, however, a visionary. He was convinced that he had received a direct call from the Almighty to serve his King and save his country from atheism and revolution, and he was apt to choose his friends and colleagues with reference to their piety rather than their powers as politicians. In the hectic discussions of the days before 5 August he found that he was not to be Prime Minister or to have a free hand, and that the far from pious de la Bourdonnaye was to be his partner.

When on 9 August the names of the new ministers were published even the royalists were taken aback. Polignac had the Foreign Office and de la Bourdonnaye the Interior. For the War Office a most extraordinary choice had been made. De la Bourdonnaye had wanted Bellune, but the Dauphin's dislike for him over the Spanish fiasco prevented it, and de Bourmont was appointed. He was known to the world as the general who had deserted to the enemy three days before the Battle of Waterloo. These three names were a sensation in themselves.

Courvoisier, the Minister of Justice, was nominated by Polignac simply because of his piety. Montbel was given Education to win the support of de Villèle and his friends. Finance had been offered to Roy, but he refused, so Chabrol moved to that office from the Navy His experience under Martignac was most useful to the new Cabinet none of them had held office and he had to teach them the elements

1 Ibid., p. 504.
2 Ibid., p. 549.

of procedure. The King had wanted de Rigny, the Admiral of the Fleet that shared in the victory of Navarino, for the Navy, but again met refusal and had to appoint d'Haussez, the Prefect of Bordeaux, who hesitated before accepting this promotion. Doubt, in fact, seemed to be the note of the minor members of the ministry; as Montbel wrote to de Villèle, 'No one can have confidence in us for we have none in ourselves.'[1]

The two leaders disagreed entirely on the main lines to be taken. De la Bourdonnaye wanted to break through all constitutional checks on the King's powers; Polignac wanted to keep the law. He hoped for a close alliance between Church and State; this de la Bourdonnaye strongly opposed. Both men were busy making appointments; here the Minister for the Interior scored, and he found plenty of jobs for the ultra-royalists; vacancies in the Foreign Office went to men of more moderate views. Yet Polignac, too, was suspected of planning revenge on the liberals; the liberal paper, the *Journal des Débats*, published a quotation from a very violent speech he had made in the Matchless Parliament of 1815 in which he declared that 'chains, tortures and death' were needed to deal with the Bonapartists.

Some important people resigned their offices rather than serve the new Government; the Prefect of Police was one and Chateaubriand another. He was persuaded by his more liberal friends that it was his duty to give up the embassy in Rome, and he had to suffer not only loss of income but violent attacks from the Right-wing papers, which called him a traitor.

Polignac in the Foreign Office dreamed of great successes as a means of satisfying the country. He planned a Franco-Russian alliance as a result of the co-operation between the two countries in Greece. He even contemplated the acquisition of Belgium by France with Russian help. It was true that there was unrest in Belgium, and a good deal of pro-French feeling, but that a man who had been Ambassador in London could imagine that the English Government would accept such a plan is a surprising proof of that 'incapability' to which Charles had referred.

During the autumn the Dauphin went on tour to Rouen and Cherbourg. Little enthusiasm was shown; the townsfolk of Cherbourg would not even get up a subscription ball in his honour. As a contrast, the reception given to Lafayette in Auvergne and in Lyons was a great triumph. Even more menacing was the formation of a society in Brittany of men who pledged themselves to refuse to pay any taxes that had not been properly voted by Parliament. The idea was not very widely supported, in spite of the claims made by some of the liberals, but it was sufficiently disconcerting.

[1] De Villèle, op. cit., Vol. V, p. 395.

Charles became aware that the quarrels between de la Bourdonnaye and Polignac made it impossible for the Cabinet to draw up any plans at all. De la Bourdonnaye produced all sorts of wild ideas Polignac and the others pulled them to pieces. One or other had to go. When Charles made up his mind that there must be a Prime Minister, the Minister for the Interior resigned, and on 17 November Jules Polignac became Prime Minister. De la Bourdonnaye was reported to have given as his reason for resignation: 'When one's head is the stake, one must hold good cards.'[1] Montbel was persuaded to take over his position.

The only really bright point for the Cabinet was the successful floating of a loan bearing 4 per cent interest at a price above par 102 francs were paid for each 100-franc certificate. Otherwise the economic prospects were poor. A very wet autumn was followed by a severe winter; food was dear and there was a good deal of unemployment in the industrial areas of the north and east. By contrast, the Paris season was unusually gay with parties and balls and many new plays by Victor Hugo and other coming authors.

The Press was most active. A new liberal paper, the *Temps*, was started and the *Globe*, which had been a bi-weekly, became a daily. Constant references were made to the English revolution of 1689; there were many prosecutions and sometimes acquittals. The Government subscribed to the royalist papers, and a new one, the *Universel*, was started, but they suffered from having nothing very positive to say.

This was the fundamental weakness of Charles' government. It was negative in its attitude. The main positive actions suited to its conception of the good of the country had already been taken; the Church was secure, the compensation had been paid. The royalists wanted to prevent weakening of the royal powers but had no idea to what end these powers should be employed, so the hold of the liberals over the electors once again began to grow tighter. In a by-election in January 1830 Guizot entered the House which earlier he had indirectly influenced; Berryer, the clever son of the lawyer who had defended Ney, was also elected, but he was a strong royalist. Seven new peers were created in January, including de la Bourdonnaye and de Vitrolles, who said pessimistically: 'I know quite well that if the house is on fire, it doesn't matter much if one is sitting in an arm-chair or an ordinary one.'[2] This curious cynical acceptance of some inevitable conflagration was very common among royalists at this time.

[1] Viel-Castel, op. cit., Vol. XX, p. 81.
[2] Viel-Castel, op. cit., Vol. XX, p. 175. See also Vitrolles, op. cit., Vol. III, p. 347.

There was one field in which action was clearly necessary, and here Polignac had in the end a real success. The quasi-blockade of Algiers had been going on without result, and the generals had been suggesting a full-scale attack by land. The navy disliked the idea, holding that the nature of the African coast made successful transport and landing of troops unlikely. There were long discussions; the decision to invade was taken, then the commander had to be selected. Two ambitious men wanted the honour: Marmont, the Duke of Ragusa, and de Bourmont, now head of the War Office. Neither was popular with the army, which, though it no longer looked for a Bonapartist revolution, still felt a grudge against men who had not supported Napoleon. Marmont was disappointed, for de Bourmont was selected.

The European Powers on the whole approved of the plan, for the Algerian pirates were an international nuisance. Only England looked with disapproval at any French action in Africa. Polignac was often accused by the liberals of subordination to England, especially at the time when the Algiers plan was being made in February 1830. The charge was brought in connection with the offer of the crown of Greece, now liberated, to Leopold of Saxe-Coburg-Gotha, who was related to the English Royal Family, but it was really baseless. For France, a success in Algiers after her efforts in Greece would be a proof that she was capable of independent action, and Polignac was willing to lose the friendship of English statesmen for the sake of a victory for the King of France.

By the end of April preparations were complete. Polignac took charge of the War Office while Bourmont was away with the army; 37,000 men were assembled, with 103 assorted naval vessels and transports in addition. Bad weather delayed the expedition, but the coast near Algiers was reached on 13 June. A brief campaign ended on 5 July with the surrender of the Dey and the capture of the city; treasure hoards were found which it was calculated would pay the whole of the costs of the expedition and leave seven million francs profit. Tunis and Tripoli also surrendered. At any other period such a success would have brought popularity to the Government, but for Charles' cabinet the timing was all wrong. In July 1830 the people were so preoccupied with internal affairs that little attention was paid to Africa.

The Chambers had been summoned for 3 March, and a King's Speech would have to announce the Cabinet's programme. Various ideas had been discussed, such as new electoral laws, but in the end the only definite legislation proposed was the highly necessary budget. The Government expected the support of about 200 deputies, but so few attended the solemn mass which the King, as usual, went to in procession on 2 March, that the calculation seemed rather too optimistic. It was known that whatever went into the Speech it would be opposed by the liberals, who were busy organising. What was needed to conceal the weakness of the programme was a magnificent emotional appeal; instead the oration was a synthesis of drafts submitted by all the members of the Cabinet.

When Charles appeared to deliver the King's Speech he dropped his hat, which was picked up by Orleans. This was at once looked on as an omen. He then read the colourless oration, in which hints were given of a possible further conversion of debt which would free funds for public works and so forth. The only phrase which excited real attention was 'The Charter has placed the liberties of the people under the safeguard of the rights of the Crown. These rights are sacred, and my duty to my people is to transmit them intact to my successors.' It was felt this was significant, but precisely how no one could say.

What was at once clear was that there was no Government majority. The election for the President of the Chamber resulted in liberals obtaining the most votes, with Royer-Collard well ahead. With great reluctance Charles accepted him. The Peers made a rather colourless Reply to the Speech on 9 March, Chateaubriand was alone in opposing it after making a speech in which he referred to the danger of revolution from above. The deputies took longer. Royer-Collard was mainly responsible for the draft submitted to the House. It was severely critical in tone, and included a clear statement of a constitutional theory. The Charter, it was said, made 'the permanent harmony of the political views of your Government with those of your people indispensable. Sire, our loyalty, our devotion, condemn us to inform you that this harmony does not exist.'

For the Government, Montbel was able to quote Lainé as saying in 1816 that it was not right to demand that the Cabinet must represent the majority in the Chamber. This was a good debating point but no more. The Cabinet was weak on oratory. Some of the royalists came to its support, including Berryer, who called the Reply an insult to the King. The centre-Right tried to water down the more stringent words, but Guizot made an effective speech against them. On 16 March the Reply was carried by 221 votes to 181.

Polignac's cabinet saw clearly that they had no hope of getting any law whatever through the Chamber. In discussions on 17 March an immediate dissolution was suggested, but this seemed a complete surrender to the liberal demands and it was not to be expected that the small electorate would so soon have changed its opinions. On

19 March, therefore, the King announced that the newly-assembled Chamber would be prorogued until 1 September.

The 221 who formed the majority on the Reply immediately became a symbol. A banquet was arranged in Paris with 221 garlands of flowers, and similar festivities organised in other large towns. The liberal Press was full of discussion of the situation and many papers were prosecuted for attacking the prerogatives of the Crown. In some cases there were acquittals; in none were the sentences severe. The liberals were sure that new elections would be held before September, and began their preparations; as a sort of rallying point they determined that all the 221 must be re-elected.

Polignac seems to have been pinning his hopes on the outcome of the Algerian venture. De Villèle was seen by the King and later left Paris on 12 April for Toulouse. That either he or Polignac ever seriously considered his joining the Cabinet seems unlikely; the only result of the interview was to add to the mass of rumour flying round Paris, and still further to divide the various sections of the Right. A summary of the finances of the whole period of the Restoration was published; it was an impressive record of common sense and steady improvement, though critics said that far too much had been spent on the Court and far too little on the navy, education, the roads and so forth. In any case it was not likely to rouse the powerful emotion which was the only hope for the monarchy.

The Cabinet went on discussing schemes. Several members seemed to wish to resign, but felt it would be disloyal and cowardly. The prefects were asked to report on probable electoral results; naturally they wished to be as optimistic as possible, but even so they could only forecast a majority for the Government of thirty to forty. In many districts they were being pestered by a curious outbreak of incendiarism; barns and stacks were set fire to and peasants had serious losses. Neither contemporary nor later investigations have discovered the reasons for this malice; it was of no advantage to any political party. In some places the reinstatement of the National Guard was asked for as additional protection, for though it was only the Paris Guard that had been formally disbanded it had ceased to function in the provinces too. Certainly the fires were yet another worry for Polignac, but to disturb the countryside was not at all what the liberals wished when an election was anticipated. It seems likely that after the hard winter some miserable people had found this way of expressing their dislike of society, and had been imitated by others.

Two courses seemed open to the Government. One was to wait for good news from Algiers and then hold a snap election in the hopes of a majority, though Polignac was reported to have said that he didn't know what he would do with one if he had one. The other was to have a dissolution soon and be prepared for arbitrary action if the new Chamber too closely resembled the present. When the second plan was adopted, and a dissolution announced on 16 May, two of the ministers resigned, Courvoisier, the Minister of Justice, and Chabrol, the experienced Minister of Finance. Charles insisted on Peyronnet being given office, another extremely unwise move, for he had recently been accused of malversation of funds and was in any case detested by all who followed de Villèle.

The new elections were ordered for the end of June. Several officials suspected of liberalism were dismissed, and some of the more foolish bishops wrote letters to their flocks which were practically election manifestoes. Yet there was little disorder. As the first results, the election of those nominated in the local electoral colleges, came in, it was clear that the liberals were improving their position. There were rejoicings in Paris and the large towns, while the various factions of royalists blamed each other for their disappointment.

Before the election was over the Government decided not to allow the Chamber to meet. One minister uttered a note of warning; he said that before any decisive action was taken strong bodies of troops should be prepared not only in Paris but also in Lyons, Rouen and Bordeaux. Peyronnet was full of ideas. One plan was for a sort of constituent assembly to be nominated by the King. When this was rejected, he suggested that simultaneously with the dissolution of the new Chamber a fresh system of election should be proclaimed by an ordinance issued under the powers given the King by Article 14 of the Charter, and all newspapers be suspended. On 7 July this scheme was adopted. Charles was determined not to surrender to the middle-class electorate. The final results confirmed his distrust of the 'new men', for the Opposition had won 274 seats to the Government's 143, with 12 others held by a group whose support could not be counted on. Of the 221, 202 had been successful.

The really astonishing thing is the calm way in which Charles faced the situation. That Paris might be dangerous had been shown by a nasty little incident on 31 May, when a crowd had invaded the gardens of the palace where the Duke of Orleans was entertaining the King and Queen of Naples at a ball, and had done a lot of damage. Possibly he thought it was Orleans who was unpopular, though all through the visit of the royal pair complete indifference had been shown; not even, as was noticed, were there gibes and caricatures. They were returning from Spain, where their daughter had just been married to Ferdinand, and the Government had had some hopes that the brilliance of the festivities might distract the people of Paris.

Warnings were coming in from men like de Villèle, and de la Ferronays at the embassy in Rome, who could not be suspected of disloyalty. A liberal paper, the *National*, published an article in which it was suggested that Charles might be thinking of a scheme of revolution under the constitutional guise of ordinances, which was extremely close to that actually decided upon. In spite of this, the King demanded absolute secrecy, for he believed that the people were really on his side and he did not fear resistance, except from the middle-class liberals. As the members of the newly-elected Assembly came to Paris, to settle down before the session, there was a constant and growing stream of discussion and of rumour. Foreign representatives warned the Cabinet of probable dangers from any *coup*, but it was impossible for them to make the King understand. His view was that his brother, Louis XVI, had died because he had given in to the pressure of a hostile minority, and that he would act now as he would have done in Louis' place in 1789—resist at once.

The narrow streets of the old city of Paris had often been blocked by barricades during riots, and to ensure that they were kept clear was essential. Troops must be available, but Charles refused to bring in additional forces as this would betray his plan. The Government decided to place the garrison under Marmont. Two things about this decision were odd: one, that he was known to be hurt by de Bourmont's appointment to the Algiers army; the other, that he was not told of the King's plans. Had he been consulted, some reasonable precautions might have been taken. Not even the Prefect of Police in Paris or the under-secretary at the War Office were informed until the general public was itself. The King was at St. Cloud, a palace near Versailles, some little distance from the city. The ministers had to drive or ride to and fro to see him, but he was not at all bothered about this.

On Saturday, 24 July, the ordinances were brought to him for signature. A long justificatory report signed by all the ministers preceded them. It was primarily concerned with the wickedness of the newspapers which stirred up hatred of the monarch and the constitution and wound up by declaring that a return must be made to the 'spirit of the Charter' which in Article 14 had given emergency powers to the King. The first ordinance was directed against the Press; no periodical was to appear without Government leave, granted for three months only and revocable at will. The second, signed only by the Minister of the Interior, dissolved the new Chamber. The third contained a new electoral law reducing the number of deputies, narrowing the franchise and restoring partial renewal. There were other alterations, including abolition of any secrecy of the ballot, but of comparative unimportance as they never came into effect.

On Sunday Charles went hunting and the ordinances were taken to the printer of the *Moniteur*. To scrap the type already set up and print all this new material meant working all night, but on Monday morning the paper duly appeared. The police were given orders to tell all other newspapers that they were not to appear. As it happened, Marmont left St. Cloud in the morning without bothering to look at the *Moniteur*, and went to attend a meeting of the Academy of Sciences in Paris. He was horrified when a friend there gave him the news. Many other people, too, did not read their paper till the afternoon, so the news of Charles' *coup* was not widespread till late on the afternoon of Monday, the 26th.

Meantime, the other papers had received their prohibition. Some of the editors of the liberal papers got together and decided to ignore it, and agreed to a long protest drawn up by Thiers. This was printed for publication. By the evening small groups were demonstrating in the streets, and stones were thrown at Polignac's carriage. There were few signs as yet of serious trouble, and it looked as if Charles' hopes were justified. He had spent the day hunting; when he returned he asked Marmont how things were; he reported that there was a good deal of panic and prices were falling on the Stock Exchange. Charles even now did not inform the Marshal that he was in charge of the Paris troops. The Duchess de Berry congratulated her father-in-law in being truly king at last, and they all went peacefully to bed.

Next day, Tuesday 27 July, the Duke of Ragusa was just about to leave for the country when the King sent for him. He was told to go and take command of the troops in case there were any trouble. Polignac, meantime, in his capacity of acting head of the War Office, was quietly discussing contracts for the army. Marmont knew well enough that the forces at his disposal were completely inadequate for dealing with serious riots. The best regiments were in Algiers and considerable forces were on the eastern frontier, where agitations in Belgium had led to some alarm. The Paris garrison was nominally 11,000 men and another 5,500 were at Versailles and other bases not far from Paris. Polignac had counted on 18,000, but had forgotten allowances for men on guard at St. Cloud and those absent on leave or sick or on special duties. Marmont had the Royal Guard, which would be sure to fight for the King but whose efficiency was dubious, but he was not at all sure how the ordinary line regiments would react to being used against the people of Paris.

Even before he could start his organisation, the situation was getting out of hand. Some factory owners had closed their works and their men were wandering in the streets ready to join in anything that went on. Crowds had collected round the closed newspaper offices, and clashes with the police brought more people into the streets. Undergraduates and students from the technical colleges were more than ready for action. There was no concerted plan, no one to give orders, but a general atmosphere of resistance. Barricades were raised and demolished by soldiers; one old man was killed and in the best revolutionary tradition his body was paraded round the streets to excite pity and horror. But by nine o'clock in the evening there was comparative calm.

During the night, paving stones were torn up and solid barriers made. Small outposts of troops were overrun, the arsenal was seized and other stores of munitions, and on the Town Hall the tricolour flag was hoisted. Marmont sent an urgent message to the King, saying that this was no riot but a revolution and that some means must at once be taken to pacify the people. But Charles preferred to believe Peyronnet and other ministers who had got away to St. Cloud before the more serious risings, and sent orders to Marmont to arrest the liberal deputies who had issued proclamations. The General was not at all pleased; already his troops had suffered casualties as the columns passing down narrow streets were fired on from the houses. Some of the deputies called on Marmont, and he tried to get Polignac to see them. The Prime Minister said such an interview was pointless. The Marshal then told him that some of the soldiers were fraternising with the crowds, and Polignac replied that in that case they must be fired on too.

One cannot but doubt whether Marmont hoped for much from the Government he was trying to preserve. He sent an urgent dispatch to St. Cloud; his messenger was kept for some hours and then brought back a reply telling the Marshal to promise the troops six weeks' pay as a bonus and to be sure to guard the Government offices properly and see that the ministers got safely to St. Cloud the next morning. Further orders would then follow. During these hours the possibility of action was getting less and less. Small bodies of men alone could clear the streets, but small bodies were often overwhelmed and sometimes surrendered. The Marshal had to order a concentration of the forces, even withdrawing the men who had succeeded in recapturing the Town Hall; 2,500 men had vanished, some killed, some wounded, some deserted. Marmont's only hope was to hold the Tuileries and the Louvre and negotiate with the rebels, before his munitions ran out.

By now the sound of the firing could be heard at St. Cloud, yet Charles still believed all would be well. It was later reported that

Polignac had told him he had had a vision of the Blessed Virgin and that she had promised her help. Some such confidence alone can explain the extraordinary scenes that took place at St. Cloud; a constant stream of people escaping from Paris found that no courtier dared to show alarm to the King, who was quietly playing whist as usual.

Early on the morning of 29 July even the members of the Cabinet began to see that unless something were done rapidly the days not only of the Cabinet but of the monarchy itself were numbered. The best that Marmont could offer was to hold out for a fortnight; that order could be restored was now impossible. Some of them got to St. Cloud, and one of them, weeping bitterly, told Charles that the only thing to be done was to recall the ordinances and appoint a liberal cabinet. Charles said that he would discuss the matter. As the Duke of Ragusa had expected, everyone now began to blame him. While this talk was going on, two of the remaining regiments deserted, completely disorganising the defences.

Still no responsible leader had appeared with whom negotiations could be carried on, and the violence in Paris was getting worse; 200 of the Swiss Guard who refused to surrender their barracks were almost all burnt to death when the attackers set fire to it. The palace of the Archbishop of Paris, a Jesuit house, and a monastery of missionaries were all sacked. Various cries were raised by the rioters, some for a Napoleon, some for a republic, but all were demanding the fall of the Polignac cabinet.

There are varying and sometimes contradictory accounts of the various envoys sent by Charles to try to obtain support from some of the politicians. What is perfectly clear is that there was no one in the royal circle capable of dealing with an emergency. The Dauphin thought only of resistance, but as news came in Charles gave way. On the night of the 30th he withdrew the fatal ordinances and signed others, reinstating the National Guard and so forth. But it was now much too late.

Marmont came to St. Cloud to assure himself of the safety of the Royal Family and receive instructions. He found that man by man the less enthusiastic soldiers were slipping away. To retain them he drew up a sort of proclamation praising the troops and telling them that the ordinances had been withdrawn. This was not approved by the ministers or by the Dauphin, the nominal Commander-in-chief; the Duke of Ragusa's excuse was that they were not available and the matter was urgent—whether correct or not, that this could be said was a clear indication of the utter confusion at the Court. When he heard of the proclamation the Dauphin went almost out of his mind with rage; he accused Marmont of treachery and attacked him, seizing him by the collar and hurling him on to a sofa. With great difficulty Charles brought about a formal reconciliation.

From excess of optimism the King and his friends went to the other extreme. They were sure the Paris mob would march out and attack them, so they decided to move away. Early in the morning of 31 July the flight began. With Marmont in charge of the guard, Charles went to the Trianon, in the park of Versailles; in the little town the tricolour flag was already flying. Later in the morning the Dauphin followed with his forces; when on the way the men were ordered to charge some insurgents, they did not obey. So great was the indiscipline that a gun was actually abandoned on the way.

At Trianon Charles said good-bye to his ministers, giving them a little money—for they had got out of Paris leaving their goods behind—and blank passports. He went on to Rambouillet, where he was joined by his son's wife on 1 August. He tried to enrol Orleans' help but received vague replies; and on the 2nd three cavalry regiments went off to Burgundy with a permit from the revolutionaries to serve as safe-conduct. He now believed that abdication was the only dignified course. The Dauphin at first resisted, then agreed, and they both solemnly abdicated in favour of the little boy, de Berry's son. Orleans was asked to proclaim him and act as Lieutenant-General during the minority of Henry V.

Meantime, all sorts of rumours were current, and the crowds in Paris thought that Charles was coming with powerful forces. Orleans sent to beg him to withdraw, but not until 3 August, when in fact revolutionaries were drawing near, did he accept the situation fully. Then slowly and sadly the Bourbons returned to England, once again exiles from the land to which they had come rejoicing in 1814.

Chapter XV

THE MONARCH OF JULY

'WHEN the *coup d'état* burst over Paris it encountered there neither secret societies nor a Committee of Direction, nor open or hidden preparations for war; at most there were a few deputies and Peers who were habitually kept in the capital by their business or who had anticipated the opening of the session by a few days, who were, however, scattered and not grouped and without any understanding among themselves.'[1]

The Duke de Broglie's statement seems to be borne out by all of the many people who were present in Paris during the 'Three Glorious Days' and who recorded their memories. It is, of course, always true that memories fade and become selective, and that memoirs are printed usually with the aim of justifying the actions of the author and his friends. But in this case the extraordinary confusion seems adequate proof that there was no definite plan to overthrow the Bourbons at that time. The fighting was like all Paris riots, but on a larger and more persistent scale. The number of killed was considerable; the *Moniteur* on 4 February, 1840, gave them as 163 soldiers and 504 civilians. It seems likely that these figures are an underestimate, so far as the soldiers are concerned; but the number of civilians is probably correct, since civilians were given pensions and rewards. In addition, there was a very large number of people wounded. People who wished to make plans had to run considerable risks in getting to each other's houses.

There were at least three groups of people who wanted to take up the government that Charles X had lost, the republicans, the radicals, and the conservatives. Both the latter were called liberals. The republicans were led by Lafayette, that veteran conspirator. He and some of his friends seized the Hôtel de Ville, the centre of the government of the city, declared themselves to be a provisional government, and allotted themselves offices. They had no political experience; they could count on support from the discontented workers and old soldiers, but they would have to invent a constitution. It is probable they could have held Paris for a time; it is certain

[1] Broglie, Duke de: *Personal Recollections*. Trans. Beaufort. London, 1887, Vol. II, p. 350.

that they would not have got a majority if they had held elections with universal suffrage, for outside the towns they had little support. For the moment, however, they held a key position.

The radicals were not very numerous; they had no strong organisation. Their main aim was to extend the franchise and to reduce the power of the central government by prohibiting State officials from being members of Parliament. Many of them wished to strengthen local institutions and reduce the power of the prefects. In July they could do little, but their hopes were high.

The effective group was formed by the journalists and members of the Chamber of Deputies. They were greatly alarmed at the anarchy prevailing, and wanted a rapid solution. To retain the existing system and simply change the policy of the Government seemed to them the right course. What was needed was a figurehead, and there was one obvious person to whom to turn, the Duke of Orleans. Many of the Peers, and some of the more conservative deputies, wanted him to act as Regent for the little son of the Duke de Berry, as his ancestor had acted for the young Louis XV. Others, his personal friends, wished that he should play the part of William III of England and become king. Both groups had a serious practical difficulty: the chief actor was not available for discussion. He was out in the country, some miles from Paris, at Neuilly.

Laffitte, the banker, had no doubts that Orleans must take over control. He was on intimate terms with him, and had advised him in his money affairs. Several of the journalists were in Laffitte's house on 29 and 30 July, and prominent among them was Adolphe Thiers. He had made his name and fortune through the *National* newspaper, financed by Laffitte and partly by Orleans himself, and he and his friend Mignet hastily wrote out and posted up placards. One of them ran as follows:[1]

'Charles X can never return to Paris; he has caused the blood of the people to be shed.

A republic would expose us to terrible divisions; it would embroil us with Europe.

. The Duke of Orleans is a prince devoted to the cause of the Revolution.

The Duke of Orleans has never fought against us.

The Duke of Orleans was at Jemappes.

The Duke of Orleans bore the tricoloured flag under fire; the Duke of Orleans alone can bear it again; we will have no other flag.

[1] Gérainville, A-E. Billault de: *Histoire de Louis-Philippe*. Paris, 1871, Vol. II, p. 299.

12

The Duke of Orleans has declared himself; he accepts the Charter
as we have always wished and understood it.

It will be from the people of France that he will hold his crown.'

This was a daring pronouncement. Orleans was little known to the
people; he had not consented—he had not even been consulted—
to be a candidate for the monarchy. Many people hoped that he
would be Regent only. The authors of these proclamations had no
right whatever to compromise him in this way. They were, however,
very skilful. The constant reiteration of the name of Orleans, the
appeal to the traditions of the Revolution, had precisely the effect
they planned. When at length the Duke appeared, his presence was
looked on as inevitable.

Thiers himself, though a very bad horseman, rode out to Neuilly
to bring the king he was making to Paris. He found him absent. The
Duke seems to have been in a state of profound indecision; he had
gone to Raincy, some miles away. His sister, Adelaide, sent a messenger to him, telling him to 'make it clear to my brother, there is no
middle way; he must choose at once between a throne and exile.'[1]
The Duke started out in his carriage when he got this message,
turned back again, and then finally came to Neuilly, where he would
not enter the house, but went to one of the little summer-houses in
the park.

Meantime, a hasty meeting had been called of such deputies and
Peers as were available. At half-past twelve on 30 July about sixty
deputies met under Laffitte as President of the Chamber. After
some discussion it was decided to ask Orleans to come to Paris; the
understanding was that he should be invited to act as Lieutenant-
General for the time being. A message to this effect was submitted
to the few Peers who were in session. While they were debating, a
very belated message from Charles was brought to the Deputies'
Chamber, where by now only a few remained; this gave Laffitte
the excuse he needed to refuse to receive it officially. Lafayette, too,
sent messages urging that full guarantees should be demanded before
any offer was made. The debate was cut short by the return of the
messengers sent to the Peers, who reported that they were agreed to
the invitation to the Duke. With three abstentions only, the Deputies
carried a motion, and twelve deputies were selected to convey the
nomination to the Duke. There is no doubt that many of them, like
Talleyrand, hoped that he would accept the office simply as representative of Henry V, de Berry's son.

The Duke's delay in coming to Paris was, there seems every
reason to believe, due to his own very grave doubts as to whether

[1] Gérainville, op. cit., Vol. II, p. 327.

he could honourably accept the throne. Merely to act as Regent would give him all the labour and no reward. The royalists would resent him, the opponents of Charles would feel they had been cheated. He was himself a Bourbon and had a keen sense of the historic dignity of the family; while he had with justification resented the way in which Louis XVIII had treated him, he had no quarrel with Charles. The King had granted him and all his sons the title of Royal Highness; he had given him free access to the Court.

On the other hand, he had a large family and was intensely ambitious for them. His personal friends were drawn from the 'new' men, who had made and were making money. He was proud of the part he had played in the early days of the Revolution; he remembered well the bitter poverty and frustrations of his youth. In 1814 he laid claim to the great estates of his family, which in theory were still the property of the crown of France though the Orleans family enjoyed their use so long as there was a male heir to succeed to them. The Duke entered upon a series of law cases to regain this property and was on the whole successful. In Paris itself the Palais Royal was Orleans property; it had been a good deal knocked about during the Revolution, but a great deal of land surrounded it. Some of this had been sold by 'Égalité', his father, and a theatre built on it; the Duke's lawyers claimed that the sale was invalid, and after a long-drawn struggle in the law courts the proprietor of the theatre had to pay 100,000 francs to retain it. The palace was put in order and the ground floor let out in shops at high rents, while the family occupied the upper stories. In another case he laid claim to land on the Channel coast, mostly heath and dunes and rough pasture, which generations of local peasants had used freely. A number of suits were brought against these humble farmers, and the tenacity with which they were pursued led Charles X to ask his cousin to abandon them. He thereupon transferred his claims to a company, so that he could get the profit without the scandal.

Other peoples' claims were treated with something a good deal less than justice. His father had left great debts; after long negotiations the creditors accepted a settlement which gave them only about 5 per cent of their money. His father's former mistress, on whom 40,000 livres a year had been settled, was induced to accept 6,000 francs a year, the equivalent of about 240 livres. But when the distribution was made of compensation to the émigrés and others in 1825, Orleans was awarded 17 million francs, greatly to the anger of de Villèle.

The money and lands acquired by various means were most skilfully managed. With the advice and help of Laffitte and other financiers, the Duke invested in shares at home and abroad, buying and selling to great profit. These and rents from land and houses brought him a very handsome income, which was not wasted. When necessary, as on the occasion of the ball for the King and Queen of Naples, he could entertain magnificently, but as a rule he and his family played little part in society. The personal expenses of the family were rigidly controlled; the future Queen, Marie Amélie, herself was known to have checked laundry bills, and her husband drew up frugal menus for his children; in 1828 a midday meal for eleven people was to cost under 20 francs, excluding coffee.[1]

Both the Duke and the Duchess were genuinely, if perhaps a little indiscriminately, charitable. It was estimated that they and Madame Adelaide, the Duke's sister, gave away about 500 to 700 francs a day to charitable institutions and in personal gifts, yet the children were kept very short of pocket-money. Something of a parade was made of the elder boys going to an ordinary school. In fact, though they attended the most fashionable of the Paris schools, the College of Henry V, they merely went to the classes; at the school lunch they were served apart with special dishes, and if they went into the playground were always surrounded by a group of boys chosen by their father. Each boy had his own private tutor, each girl her governess.

The children were very strictly brought up. They had to rise at 5 a.m. and follow a rigid time-table; even on Sundays there were lessons in dancing, fencing and so forth. Only in holiday time, when they were in the country, had they any freedom, and even then their tutors had to submit a daily report to their father. The family very rarely separated; when visits were paid to relations they travelled in a vast carriage which held twelve people and was drawn by six horses; one of the sons said it was 'very like a travelling menagerie van'.[2] When one reads of the intensity of the family life one can understand why Louis-Philippe and his wife got on so very well with Queen Victoria and Albert.

In 1830 the eldest son, the Duke of Chartres, was twenty years old. He was very popular, both with his brothers and sisters and in the regiment which he joined. Nemours, born in 1814, also went into the army; Joinville, who was only twelve in 1830, later joined the navy; he had to be specially crammed to pass his examinations. There were two other boys, Aumale and Montpensier, who in 1830 were eight and six years old. The eldest daughter, Louise, was born in 1812 and her father was already thinking about her matrimonial

[1] Gérainville, op. cit., Vol. II, p. 494.
[2] Joinville, Prince de: *Memoirs*. Trans. Loyd. London, 1895, p. 23.

prospects; Marie was a year younger, and Clementine was thirteen years old.

When the father of this large family received the message from the Deputies, his sister Adelaide gave him a tricoloured ribbon and urged him on. It was night time, and the Duke went to Paris in ordinary clothes, reaching his palace with difficulty, climbing over the barricades in the middle of the night. He sent two messages, one to Laffitte and one to Lafayette, to congratulate them. About three in the morning of Saturday, 31 July, Charles X's envoy reached him. He reported later that the Duke had told him that he had been forced to come to Paris and that he would never consent to be king.[1] This is quite likely to be true; it is clear that the future monarch was still very unhappy and undecided. Chateaubriand was very likely right when he said that if Charles had sent for Orleans to join him at St. Cloud, he would have come; but here again Charles could not realise the dangers about him.

About eight in the morning a deputation from the Parliament arrived. They painted a terrifying picture of the dangers of republican anarchy if Orleans did not at once accept the rôle of Lieutenant-General. Eventually Orleans agreed to a proclamation addressed to the people of Paris, in which he said that he had not hesitated to come and share their perils, and had accepted the office of Lieutenant-General.

When the deputies received the proclamation, they ordered it to be printed and posted all over Paris. There was still a good deal of republican demonstration going on, and Guizot drew up a document, a sort of equivalent to the promises given in 1814. It pledged the new Government to certain definite reforms; the re-establishment of the National Guard, who were to participate in the nomination of their officers; some part to be played by citizens in local government; juries to be used in Press trials; guarantees for the responsibility of ministers and officials; deputies appointed to official posts to seek re-election; and a general promise of 'developments'. It ended with the words 'The Charter will henceforth be a verity.' Ninety-one deputies signed this manifesto.

Laffitte then led them to the Palais Royal, where Orleans approved the document and went with Laffitte on to a balcony, where the crowd milling round the palace cheered wildly. He and the deputies then formed an odd sort of procession. A drummer went first, then four of the ushers of the Chamber of Deputies. Orleans came next, on horseback, with some former National Guardsmen; Laffitte was carried in a chair and a crowd of deputies followed behind. In great heat, through crowds and over barricades, they went slowly to the

[1] Mazas, M. A.: *Mémoires pour servir à l'histoire de la Révolution.*

Hôtel de Ville, Orleans constantly leaning down to shake the hands of those near by. It took a long time.

Lafayette knew well that if he accepted Orleans, it meant the end of his dream of a republic. But he was seventy-three years old, and was persuaded that a sovereign who owed his throne to the people was the best solution for the moment. The proclamation was read to him, Orleans spoke to him, and then they went together to the window, the old revolutionary holding a tricoloured flag in one hand and the Duke's hand in the other. As the crowd cheered, Orleans turned and embraced him. This was a master stroke, recorded in endless pictures and caricatures. The period of doubt was at an end; that France would remain a kingdom was now certain.

Slowly the prince returned to his palace, where his family was assembling. The big omnibus carriage had left Neuilly at about eight o'clock on the night of Saturday, the 31st; the younger children with their mother and Aunt Adelaide had to get out before they reached their destination and scatter. Joinville was most impressed by the number of tricolour flags and cockades that had appeared as if by magic; 'how people found time to make up so many emblems in those two days is a mystery!'[1], he wrote. The eldest son, the Duke of Chartres, had been arrested when he came to Paris from Joigny, where his regiment was stationed, and when he escaped decided to return to his barracks. It seems clear that whatever their father's reactions were, the sons and daughters took a very poor view of the crowds who invaded their rooms, and the many applicants for positions under the new régime.

The Duke was constantly engaged with the politicians who were making arrangements for taking over the government and for getting formal recognition of the new ruler. Charles had summoned the two Chambers to meet on 3 August and it was simplest to allow this session to take place. It was hardly a full meeting; only a fraction of the deputies were in Paris, and many Peers abstained. They were assembled together in the Palais Bourbon, where an empty throne was erected with a tricolour flag floating above it. The Duke came in and sat down on a chair to the right of this throne and made a little speech. He declared himself ready to do all he could, with the guidance of the Chambers, to restore order and secure the liberty of the people and the full observance of the Charter. He referred to the points made in his proclamation. The speech was greeted with applause.

Next day, Wednesday, 4 August, the Chambers had formal meetings. It was now known that Charles X had left the country, and this was a great relief to everyone except the loyal royalists. It

[1] Joinville, op. cit., pp. 34 ff.

allowed the adoption, during the discussions on the modification of
the constitution, of that convenient formula used by the English in
1689 that 'the throne was vacant'. On 7 August the debate took
place, and a revised Charter was accepted by 89 deputies to 10, with
15 abstentions. Without waiting for the Peers' consent, the deputies
then went to the Palais Royal and offered the crown to the Duke.
Emotional scenes culminated in another embrace on a balcony in the
sight of a cheering crowd; Lafayette with his arms round the new
King, spoke the often-repeated words: 'This is the prince we
needed! This is the best of republics!'

The amended Charter was preceded by a declaration, which after
speaking of the 'heroic resistance of the citizens of Paris' to the
violation of the constitution, and declaring the throne vacant because
Charles and the Dauphin had left France, annulled the preamble
which had 'appeared to grant' the French people their rights,
declared all nominations of Peers made by Charles to be void, and
offered the throne to Louis-Philippe. It was carefully stated that he
would have to accept definite engagements, and that his title was to
be King of the French, not of France. The theory of Divine Right of
Kings was thus explicitly abandoned.

Modifications in the Charter itself were not nearly as great as the
more advanced liberals would have wished. Censorship of the
Press was never to be re-established. After the formal statement of
the King's duties it was declared that he had no power to suspend
laws or dispense with them. The Chambers were given the same
right as the King to propose new legislation. The creation of extraordinary courts was prohibited, the tricolour declared the sole
national flag. Laws were to be made with regard to Press trials, the
national guard and so forth, as promised in July.

The liberals were most interested in the clauses regarding the
election of deputies. The only serious change in the Charter itself
was that the age limits were lowered; voters must be twenty-five and
members thirty. Partial renewal was abolished, and the Chamber
elected for five years. Presidents of electoral colleges were to be
nominated by the electors. The amount of tax qualification for
voters was not stated; that thorny problem was left with the other
disputed matters for future decision.

Whether the new King would have liked a grand coronation in
Rheims we do not know, but he had no chance. It certainly would
have been inappropriate, but the contrast was very marked. There
was no great religious ceremonial, no splendid procession. On
9 August, at 2 p.m., the deputies and the remainder of the Peers
who still had the right to attend and wished to do so assembled in
the Commons' usual debating hall in the Palais Bourbon. Orleans

took his place before the throne; behind him stood four marshals bearing cushions with the royal insignia laid on them. The declaration laid down in the Charter was read and the prince took the oath to govern by the law, to obey the Charter, to give justice to all and to act in the interests and for the glory of the people of France. Three copies of this oath were then solemnly signed by the new King, who took his place upon the throne. The crown and sceptre were handed to him by the marshals, he made a short speech and then returned to his house through the cheering crowds.

So ended the ancient monarchy: so began the new. Neither had been the deliberate choice of the people, probably no government ever has been. The foundations of the rule of Louis XVIII were much more solid than those of his cousin; they were dug deep into the past. The superstructure of both was built hastily by the politicians who were on the spot at the moment; the new one was but a modification of the one it supplanted. The differences were real, however. The new King stood for tendencies, not for a tradition. His coronation was a civil ceremony, as suited the anti-clerical tone of the wealthy middle class to which he belonged by adoption, despite the ancient lineage of which he was so proud. Bankers, journalists, professors had placed him on the throne left vacant by the folly of a man who thought in terms of days long gone by; their act was ratified by an assembly, elected for normal business by a small fraction of the people, and a House of Peers shorn of many of its members. Yet no other basis of power was possible. A plebiscite was suggested, but its organisation would have taken a long time and, as is usually the case with plebiscites, could hardly have had any result but to ratify the accomplished fact. To vote against a government when there is no clear alternative is merely a gesture and one which few choose to make. Even the men who had fought in the streets had no clear idea of what they wanted save the fall of an unpopular Cabinet; their loudest cry was for revenge on Polignac and his associates. In the provinces there were in the larger towns demonstrations against clerics and unpopular royalists, but there were no widespread demands for any new type of government.

Louis-Philippe's first aim was to restore order and show that he was a genuine king, strong enough to control the revolution to which he owed his throne. His first Cabinet, hastily appointed, included two men whose political experience went back to Napoleon's era, Molé at the Foreign Office and Baron Louis at the Exchequer. Guizot, responsible for the Home Office, and de Broglie, in charge of Education, represented the doctrinaire liberals. There was no Prime Minister.

During August several changes were made in the administrative services: royalist prefects, mayors and even generals were dismissed. All the 'regicides' and others banished by the Bourbons were invited to return to France, and early in September the death sentence for political crimes was abolished. Such demonstrations of a liberal outlook seemed essential. The new King was cautious in his reforms; even if he had wished to be democratic, and he certainly did not, he needed first to be accepted by the other monarchs.

Louis-Philippe sent autograph letters to the European courts in which he justified his acceptance of his crown. He chose well-known generals as his special envoys; the 'new men' might have given offence, and Charles' diplomats would hardly serve. They were coldly received, for the year 1830 was one of political excitement and unrest in many parts of Europe. After the death of George IV in June the agitation for parliamentary reform in England rapidly increased. In many of the German states there were demands for constitutions, sometimes leading to rebellion. Even in Switzerland the smaller towns were revolting against the domination of the larger, and the constitution of the Federation had to be amended. In Naples in November the new king, Ferdinand II, had to agree to a constitution, and in the same month the Poles revolted against Russian rule.

Far the most important for France of all these agitations was the Belgian demand for independence from Holland, to which she had been joined by the Treaty of Vienna. The temptations offered to an ambitious ruler of France were very great indeed. Save for Flanders, on the Channel coast, the Belgian provinces bordering on France were French in speech and culture and naturally looked to their neighbour for help against the Dutch. Louis-Philippe knew well that it was a long-standing tradition in England that France should not control the southern Netherlands. Before he could decide on a line of action, he must have an understanding with the British Government, and Wellington, the Prime Minister, in spite of his conservatism, had been most suspicious of the Bourbons' policy in Spain.

The aged but still immensely alert Talleyrand was sent to London in September 1830; a wiser choice could not have been made. The salutes from the guns of the fortress at Dover that greeted his arrival symbolised for once a genuine admiration felt for him in England. Talleyrand was most anxious that Belgian independence should be secured, but that the initiative should come from England; he found Wellington reasonable; though plainly showing that he thought the July revolution had been 'unhappy', he seemed not at all unfriendly to the new Government.[1] The King of Holland had asked Prussian

---

[1] Talleyrand, Prince de: *Mémoires*. Ed. de Broglie. Paris, 1891, Vol. III, p. 336.

help to subdue the Belgians, but Prussia, too, was waiting for a lead from England. A conference of the Great Powers was, therefore, opened in London in November; hardly had it begun when Wellington was forced to resign and Lord Grey's ministry, pledged to reform of the suffrage, took over control. Talleyrand was pleased; he wrote to Adelaide, the King's sister, on 19 November: 'This administration will be strong, and favourable to us . . . they all speak of the King with great respect.'[1]

By 20 December the Powers had agreed to recognise the independence of the Kingdom of Belgium, for that was the announced determination of the assembly in Brussels. The choice of a monarch was by no means easy. A strong party wanted to have the Duke of Nemours, Louis-Philippe's son, and the offer was very tempting. Talleyrand knew well, and so did his King, that acceptance would meet with immediate resistance not only from England but from Russia and Prussia as well, so it was regretfully declined. There were always German princes available of sufficient rank to be candidates, and the French supported Leopold of Saxe-Coburg, who had refused the less attractive throne of the newly-independent Greece. In June 1831 he was adopted by the Belgians with the consent of the Powers; he was a man of forty-one, the brother of the Duchess of Kent and so the uncle of the future Queen Victoria. When he was firmly established he showed his gratitude for the aid given him by France, not only in the conference room but by the sending of troops to drive out Dutch forces, by marrying Louise, the eldest daughter of Louis-Philippe. One, at any rate, of that large family had been admitted to the charmed circle of the crowned heads of Europe.

Talleyrand's negotiations had not been made easier by the instability of the Government in Paris. In 1852 Thiers was discussing this with Nassau William Senior, Professor of Political Economy in Oxford, who travelled over Europe interviewing distinguished persons and recording their views. His view was that Louis-Philippe 'never would consent to be a constitutional king', that he was constantly nearly upsetting the boat 'by getting up to seize the rudder'. Thiers' own ideal of a monarch was that he should reign, but not govern; in fairness to Louis-Philippe it must be admitted that it is doubtful whether even Queen Victoria, often looked on as the first true constitutional sovereign, would have accepted this definition. Thiers went on to say that 'until he found an instrument in Guizot', the King delighted in a ministerial crisis, 'which gratified his love of power and his love of intrigue'.[2]

[1] Talleyrand, Prince de: *Mémoires*. Ed. de Broglie. Paris, 1891, Vol. III, p. 460.
[2] Senior, N. W.: *Conversations with M. Thiers, M. Guizot and others*. Ed. Simpson. London, 1878, Vol. I, p. 127.

Certainly his refusal to appoint a President of the Cabinet greatly weakened his first ministry and made it harder for it to deal with the continued agitation in Paris during August and September. Lafayette's National Guard was more apt to fraternise with than to repress rioters, and reports of disturbances had a bad effect not only on the country but also on France's reputation abroad. In October elections were held to replace 113 deputies who had resigned or whose election had been declared invalid. To meet the renewed Assembly, the King chose a new ministry on 2 November.

His friend Laffitte was made Prime Minister; most of his colleagues were not experienced politicians. They were much more conservative than the men they replaced, and were joined on 17 November by Soult, who had the name of being a 'strong' man. Agitation was kept alive by the trial before the House of Peers of Polignac, and such others of Charles' ministers as were available, for breaking the constitution by issuing the July ordinances. The formal proceedings did not begin till 15 December; Martignac showed his courage and lack of personal rancour by undertaking Polignac's defence, although he was so ill that he could well have been excused so arduous a duty. The House was now reduced to 163 members and they carried out their task with fairness and dignity. Outside the Luxembourg Palace, where they sat, crowds were shouting for the death of the accused; when on 21 December the trial ended the prisoners were smuggled out of the Chamber and safely lodged in the fortress of Vincennes. They were sentenced to deportation, and Polignac to 'civil death', which meant loss of all rights. The word 'death' was misunderstood by the mob, who dispersed.

The rioting gave the King the excuse he needed to break with Lafayette. On 24 December the Parliament passed a law which abolished the office of Commander-in-Chief of the whole of the National Guard. This led, as was hoped, to Lafayette's resignation of the minor post of Commander of the Paris National Guard. The corps was reorganised; it had had some cannon, but these were now transferred to the army. Louis-Philippe had made his attitude clear: a revolution had made him King but he would not be the King of the revolution.

Chapter XVI

THE STATE AND THE WORKERS

THE first need for the Government was to pass a budget. The custom had been for an estimate to be presented for the expenses of each ministry, and a block grant made. A considerable increase in the control of the Chamber of Deputies over the Cabinet was given by a law passed on 29 January, 1831; in future, each department of the executive had to present its estimates under a series of headings and sums granted for one purpose could not be transferred to another within the same department. The deputies therefore could challenge the details of State expenditure. The Government retained the right to permit additional expenditure, should the money voted for any purpose prove inadequate or some unforeseen expenditure be necessary; these extra credits had to be approved later by the Parliament.

On 8 February, 1831, a law gave the 'ministers of the Jewish religion' the right to State incomes already held by the Catholics and Protestant pastors. The theory behind this law was of more importance than the actual money given; France ceased to be nominally an entirely Christian state: all religious organisations were equal in the eyes of the law. To contemporary observers, as well as to later commentators, the July monarchy seemed to be taking an anti-Catholic line, in harmony with the views of the liberals. That religious observances still had political implications was clearly shown soon after the law was passed on 14 February.

The legitimists decided to hold their customary requiem mass for the anniversary of the death of the Duke de Berry. There was no procession or other public demonstration, but the number of grand carriages going to the church of St. Germain l'Auxerrois, a four-teenth-century building opposite the colonnade of the Louvre, attracted attention. Some people managed to get inside, and found that not only was a portrait of his son, the pretender to the throne, exposed but that a collection was being made for soldiers wounded in July in resisting the revolution. It was felt that this was an insult to the people of Paris, and the National Guard was summoned and ordered the congregation to leave.

A crowd soon collected, dashed into the church and tore down not only the royalist emblems but the decorations of the altars, smashing statues, breaking windows, looting, and profaning the sacred vessels. The priests' house adjoining was pillaged, and next day the rioters invaded the house of the Archbishop of Paris, stripping it of furniture and damaging the structure. Other churches, too, were attacked. It was perfectly plain that the sympathy of the authorities lay with the rioters, for the Prefect of Police himself had been present and had done nothing to stop the attack on the church. When on 17 February the riots were discussed in the assembly, the prefect, who was himself a deputy, so far from apologising for his failure to keep order, attacked the very Government he served. He said the people were discontented as the Government had done nothing for them, and demanded a variety of reforms, including a new electoral law. Odilon Barrot, a radical, defended the rioters. Even the minister in charge of the Department of Education and Religion laid the blame on the royalists. Guizot pointed out that the Government had a duty to keep order; in the Peers, the Minister of the Navy declared that the prefect had not done his duty. The weakness of the Cabinet could scarcely have been more clearly shown, yet the deputies refused to pass a vote of censure.

The excuse was made that the blame lay with the Archbishop of Paris for permitting the service, and he and the parish priest were charged before the courts for provocation of disorder. Several prominent royalists were arrested, and in their private papers was found correspondence with the exiled Royal Family. Former officers of Charles X's Royal Guard were ordered to leave Paris, and many of the men who were hoping to restore the Bourbons left France. Louis-Philippe was not at all pleased with his Government; he did not want to go on living in an atmosphere of turbulence and demonstrations, or employ radical politicians as policemen. He dismissed the prefect, and on 13 March Odilon Barrot and Laffitte lost their posts in the Cabinet.

A 'strong' man was needed, and the King chose Casimir Périer. A man of fifty-four, he came from a family of manufacturers, and in 1801 had founded a very successful discount bank in Paris. All through the period of the Restoration monarchy he had been a severe critic, especially of de Villèle's financial policy. He had joined in the attack on the Congregation, he had been one of the '221' opponents of Polignac, and one of the group of deputies who took control in July 1830. He now took office as Prime Minister and Home Secretary. Baron Louis was back at the Exchequer, and Soult was at the War Office. The controlling force was Périer himself; his colleagues found that he insisted on full information from them and was determined in his enforcement of his ideas.

The necessary constitutional changes were now put through. Ever since July the fulfilment of the pledges to modify the Charter had been a subject of debate; how much more democratic would the State become? Ever since December the question of the suffrage had been discussed. One plan put forward had been that of 'capacity', professional men were to have the vote irrespective of their wealth. There was strong division of opinion as to which professions should be included in this privilege. Finally, the tax basis was preserved and at a high level (200 francs), though the 'capacity' idea lingered in that all members of the Institute (the original Academy and four others, for History and Archaeology, Moral and Political Science, Natural Science, and Fine Arts) and retired officers with a pension of 1,200 francs and over had the vote even if they did not pay the tax of 200 francs a year. If any local district had less than 150 qualified electors, a few men paying less could be added. In the year 1831 the total of qualified electors was under 170,000, or about five in every thousand of the people; the corresponding figure in the English Reform Bill of 1832 was about 32 per thousand. The electoral districts had been arranged so as to minimise as far as possible the influence of the large towns.

Another desire of the radicals had been to reduce Government influence in the deputies by forbidding officials to sit. The qualification for a deputy was that he should be thirty and pay 500 francs a year in taxes, and it could be argued that, if State employees were excluded, the number of possible members of the Lower House would be greatly reduced. The only concession made to the opponents of 'place men' was that prefects and other officials with important functions in the administration could not be elected in the department in which they actually worked, though they were eligible anywhere else and, if they resigned their office, within six months of their retirement in their own district. Louis-Philippe's cabinets took full advantage of their right to nominate deputies to office or to encourage official candidates; it was calculated in 1842 that out of a Chamber of 459, 149 held Government posts. With such solid support, a Government majority was easily obtained.

The view that good citizenship and wealth went hand in hand was reflected in new arrangements for the National Guard, embodied in a law passed in the spring of 1831. All Frenchmen between the ages of twenty and sixty were liable to serve, but only citizens paying direct taxes and volunteers were placed on the active list; everyone else was on a reserve list. The pledge that the guardsmen should elect their officers was nominally fulfilled by allowing them to choose their own N.C.O.s and junior officers, but their tenure of command was for three years only. Senior officers were chosen by other officers, not by the men, and commanders were selected by the Government. The law itself as well as the debates that preceded it showed that the new King and his Cabinet were most distrustful of this force with its revolutionary and popular tradition.

This spring of 1831 may be looked on as the most important period in the history of the July monarchy. The decision to keep political power in the hands of the upper middle class gave the Government far too narrow a basis. As industry developed, the number of voters increased, but there arose another class of 'new men', the smaller factory owners and shopkeepers, who greatly resented their lack of the vote. Such men are slow to combine and to agitate, but their numbers were such that when they felt they had real cause for dissatisfaction with the policy of the State they had the means to publicise their demands. It is conceivable that, as some contemporary observers thought, spectacular achievements in foreign policy might have kept them happy, but such victories would have involved risks and expenditure which might equally well have frightened them.

The fear of popular risings and agitation was already clearly shown. Louis-Philippe, like Louis XVIII, had to face plots to turn him off the throne, but at any rate in the early years they were not dangerous for they had little support from the country as a whole. To him, and on the whole to his ministers, unrest among the workers was ascribed to the legitimists and Bonapartists, and the basic causes of discontent, never adequately investigated, were looked on as temporary or as a field for private rather than State action. Theories of radical reform were being freely discussed, but in the earlier years of the reign there were reasonable grounds for thinking that they were so high-flown and impractical that they could safely be ignored.

The works of two writers in particular were being read and discussed, especially by science students and by young engineers. Most of the books had been published well before 1830, but their effect seems to have been noticeable only after the July revolution. One interesting point in the history of French socialist ideas is that the criticism of modern industrial organisation preceded its appearance on a large scale; when the phenomena of modern proletarianism began to show themselves, they were met by antagonism partly due to the ideals publicised by two very different men, Saint-Simon and Fourier.

Their theories sprang from the combination of science and romance which characterised the intellectual revolution in Europe. Though Fourier, in particular, could be very practical in points of detail, Marx was justified in dubbing them 'Utopian', dreamers rather than planners of a practicable scheme. Both wanted a radical transformation of political and economic life; both thought that an experimental state could be founded whose outstanding success would convince all reasonable men of the truth of their theories. Both believed in themselves with an intensity that led them to pour out books full of startling and challenging ideas. Their coincidence in time and in attitude has led to their being coupled almost automatically, like Damon and Pythias, yet they were extremely different in class, in character and in ideals.

Saint-Simon was born in 1760 and died in 1825. He was an aristocrat not only by birth but in mind. His personal extravagance led him to great poverty, but he never lost his belief in himself. His work was apt to be haphazard, but his disciple, Enfantin (1796–1864), had the power of organisation he lacked, and ran a successful publication, the *Globe*, and lectures attended, it was claimed, by 40,000 men. Enfantin was an engineer, and the notion of great canals for international traffic was said to have been born in the discussions of the Saint Simonist school; certainly de Lesseps, the builder of the Suez Canal, was a member.

Saint-Simon's fundamental doctrine was that love was the mainspring of human activity, love for oneself which, if adequately satisfied, would mean love for others. Such love would find its natural channel in one of three major types of activity, according to the characteristics of individuals: philosophy and morality—the priest type; speculative thought—the scientists; physical action—the workers. There was thus a natural division of mankind into three classes. The idea of love, not excluding self-love, as the sole motive force was very attractive; unfortunately in the eighteen-thirties many of the organised Saint-Simonists interpreted the word very narrowly in a purely sexual sense, and their practice of 'free' love led to their institutions being closed by the police.

The State, it was held, was essentially a means of organising society and attaining the happiness of men by an immense increase in wealth. Like many early socialists, Saint-Simon took the materialist and evolutionary view of history; modern political organisation was needed to replace one based on outworn economic ideas. Wealth increases through the association of workers in labour intelligently directed, so those who do not work have no right to own; a man may keep the fruits of his own work, but the State is the universal inheritor of all property. At its head should be the Supreme Distributor, drawn from the ruling class of priests, who are the constant source of inspiration, teaching a simple and undogmatic form of Christianity.

The scientists would direct the activities of production and distribution, continually adding to the sources of wealth. The workers would be happy, making the goods for themselves and others. All children would be educated and trained as members of whichever class they were naturally suited for. Such a society could be founded on an experimental scale; Saint-Simon had thought that Louis XVIII or perhaps the Pope would be a suitable person to put up the money. In fact, a few groups of people did get together and try to found a model state, but, not surprisingly, these experiments collapsed.

It was not the scheme which influenced people; it was the attack on the conditions of the time. That men should be individuals happily co-operating for the good of all, not slaves of a master; that science and not tradition and prejudice should organise production; these were conceptions widely at variance with existing political and economic facts. Even men who had no sympathy with Saint-Simon's philosophy were led to question the bases of their life. When they preached to the actual workers they usually met with incomprehension, which, however, could easily be explained by the lack of education.

Fourier, who was born in 1772 and died in 1837, was a man very different in birth and outlook from the aristocrat Saint-Simon. He came from the lower middle class and his ideas came from practical observation, not from study. Engels called him a great satirist, and indeed his works are as full of challenges to accepted customs as was Sir Thomas More's *Utopia*. He wrote several books, using peculiar words of his own invention, and mixing together startling psychological theories, practical plans for economic organisation, shrewd analyses of contemporary society, and penetrating forecasts of future developments. He seems to have deliberately made his books difficult for the reader, but even to-day they stimulate thought.[1]

Like Saint-Simon, Fourier believed he had a great rôle to play in the world, and confidently expected some millionaire to come and give him money to found a model state. His conception was much more practical than the aristocrat's, and founded on a wider basis. He recognised that there were many facets in human characters, and believed men must be given the chance to develop them all, though some would be stronger on one side than others. He accepted property and the acquisitive and competitive instincts as natural, but also as dangerous if over developed. In his model state, which he called a phalanstery, perfect harmony was to be attained. It was to consist of about 1,600 people and be quite self-sufficient; the description reads like the prospectus of a first-class residential holiday hotel. Each citizen was to work, but at a variety of tasks, so

[1] An excellent brief selection was made by C. Gide: *Œuvres Choisies de Charles Fourier*. Paris, n.d.

13

as to avoid both monotony and lop-sided development. Each worker
would put part of his income into the enterprise and receive interest
on it; this would give him property which was both individual and
communal. Teams of workers would compete against each other to
raise output and give natural expression to the passion of emulation.
Many types of personality must be included among his 'Har-
monians', but no one would be admitted who had not excellent
manners. Fourier's state, therefore, did not conflict with normal
religion and morality.

His criticism was not so acceptable. He hated what he called
'parasites', which term included children (who ought to work and
were specially well suited for dirty jobs), soldiers, officials and,
above all, middlemen. He knew a lot about the distributive trades,
for he had been a commercial traveller, and thought the waste of
labour they entailed and the attitude they fostered quite deplorable.
He pointed out the danger of misuse of the land, especially the
destruction of forests; he was laughed at for saying the Sahara might
be made fertile, but modern scientists now believe this quite
possible. He foretold that fierce individualist competitive capitalism
would lead to a 'new feudalism' of trusts and combines. An extraordinary number of ideas put forward by modern writers can be
found in Fourier's works.

Considérant (1808–93) tried to make his work more accessible.
He had some success; Mill, in his *Principles of Political Economy*,
expressed the wish that it should have a trial[1] and some Fourierist
colonies were attempted in the United States. They all failed dis-
mally to fulfil Fourier's basic conditions; they were far too small to
hope for any success. That they were tried at all does indicate that
his ideas were attractive to many educated people; and the sharpness
of his criticism found a wider hearing than his schemes for an ideal
pattern of living.

Save for the 'free love' of Enfantin's followers, these theorists
seemed harmless to the Government. Yet it may be argued that so
much and such pointed attack on the economic foundations on
which the July monarchy rested contributed seriously to its weakness. Later socialists produced writings more intelligible to the
workers than the Utopists, but Saint-Simon and Fourier had helped
to form the atmosphere which moulded their minds. Louis-Philippe
himself shared the outlook of those very capitalists and middlemen
and speculators whose activities were leading to the changes in the
pattern of living in the towns of France which the theorists criticised
and the workers resented.

[1] Mill, J. Stuart: *Principles of Political Economy*, 3rd edition, 1852. See
Ashley's edition, London, 1909, p. 211.

Throughout his reign, population in the towns was rising faster than in the countryside, though population was not increasing as fast in France as in some other countries.[1] Agricultural production was rising slowly, and as a protective barrier excluded foreign foods, a bad harvest was apt to cause a rapid rise in the price of bread. Poor communications, too, played their part in such circumstances, for rapid transfer from one district to another was not at all easy. It was noticed that between 1835 and 1845 a trend in national physique had been checked; the average height of recruits for the army had been rising, but this was no longer the case.

The living conditions of the town workers were on the whole bad, not only by modern standards. In the industrial towns most families occupied one room only, and as much work was still done at home the congestion was extreme. Wages were irregular, and the rooms were rented by the week and paid for in advance, so dispossession was common. It was calculated that rent absorbed 10 per cent of the average family's income, and food 75 per cent; as in England, the miseries of the workers were often ascribed to their improvidence, but it was quite impossible for most men to save. Wherever it was possible, the children worked, but by no means all French industries had adopted the factory system which gave them employment.

Apart from the mines and heavy industries, much French production was concentrated in the luxury trades, which were highly profitable but also very vulnerable. Any fall in demand led to immediate unemployment. In Paris in 1836 it was calculated that there were 30,500 men who never had regular work out of a total labour force of 250,000, and in that year there were another 55,000 unemployed and therefore ready to demonstrate in the streets. That the State should come to the help of these men was looked on as positively wrong; the care of the poor was the duty of the charitable well-to-do. Yet a good deal of the unemployment has been attributed to the State's own action in maintaining high import duties; the import of raw materials was made more difficult and sales abroad were lessened when no corresponding foreign goods were bought by French traders. When the Government suggested a freeing of foreign trade, opposition was immediate, especially among the wealthy men, who alone had the vote. In the late 'forties a movement for Free Trade began in imitation of the English Manchester school, but it had no great success.

In the autumn of 1831 Périer's government had to deal with a serious disturbance in that home of revolutionary activity, Lyons. The population of about 180,000 was mainly dependent on the silk

[1] Morazé, C.: *La France Bourgeoise*. Paris, 1947, Ch. I.

industry, though there were also a good many manufacturers of hats. The organisation of the manufacture of silk, satin and velvet was peculiar. The capitalists were not themselves manufacturers; they were dealers who imported raw silk and gave it to the master employers, ordering a specific amount of material of some special pattern. The master craftsmen owned the looms, which were mostly of the type invented by the Lyons mechanic Jacquard, which were far larger than the old small looms and therefore more expensive. They themselves worked with the help of hired labourers, often only three or four. Hours were long and conditions unhealthy; tuberculosis was common and the poor physique of conscripts from Lyons was notable.

There was a certain amount of quasi-trade union organisation among the hatters and even among the silk-weavers; under the cover of a friendly society, the law prohibiting combinations could be evaded. A *Conseil de Prud'hommes* was often called in to arbitrate over wage rates; in 1817 the local prefect had enforced its scale. There were three sources of trouble in the city; the fundamental one was the erratic cycle of great demand for silks, which led to workers coming in not only from districts round about but from Savoy and Italy, followed by a sudden decline when there were many idle looms and hungry men. Secondly, the masters who owned the looms were at the mercy of the capitalist dealers, and found it hard to co-operate with each other and put up a common demand for reasonable prices for the silk they made. Thirdly, the hired workers struggled for better wages from their immediate employers.

In 1827 there was a serious crisis in the silk-weaving trade and in 1828–29 the Government had to give substantial relief as well as giving some employment by rebuilding the fortifications round the town. In 1830 the *livret* system[1] was used to expel all workers who were not strictly citizens of Lyons, though this was not really legal, so the July revolution was tremendously popular, as any change of government would have been. Instead of immediate prosperity, the result of the political change was a general falling off in demand for rich fabrics both in France and among foreign buyers, so in January 1831 there were demonstrations in the streets.[2]

All types of revolutionaries were active in so hopeful a field. Legitimists thought there was a hope of overturning Orleans; Saint-Simonists preached socialism; men who belonged to the Carbonari tried to organise a corps of volunteers to enter Savoy and help the

[1] See *supra*, p. 3.
[2] Rude, F.: *Le Mouvement Ouvrier à Lyon de* 1827 *à* 1832. Paris, 1944. This exhaustive study of over 700 pages gives a detailed account of its interesting subject.

revolutionaries there. The prefect was ordered to stop this; but in February 1831 a pathetic band of men, without arms and many in rags, marched out of the town. They were pursued by 100 dragoons and 20 gendarmes, who persuaded them to return, and the local authorities pushed on the building of the fortifications to give employment. They also sent reports to Paris which minimised the whole trouble; it seems likely that about 500–600 men actually took part, though the number may have been higher. In the end it was Savoyards who came to Lyons, to earn the wage paid to labourers on the forts which, though very low, was more than they could earn at home.

During the spring and summer there was much restiveness but little serious trouble. In May there were riots, which were neatly handled by the authorities, who pointed out to the workers that trade was seriously damaged by disturbances that frightened foreign buyers. Ringleaders were arrested, but sentenced to only two or three days' imprisonment. The notion of a corps of volunteers was not dropped; at times during the summer it was proposed to march to help the Belgians, or later the Poles. The fundamental reason for unrest was not political; it was that the average day's work for weavers was 16–18 hours, with only one hour off for meals, and the average wage earned by a good worker on piece rates was 1 franc 50 centimes. Unless there were children in the family who could earn, it was really impossible for a married man to live on these wages.

In October 1831 the master craftsmen began to organise, in the hope of raising the price paid them by the capitalist middlemen. On 25 October representatives of the master craftsmen met to discuss prices and wage rates; about 6,000 workers assembled and marched in regular squads to the square outside the building where the arguments were going on. They stood, surrounding a tricolour flag, in perfect order, until after four hours they heard that a scale had been agreed on. They then marched off after cheering the prefect.

When the news of this demonstration reached Paris, Casimir Périer was greatly relieved; Soult, however, took a different view. He did not at all like the clear signs of organisation among the workers. Had the new wage scales immediately been put into force it is likely that the various groups behind the organisation would have dispersed or become weakened, but unfortunately without some definite sanction it was impossible either to make all the small individual masters insist on the scale being paid to themselves or to insist on their paying it to their men. In November there were frequent meetings to demand that the wage scale should be enforced by law; on the 17th the prefect announced that the agreed tariff was merely an honourable engagement not enforceable at law. The result was both lockouts by some of the masters and threats of strikes by the men.

On 1 November serious trouble began. The National Guard contained a number of workers and ex-soldiers, and could not be relied on to put down insurgents. Some of the workers made a little fortified post on the outskirts of the city; they had few arms and less ammunition, but they made bullets for themselves using thimbles as moulds. Paving stones and tiles were collected; some streets were barricaded. Some shots were exchanged between the workers and the National Guards who were ordered by the prefect to break up the assemblies, and some of the Guard went over to the workers.

As had happened before, the authorities were handicapped by bad relations between the civilian officials and the general in command of the troops. The soldiers were sent too late, and when the prefect had been fairly successful in negotiating with the men, artillery fire from the garrison made the men think they had been deceived. They took the prefect and the commander of the National Guard into a kind of custody, thus paralysing the civilian authorities. The attitude of the workers became more revolutionary; they displayed black flags and banners with the slogan '*Vivre en travaillant ou mourir en combattant*', which was meant as a claim for a living wage. The leaders were now asking for revolution, but when one speech ended with the phrase 'Long live the Republic!' some of the older men said 'We want the wage scale, not a republic; let's go' and went off.[1]

The attitude of the soldiers was often sympathetic to the men, and in any case the number of troops was not large, not over 4,000. By midnight on the 22nd most of them had been concentrated on the Town Hall, and the workers were in control of the city. Early on the morning of the 23rd the remaining troops were withdrawn, the people throwing bits of furniture at them out of the windows.

It is probable that about 600 casualties had resulted from the scrappy fighting. Once the troops had gone, the prefect succeeded in restoring order. The men were far better organised than the Paris revolutionaries of July; their patrols stopped all looting. Numbers of proclamations were issued by various groups, but the silk weavers on 24 November turned out a Revolutionary Committee that was claiming authority, and next day set up an organisation of their own to send two deputies to Paris to ask for legal sanction for the new wage scale. Shops reopened, life slowly returned to normal. On 27 November the prefect announced that the King had ordered 640,000 francs' worth of silk for covering furniture, and many of the

[1] Rude, op. cit., p. 411.

men returned to work, confident that the new wage rates would now be paid.

Meantime, the Government in Paris had become seriously alarmed. Soult himself, with the Duke of Orleans, the King's eldest son, and a large body of troops marched towards Lyons. The Duke was full of anger; he wanted to strike a 'terrible blow' at the revolutionaries, but also thought a good plan would be to bribe the leaders and make ample promises of better conditions.[1] Soult seems to have felt that the workers had a case and that it would be right to enforce the new wage scale.

Before the troops actually entered the city, delegates from the workers saw Soult, who gave them to understand that the agreed wages would be paid if no further disorder occurred, so they in turn promised that all arms would be handed over. Now he was on the spot, the Marshal seems to have modified his views; he thought incorrectly that life and property had been saved by the intervention of the middle-class citizens. Soldiers were sent to collect the muskets and occupied the suburbs of the town, but there were no demonstrations. On 2 December the ringleaders of the rising were arrested, and the National Guard disarmed and disbanded, with a promise that it should be reorganised. By now about 20,000 troops had assembled, and Soult and Orleans marched into the city on 3 December. Soldiers were housed in all the public buildings; there was no demonstration but the people watched gloomily. Orleans handed out medals, but without rousing any enthusiasm; instead the richer people were alarmed at the good terms which were rapidly established between the soldiers and the workers.

This may explain the actions of the Marshal, who on 7 December announced that all the workers' *livrets* were annulled and that new ones could be had only by men who had a 'good conduct' certificate from the police. This involved permanent unemployment in Lyons not only for the outsiders, who were not known to the Lyons police, but also for anyone with whom they were on bad terms. Next day, on 8 December, he declared the wage scale to have no binding force. Every worker had understood that the fundamental aim had, in fact, been won, and that Soult had promised the new wages. Demonstrations were not possible, but bitter anger spread.

On 9 December the Marshal and the heir to the throne left Lyons. So far from attempting further revolution, on 30 December one of the workers' leaders sold to the prefect 512 muskets, at 5,000 francs below their cost price, yet that did not mean all was well. In January 1832 the *Conseil de Prud'hommes* was reconstituted, but only one

[1] Rude, op. cit., p. 598.

quarter of the master craftsmen were allowed to elect members and the workers were wholly unrepresented. Through the winter and summer of 1832 men who had been arrested for agitation during or after the November risings were brought to trial; the majority were acquitted and only tiny sentences imposed on those found guilty. This greatly disturbed the Government. In January 1832 a special grant was made to the city to 'meet urgent needs'. One third of this was used to rebuild public buildings damaged during the riots, and part of the remainder absorbed in paying bills for food distributed in November, so not much was left for the people who were hungry and out of work.

The Lyons 'revolution' had settled nothing, but because of this its effects were widespread. The Government had had a serious fright, but believed that workers' risings could be put down; the idea that wages and conditions of work were private matters in which the State should not interfere became firmly established in the governing section of the community. Some of the middle class held that men had a right to a living wage, but even the more liberal Press tended to oppose any element of compulsion in economic life, whether by organisations of workers or by law. The workers, especially in the Rhône valley and in Paris, felt they had been betrayed and remained restless and dissatisfied.

The Lyons garrison was greatly enlarged, and the presence of the soldiers demonstrated by frequent drills in the squares of the city. The republicans and other men of the opposition began to organise, and in May 1833 planned a banquet as a demonstration. The authorities suddenly prohibited this party, and though the organising committee got legal opinion that no law forbade such a meeting, troops occupied the garden where it was to take place on 12 May. Editors of local papers were tried and sentenced severely for their criticisms. Leaders from Paris came to try to organise the revolutionary groups, but the difference in outlook between the middle-class theoretical Carbonarists and the workers prevented any solid combination. A revolutionary Society of the Rights of Man was the most important of the associations, and it secured members in the surrounding districts as well as in the town.

A sharp decline in the demand for silks led, early in 1834, to a cut in the price paid for plush, and the consequent reduction in wages led to a strike on 12 February. The Society of the Rights of Man did not support the strikers, and without funds behind them the men were forced to give way. After the trouble was over, six of the workers' leaders were arrested, and when they were brought to trial in April excitement was widespread. Soldiers were in position at various key points, so resistance was really hopeless; the workers had hardly any weapons and their organisation was of the poorest. On 9 April, when the trial began, a shot was fired, probably by an excited soldier, which killed a man who, though dressed as a worker, was actually a policeman.[1] Immediately a general struggle began; some of the troops seem to have used quite unnecessary brutality, while others showed sympathy for the workers. By the evening of 10 April resistance was really at an end, though complete order was not restored till the 12th. That agents of the police had encouraged the building of barricades, etc., was generally believed; whether this was true or not, the general effect was one of bitter hatred being roused against the Government. The Lyons men had hoped for a sympathetic rising in Paris, but this was not carried through; efforts there were easily put down by the troops, and again the charge was made that unnecessary violence had been used.

The Government decided to treat the rioters in such a way as to discourage all future attempts. In February 1835 the House of Peers was summoned to try a miscellaneous collection of people for treason. Several Peers refused to attend, and this, of course, made the chances of the accused far worse. The Government at first declared that only counsel appointed by the State could defend the prisoners; this led to widespread protest from lawyers all over France. The trial gave rise to great excitement, enhanced by the success of some of the prisoners in digging a tunnel and so escaping from the prison of St. Pélagie. In the end, 18 of the accused were sentenced to transportation; 88 to sentences varying from 20 years, to one year's imprisonment, to be followed by close police supervision.

This technique of prompt use of military force to quell any demonstrations by the workers was continued by the authorities during the rest of the reign. It was intensely disliked by the soldiers as well as by all liberals, but was on the whole effective in preventing any combination between the various groups of opponents. Outside as well as inside France, revolutionists developed a whole legend about the men of Lyons, while conservatives used the incidents as a proof that it was dangerous to yield to democracy in any degree at all. Both sides tended to over-emphasise the political aspects of the risings; the simple truth was that the workers would rise whenever they could, unless they could have what they believed to be decent and reasonable conditions of labour and adequate wages.

[1] Blanc, Louis: *The History of Ten Years*. London, 1844, Vol. II, p. 258.

Chapter XVII

THE CITIZEN KING

CASIMIR PÉRIER'S attitude to the troubles in Lyons had been considerably affected by events outside France. Although in the summer of 1831 the Belgians had chosen Leopold as their king, King William of Holland had refused to recognise the division of his kingdom of the Netherlands. Périer threatened to resign if Louis-Philippe refused to send French troops to turn out the Dutch forces which invaded the new State, so France played an active share in creating the first major breach in the arrangements of the Treaty of Vienna. Not until 1833 did the Dutch accept the settlement. That other revolutions would be supported was sincerely hoped by the French radicals, but risings in Italy were watched with a good deal of suspicion. Austria had taken the revolutions in Parma, Modena and other States as an excuse for intervention; when the Papal States also rose and the Austrian armies marched into them, France became alarmed. The strongest anti-clericals, who were glad to see the Papacy in trouble, did not want it backed up by Austrian force and Austrian influence; while even the best friends of the Pope disliked this subordination of Rome to Vienna.

Long negotiations went on during 1831 between the French Government and Gregory XVI. The Pope promised serious reform in his dominions to meet the well-founded complaints of his subjects, but many of the Cardinals, through whom his government was carried out, were elderly men to whom political disorder and religious disaffection seemed to be identical evils. Once again, in January 1832, the disorders were so widespread that the Austrians were called in to put down the revolutionaries.

Périer decided that if the Pope did really need protection France must join Austria in providing it. Without any formal request from Rome, or even the Pope's consent, a French fleet was sent in February 1832 to Ancona, the main Adriatic port of the Papal States. The commanding officer was sent in one of the new steamboats, so that he could arrive in advance of the troops, who were in sailing vessels, and make arrangements with the papal officials. Unluckily, the winds were exceptionally kind to the sailing ships, and they arrived well before the little paddle steamer flogging her way

ound Italy. The commanders were nearly all old soldiers of
Napoleon, who not only hated Austria but had the greatest contempt
or the Pope, so without waiting for any permission they landed their
men and occupied the town, telling the people that they had come to
liberate Italy from the Austrians. In France the anti-Papalists
rejoiced, but the Government was dismayed.

Luckily Sainte-Aulaire, the French Ambassador in Rome, was a
very able man. With extreme skill he pacified the responsible Cardinals and the Pope himself, who fortunately was not a bellicose
person. He obtained an authorisation for the French to occupy
Ancona temporarily, and so extricated Périer from a most awkward
position, even raising his country's prestige. As he wrote to de
Barante, 'I admit, however, that it is an advantage to have proved
to Europe that we were able to perpetrate an act of folly and injustice
with impunity.'[1]

By the spring it seemed that Casimir Périer was firmly established
as Prime Minister, but his career, like that of thousands of others,
was cut short by the terrible epidemic of cholera that swept across
Europe in 1832. On 26 March the first cases appeared in Paris and
the disease swept through the close-packed and insanitary streets of
the capital. Wild rumours were spread that criminals had poisoned
the water or the bread supply; inadequate medical knowledge and
sheer panic aggravated the number of victims. Between March and
September over 18,000 people died, and among them was the Prime
Minister, who succumbed to the illness on 16 May, 1832. Riots in
June made things even worse; the remainder of the Cabinet which
was carrying on the government ordered troops to fire on the
demonstrators, and the fighting which followed caused about 800
casualties, many wounded being added to the number of cholera
victims already in hospitals.

All through the epidemic the Church was shown in its best light.
Priests once again wore publicly the black cassocks which they had
not dared to show outside the churches since 1830, and, thus easily
identified, they went about with the greatest courage consoling the
sick and carrying the sacraments to the dying. The Royal Family
had moved to the Tuileries in October 1831 on the request of Périer,
though with a good deal of reluctance. There they stayed throughout
the epidemic, setting a good example compared to the many wealthy
people who fled the city. The heir to the throne, the Duke of Orleans, himself visited the sick in hospital and the whole family
gave generously to the various charitable funds.

It may be doubted whether Louis-Philippe really profited in
popularity from his donations. He had been granted 12 million

[1] Barante, Baron de: *Souvenirs*. Paris, 1894. Vol. IV, p. 496.

francs a year for his 'civil list', out of which the cost of the roya
guard, the upkeep of palaces and so forth had to be met as well a
his own and his children's households. This seemed to him inade
quate; Charles X had had 25 million in addition to separate grant
for the Dauphin and for de Berry's child, the Duke of Bordeaux
The Chambers had haggled over the grant, so it had to be accepted
but as time went on the King frequently appealed for extra sums fo
his growing family. This gave marvellous opportunities for the
cartoonists and satirists. Louis-Philippe was haunted by a fear o
poverty; when he became King he had transferred his large private
fortune to his children and most of it was invested abroad. He con
tinued to save all he could; he might order Lyons silk to help the
industry by a gesture, but he and his wife were most economical
A story is told of an American lady visiting a famous Parisian dress-
maker and seeing an old black silk dress on a chair, clearly intended
for turning and refurbishing. She was told that this tiresome sort o
work was undertaken only for the Queen.[1]

Court entertainments were usually more simple than was
customary in Europe at that time, and the King showed himself in a
friendly and informal way to his guests, chatting freely with them
and telling his favourite stories about the Battle of Jemappes. He
walked the streets with his famous umbrella, affable and accessible
It is probable that the rising middle class would have preferred a
monarch less like themselves, one more capable of rousing emotion
The old nobility naturally despised him as an upstart and a traitor
to the traditions of his race; many of them were by no means convinced that the cause of the young son of de Berry was wholly lost.
'Carlists' in touch with the exiled monarch had tried unsuccessfully
to influence the Lyons strikers. Vague associations, usually of a local
or a family character, existed all over France which aspired rather
than planned for the restoration of the Bourbons for a third time.
The death in July 1832 of Napoleon's son raised their hopes; the
people who had wanted a return of a Napoleon might now be
induced to support another candidate.

Charles himself, old and weary, keeping up in exile all the
formalities he loved, was not the man to organise a plan. That
exciting task was undertaken in spite of all discouragements by the
pretender's mother, the Duchess de Berry. In 1832 she was thirty-
four, and still kept her love of dancing and all sorts of activity;
she was bored to tears in the solemn court at Holyrood. In April
she went to Italy, and against the advice of all whom she consulted
who had any political experience decided to raise a revolution in
the old royalist regions of France. She landed near Marseilles on

[1] Latimer, E. W.: *France in the Nineteenth Century*. Chicago, 1895, p. 56.

9 April but found no support whatever from the local gentry. With a few friends she set out in a great coach and drove right across the south of France, changing her name, putting on disguises and often sleeping as well as eating in her clumsy chariot. Though on her journey, by night as well as by day driving west, she met several royalists none seemed anxious to join her. In Toulouse she found a group of young men who begged her to stay there and told her they could raise the whole town in her support, but she had by now set her heart on the north-west and pressed on. By 7 May she reached the old Château of Plassac, which she made a sort of headquarters. On 16 May she met some of the old Vendéan leaders, and dressed as a boy and calling herself Little Peter, she went about in the woods and villages trying to stir up revolt.

Most of the peasants refused to move. Small local demonstrations were crushed, and the main effort, planned for 4 June, was a pathetic rather than a tragic failure. The Government's troops scattered the columns converging on a meeting-place; gallant but foolish men made suicidal stands and were killed. In August she received in her hiding place a letter from Charles, urging her not to go on with a folly which was ruining her son's chances, but she would not obey. Her refuge was discovered by the police on 5 November; she hid in a cupboard concealed in a chimney-breast, but when a fire was lit was forced to come out on 9 November, a thin, haggard, blackened and exhausted little figure.

She was taken to a fortress at Blaye and kept in confinement while the authorities made up their minds what to do with her. Their suspicions were aroused by her state of health, and it became clear that she was pregnant. General Bugeaud, her gaoler, forced her to admit her condition and by the end of February the news was published all over France. She declared she had remarried, but would not give her husband's name.

A widow fighting for her son was a romantic heroine; the royalists for a long time refused to believe that she had been, as they thought it, 'false' to her dead husband. Actually, for a woman in her condition to have lived as she had for the past months was extremely brave, but no one felt that; she had lost her status. The birth of her child, a little girl, on 10 May was witnessed as if it had been one of the royal births of olden times, so that no one could accuse the Orleanists of inventing the story. Now at length she revealed that the child's father was a Neapolitan of good family, eight years younger than herself, whom she had known in his childhood. Count Lucchesi-Palli was now a diplomat, holding minor posts, often moved because his remarkable good looks made him too successful with ladies. On 8 June Bugeaud escorted the princess to Sicily to

join her husband. Charles found it hard to get from her prope
proof of her marriage, and wholly refused to let her rejoin he
children. She was assigned a small income, and vanished from th
political scene, though she lived on till 1870, when she died i
poverty. Though many able men in France still would have pre
ferred to see her son rather than Louis-Philippe on the throne, th
'adorable duchess' had, in fact, effectively prevented any seriou
effort at a restoration.

In October 1836 another romantic conspirator appeared as
claimant to the throne. Louis Napoleon Bonaparte was a man c
twenty-eight, the son of Napoleon's second brother, Louis, who ha
been made King of Holland. Like the Duchess, he was the only on
of the family who really believed in a restoration of the dynasty. I
1831 he and his elder brother had joined in a rising in Bologna; the
caught fever and the brother died. He went to Paris with his mothe
she to ask Louis-Philippe to help her with claims she had on th
French Government, he to ask to be allowed to join the Frenc
army. Naturally the King said that he could not possibly do so und
his own name, so he retired to Switzerland and there joined th
Berne cantonal forces as an artillery officer. He published a manu
of gunnery and sent a copy to every French officer with whom h
could get into touch. From correspondence with them he believe
that there was still a strong feeling for his great uncle, and so decide
to put this to the test. Early in the morning of 30 October, 1836, h
and a few followers appealed to the garrison of Strasbourg to rise an
proclaim him as Emperor. Many of the soldiers and even of th
townsfolk acclaimed him, but the whole affair was mismanaged an
after three hours he was taken prisoner.

A dispatch was sent to Paris by the aerial telegraph, a system c
signals. Fog led to transmission being interrupted, and for som
hours the King and his Government were very much alarmed. Whe
they heard the whole story, the very wise decision was made not t
bring the pretender to trial; he was ordered to go to the Unite
States and given back 15,000 of the 200,000 francs he had in h
possession when he was taken prisoner. His companions wer
brought before the ordinary courts in Strasbourg and, to the grea
annoyance of the Government, were acquitted. The newspapers an
cartoonists had a glorious opportunity for making fun of him and hi
pretensions. Louis probably had never any real hope of immediat
success; he wanted to publicise his aims, and he certainly did tha

His family were very angry; he had hoped to marry his cousi
daughter of his uncle Jerome, the former King of Westphalia, bu
the match was now broken off. He did not stay long in America; h
mother was seriously ill and he got back to Switzerland with a fals

passport to see her before she died, in 1837. He stayed on, and the French authorities asked the Swiss to expel him. Very cleverly, Louis-Napoleon waited till the situation was getting tense and then departed voluntarily, earning the gratitude of the Swiss and making Louis-Philippe appear to be either afraid of him or ready to bully a small country.

In 1838 he had a considerable success in English society; he appears under the name of 'Prince Florestan' in Disraeli's novel, *Endymion*. He had inherited about £5,000 a year from his mother, so could live well enough, though he wasted a good deal of money in trying to start Bonapartist papers and clubs in Paris which did not succeed. One of his companions at Strasbourg, Laity, published an account of the expedition, and again Louis-Philippe fell into a trap. His Government ordered the suppression of the book, which of course made it eagerly read by anyone who could get hold of it, and had the author tried by the House of Peers. This not only was a wonderful advertisement for the Bonapartists but indicated that an ordinary jury could not be trusted. Laity was fined 10,000 francs, sentenced to five years' imprisonment and placed under police surveillance for the rest of his life. Next year, in 1839, Louis himself published a book, *L'Idée Napoléonienne*, a most able piece of propaganda, which was sold for half a franc and went through four large editions very rapidly. It was translated into six languages and had good reviews in many countries.

In 1840 Louis-Philippe decided to ask the British Government to allow him to bring Napoleon's body from St. Helena. It seemed as if the way was being prepared for the great man's nephew to make another bid for power. He hired a steamer for a month, loaded it with boxes of uniforms, nine horses, two carriages and about fifty men, and sailed to Boulogne with a tame eagle tied to the mast. Here he had hoped for a welcome from the garrison, but again everything went wrong, the townspeople stayed quiet, he was turned out of the barracks and soon after captured.

This adventure of 1840 was even more of a farce than the one in 1836, but Louis-Philippe could not treat it so calmly. In September he had Napoleon and about twenty of his friends tried by the House of Peers. A brilliant speech from the pretender and another from Berryer, his counsel, seemed to place the Orleans government itself on trial. 'The attempt itself had been ludicrous; the trial had been rendered a serious event.'[1] Louis-Napoleon was sentenced to imprisonment for life and immured in an old fortress at Ham.

Though people laughed tremendously, especially about the eagle, Louis-Napoleon had effectually spoiled a cherished plan of Louis-

[1] Simpson, F. A.: *The Rise of Louis Napoleon*. London, 1909, p. 194.

Philippe. The King had, by his reconciliation with Lafayette, prevented a republic in 1830; the legitimists had shown their weakness in an unmistakable way; the socialists seemed too remote from reality to be capable of organising a workers' revolution. The only alternative to his own Government which seemed likely to attract a strong emotional response from the people would be one based on the Napoleonic legend. Therefore, in 1833, Louis-Philippe had Napoleon's statue replaced on the Vendôme column as a gesture of admiration and reconciliation.

Then in 1839 came the extraordinary success of Louis-Napoleon's book, which gave a new direction to the legend. In the introductory 'Napoleonic Idea' his thesis was that the social revolution of 1789 had succeeded though the political one failed, and that Napoleon had consolidated the fundamental change in society by founding 'progressive institutions on principles of order and authority'.[1] Subsequent rulers had failed to reconcile progress and order; 1830 had led only to discord. Napoleon's idea was of a state where aristocracy was based on talent, not birth; where democracy was combined with discipline; where liberty was based on broad and stable foundations. Then followed the 'Napoleonic Ideas', in which various aspects of government were dealt with and Napoleon declared to have aimed at and partially attained the desires of most types of people.

It was to counter this propaganda that the reburial of Napoleon was planned. Having obtained the permission of the British Government, in the summer of 1840 Louis-Philippe sent his son Joinville as commander of a frigate to St. Helena. The young man was ill in bed with measles when his father gave him the order. 'If I had not already been in bed, I should have fallen down flat', the prince wrote later. But on thinking it over he was reconciled to the plan. Napoleon was after all a 'matchless warrior'. 'To fetch his ashes from a foreign land was in a manner to wave the flag of vanquished France aloft once more.'[2]

After a slow voyage to and from St. Helena, the ship bearing the coffin reached Cherbourg on 30 November, 1840. There Joinville found prepared 'a frightful-looking boat on which a sort of hideous dais had been built . . . all . . . frippery and plumes'.[3] 'This masterpiece of bad taste' was destroyed, the boat painted black, and the coffin placed unsheltered under a violet pall, moving 'up the course of the river, as though to take possession of the stream'. From the river it was taken in procession to the Invalides.

[1] *Napoleon III, Œuvres.* Paris, 1856, Vol. I, p. 4.
[2] Joinville, Prince de: *Memoirs.* Trans. Loyd. London, 1895, p. 156.
[3] Ibid., p. 165.

The results of this gesture were not what had been hoped for. Even among the crowds that watched the ceremonies there were murmurs against the Government. Interest was focused on the Emperor, not the King; old pictures and busts were brought out and new ones made; old and new songs were sung, but none to the glory of Louis-Philippe. Indeed, the events of the past few years had not made it likely that in 1840 the Government could face with equanimity all the criticisms, open and implied, that were encouraged by this cult of Napoleon.

Périer's death had left the new Government without a forceful leader in 1832, and in October a new Cabinet was formed. Soult, the Duke of Dalmatia, a man of sixty-three, became Prime Minister and Minister for War. His three chief associates came from the Doctrinaire group; de Broglie, Thiers and Guizot would now, it appeared, have a chance to prove that they had learned how to translate theory into action. The King was by no means happy with such men; he liked Soult and indeed military men generally as ministers, because they might be expected to maintain order and not have any very fixed political ideas. Louis-Philippe wished to play an active part in politics, especially with regard to foreign policy; like Queen Victoria, he held that this was peculiarly a royal preserve, and the cool way in which his fellow monarchs had received him made him all the more anxious to direct relations with foreign courts. His new Foreign Minister was not likely to be in agreement with this idea; de Broglie took a rather superior attitude towards the King as well as his colleagues, and had rigid principles to which he firmly adhered. The King was most anxious that his own suggestions should receive at any rate full consideration from his Cabinet and that he should receive any credit due if they were accepted and successful. Ministerial crises were therefore not at all unwelcome; when cabinets were being formed the King's importance was obvious, and he could always hope to find new men more amenable than those lately in power.

For the first ten years of the July monarchy the dangerous tradition of frequently changing and therefore weak cabinets persisted. As Guizot later said: 'France has never been a country of true political parties',[1] and the smallness of the electorate and the great power of the bureaucracy tended to encourage individual ambitions. The advantages that could be gained from sharing in patronage were shown early in the career of the Cabinet of 1832, when sixty new peers were nominated to take the place of Charles X's peers who had been expelled in 1830. Many of the new men

[1] Guizot, F.: *Memoirs to Illustrate the History of My Time.* Trans. Cole, J. W. London, 1860, Vol. III, p. 199.

14

came from official circles, 'honourable, solid and useful supporters of the system'[1] in Guizot's view. Next year the other side of the picture was shown: an official might hope for high rank but he could also be dismissed for opposition. During the budget debates an Inspector-General of the University, who was also a deputy, was dismissed from his office for opposing the Government. Cabinets, therefore, welcomed the election of civil servants as members of Parliament.

The agitation in Lyons and other places led to the passing in 1833 of two laws which seriously diminished that freedom of expression of opinion and of association which it had been hoped would be assured by the July revolution. One placed all street vendors of pamphlets and papers under the control of the municipal authorities; the other required Government authorisation for any association for 'religious, literary, political or other purposes'. Trade unionism and similar movements were stifled at birth.

In the spring of 1834 the tension that had long been felt between de Broglie and the King and also some of his colleagues was probably responsible for a crisis which resulted in his resignation. The actual occasion was an attempt to end a situation that had lasted for over twenty years. The United States had claimed compensation for American vessels seized during the Napoleonic wars, and de Broglie introduced a bill to pay a net sum of 23½ million francs to square the old account. His handling of the Assembly was not very tactful, and the first clause of the bill was thrown out by the deputies. He resigned and the Cabinet was reorganised; some of the weaker members were eliminated and Admiral de Rigny, who had been in charge of the Navy, took over the Foreign Office. The modified Cabinet 'went to the country' in May and obtained a very satisfactory majority in the elections; this was not surprising, for the troubles in Lyons and Paris were frightening the middle-class electorate.

This very success seems to have increased rather than diminished dissension among the ministers. Soult was 'suspicious, susceptible and surly',[2] according to Guizot, and even Louis-Philippe seems to have been finding him difficult. He still clung to the idea that a soldier was best as Prime Minister, however, so when Soult resigned in July he was replaced as Prime Minister and Minister for War by Marshal Gérard.

The new arrangement lasted only till October. Gérard wanted an amnesty for the Lyons revolutionaries, and the rest of the Cabinet

---

[1] Guizot, F. : *Memoirs to Illustrate the History of My Time*. Trans. Cole, J. W. London, 1860. Vol. III, p. 185.
[2] Ibid., p. 241.

opposed him. The main holders of office resigned with him, but after various attempts had been made by the King to find other advisers, all except Gérard returned under yet another soldier, Marshal Mortier. He was not expert in politics and resigned in February 1835, after a rather unhappy time of dissension and strain. Much against his will, Louis-Philippe had to ask de Broglie to return to power on 12 March. The compensation to the United States was promptly agreed to, and it appeared as if some political stability might be secured. The Peers were dealing with the Lyons agitators, and 'resistance' seemed to be the order of the day.

It is likely that the King was disappointed. The return of de Broglie was in effect a proof that his plan for a cabinet which looked to him, not to a Prime Minister, for effective leadership had been rejected by the politicians. Soon after this indication that he had lost in the first round of his political game, he had a sharp reminder that monarchy was a dangerous profession. Assassination was a sort of occupational hazard run by many nineteenth-century sovereigns, not excluding Queen Victoria, and rumours of plots against his life had been prevalent for some time.

On 28 July, 1835, Louis-Philippe left the Tuileries on horseback, accompanied by three of his sons, four of his Cabinet and a large staff, on his way to hold a grand review to commemorate the Three Glorious Days. While he was reviewing the National Guard in the Boulevard of the Temple an 'infernal machine'—from the description of eye-witnesses it was a sort of bomb filled with musket balls—was hurled at the procession from a window. The King was slightly wounded, Mortier and five of the staff were killed outright, and many of the spectators—41 people in all—were slain or mortally wounded.

The Orleans family showed great courage. With great difficulty they brought their terrified horses under control and rode on through the blood to conclude the review. De Broglie and very many others had had the narrowest of escapes, and it was not surprising that on 5 August they introduced legislation modifying the judicial system to enable the Government to deal promptly with such attempts. The law was passed in September, and so far as repression went the Government seemed to have taken all possible measures. The author of the crime, Fieschi, a Corsican, and two of his accomplices, who were members of the Society of the Rights of Man, were captured. Once again the Peers had to try them, and they were condemned to death in January 1836. Further attempts were made; in 1836 a man fired point blank at the King, and it was amazing that he escaped with singed whiskers; and later in the year, as the Royal

Family were going to the opening of Parliament, another assassin fired into the carriage, broken glass cutting the princes who accompanied their father. One of them, Joinville, reports that after the King had left the Chamber, a deputy said: 'Ought we to congratulate the King?' 'Certainly,' was the reply, 'we always do it.'[1]

[1] Joinville, Prince de: *Memoirs*. Trans. Loyd. London, 1895, p. 79.

Chapter XVIII

THINKERS AND TEACHERS

THOUGH politics might seem uninteresting, the July monarchy saw a wonderful outburst of literary activity. The new generation of romantic writers was now in full flower; some of the finest of the lyric poetry of France appeared between 1830 and 1848. The 'singer of songs' is essentially an individualist; though some 'schools' formed around certain poets, they were no more coherent than the 'school' of the lake poets in England. As in the years between 1798, when the *Lyrical Ballads* appeared, and 1824, when Byron died, Englishmen enjoyed the outpourings of wonderful and very divergent writers, so between 1830 and 1848 Frenchmen could admire the new poems of Hugo, Gautier, Lamartine, Musset and very many others. By its very nature lyric poetry is personal and intimate; though the themes and expressions might involve political overtones, only Béranger's songs had anything of a popular appeal and seemed to embody the aspirations of the people.

On the stage the breach with the classical traditions of French drama was almost complete. Shakespeare rather than Corneille was the model of the great poet-dramatists. Historical themes were chosen, and often the persons of the drama, Cromwell, Lucretia and suchlike served as types of sovereignty, womanhood and so forth. As Hugo said, 'There will be laughter, there will be tears; there will be good, evil, the high, the low, fate, Providence, genius, chance, society, the world, nature, life; and above all that one will be aware of something grand soaring.'[1] Hugo, Vigny and Dumas filled the French stage with dramas, and they and their imitators gave their audiences marvellous spectacles, with scenery and properties to heighten the atmosphere, with secret passages for surprise entries, and disguises and excitements of all kinds, with comic relief to throw into greater prominence the superb speeches of the romantic heroes and heroines, sometimes royal, sometimes of lowly birth. Never had actors had greater opportunities. For those who tired of melodrama there were the comedies of Scribe, equally unshackled by the old conventions, where the shifts and schemes of people whose aim was wealth and position gave immense scope for wit and humour.

[1] Hugo, V.: *Œuvres*. Ed. Hetzel and Quantin. Drame, Vol. III, p. 435.

The great actors were to be found in Paris, but the novelists had an audience that comprised all literate France and many other countries too. The novel gave scope for authors of all degrees of capacity, all types of mind, all schools of thought. Historical novels made fashionable by Walter Scott could and did serve as vehicles for raising or lowering in the esteem of their readers persons or classes in Church and State. It was thought, for example, that Eugène Sue's *Wandering Jew* (1842) contributed to the anti-clerical and especially the anti-Jesuit feeling of the time. Some novels were 'escape' literature, like Dumas' *Three Musketeers*, some purely love stories, but even in these, idealised peasants or workers could be contrasted with wicked nobles or capitalists. The 'realistic' novels, especially the great series called the *Comédie Humaine*, by Balzac, exposed and analysed many of the more unpleasant sides of both upper and lower middle-class society. Such works, read for pleasure, had a cumulative effect; the ideal of the hard-working capitalist personified in the rulers of France was probably more undermined by the poets, dramatists and novelists than by the historians and political theorists.

Educated men in all walks of life found, besides the socialists and the Bonapartists, men of learning and ability whose work forced them to view their own institutions with a critical eye. In 1835 *Democracy in America* appeared and was immensely successful. Alexis de Tocqueville (1805–59) was a liberal aristocrat, of wide learning and high principles, who had travelled in the United States. His description of the institutions of America, brilliantly written, and his profound political analysis gained him not only a great reputation but also great respect for his political views. He was one of those rare thinkers who can realise that institutions however admirable may, once destroyed, be irreplaceable; he, like the liberal Catholics, would have preferred the Church to be independent of the State and to own land, and he regretted the disappearance of a landowning class such as he admired in England, but he did not think it possible that the revolution of 1789 could be reversed. What he did hope for was a breakdown of the highly centralised system of government and a building up of local institutions such as he admired in the United States.

De Tocqueville was not an active churchman, and remained apart from that interesting group of ardent young reformers who, even before the crisis of 1830, had been anxious over the apparent union between the Church and a constitutional system which they felt was out of date and out of touch with the people. They were not surprised and therefore not dismayed when anti-clericalism broke out in a violent form after the days of July. There was not a real 'liberal

Catholic' party; there were a number of ardent young Catholics all agreed in disliking the strong Gallican trend of the bishops in France, but far from united in their ideals for the future or their plans for attaining them.

Three distinct trends could be observed in their writings and discussions. One was the predominantly ultramontane tendency; international in outlook, it wished to tighten the connection between the Church in France and the Holy See, and also Catholics in other countries. The younger men had been greatly impressed by Daniel O'Connell's campaign for the freedom of Irish Catholics and his success in obtaining Catholic Emancipation from a reluctant British Government in 1829. They looked on the Belgian revolution as a victory of the Catholic Belgians over the Protestant Dutch.

A second element was the desire for liberty in all spheres. Independence for the Church from political influences was felt to be necessary, even at the heavy price of surrendering the income paid by the State in compensation for the property lost by the Church in the revolution. Freedom of association was claimed as a 'natural right'; it might lead to the rise of revolutionary groups but it would also mean that religious orders would be free to establish themselves where and when they chose. Freedom in education would allow Church schools to compete with others without intervention by the State. Even greater political freedom by the extension of the suffrage might be expected to help Catholicism by breaking the domination of the largely anti-clerical middle class.

A third, and very strong, influence was the impulse towards social reform. The many charitable institutions set on foot since 1815 had brought educated Catholics into touch with the poor and outcast of the towns. In the long run it was this trend which had the greatest effect, both immediately and in later times. All three conceptions could and did influence the same people, but as time went on individual leaders tended to concentrate on one line of action rather than another.

The first sensational demonstration of the new movement came in 1829 with the publication of a book entitled *The Progress of Revolution and of the War Against the Church*. The author was a Breton priest, Félicité de Lamennais, who had made his name in 1817 by a book on Indifference in Religion. Born in 1782, his spiritual development had been marked by doubts and hesitations. He was twenty-two before he could bring himself to make his First Communion; his elder brother had just become a priest, and his fervour was probably responsible for Félicité's decision to submit to the Church and himself to take orders. In 1818 he appeared to Vitrolles as a very nervous man. 'His outward appearance was frail and weak to the point of giving one the idea that his life could not long endure. The strength and audacity of his mind . . . were not in the least depicted in his person or his language. His timidity was excessive, his words emerged trembling, rare, brief and embarrassed.'[1] Once he had come to a decision, however, he displayed immense vigour and a pride and obstinacy which made him unwilling to accept the most friendly criticism. To his sympathisers this seemed admirable; Guérin, the author of a poem, *The Centaur*, wholly pagan in outlook, said of him in 1832: 'It is generally believed that M. Féli is a man of pride, and of fiery pride. This opinion, which has turned many Catholics away from him, is unbelievably false. What has been taken as the pride of a man is but the intrepidity of an apostle.'[2]

Lamennais' new book was a powerful attack on Gallicanism, and also claimed that political liberty was not only due to Christianity but was an essential condition for the triumph of the faith. Not surprisingly, it was severely criticised by the bishops, most of whom were both Gallican and supporters of Charles X, but many parish priests admired it and it was a great success. Within a fortnight 6,000 copies had been sold.

The revolution of 1830 delighted Lamennais and his friends of the Left wing. He and Montalembert, a man of twenty who had some money and much enthusiasm, and Lacordaire, an ardent priest aged twenty-eight, together founded a paper, *L'Avenir*, to popularise their views. It did not secure a wide circulation; there were not more than 1,200 regular subscribers, but it created a great sensation. Absolute separation of Church and State was demanded, complete freedom of the Press and of association, and an extension of the suffrage on a very wide scale.

To Catholics in 1830, especially responsible churchmen, it seemed that the authors of these articles were demanding that the Church should run great and unnecessary dangers. Abandonment of the support given by the State to the clergy would mean very serious practical problems; the laity would have to meet from their own pockets the whole costs of salaries and upkeep of churches. Moreover, complete separation meant the formal secularisation of the Government, which would no longer have even a nominal Christian basis. Freedom in education might increase the number of Catholic schools, but would also allow enemies of the Church who were wealthy and powerful greater opportunities. Freedom of association would legalise such bodies as the Carbonari, who were conducting revolution in the Papal States.

[1] Vitrolles, Baron de: *Mémoires*, etc. Paris, 1884, Vol. III, p. 283.
[2] Quoted by Leroy, M.: *Hist. des Idées Sociales en France*. Paris, 1950, p. 433.

Louis-Philippe was most anxious to avoid intervention in any quarrel between Churchmen. He said: 'One must never put a finger into Church affairs; one can never draw it out again, it will stick there.'[1] His Government, however, felt it necessary to prosecute the editors of *L'Avenir* for their attacks on the Government in its relation with the Church, but in January 1831 it lost its case.

In February 1831 a new Pope was elected; Gregory XVI was a holy man, a monk, old-fashioned and conservative but anxious for peace and good will. He recognised the genuine fervour of the men who were causing so much trouble to the French bishops, and hoped that by degrees they would recognise the dangers inherent in their policy and modify their demands. But they made things very difficult for him when they urged the men who had been nominated by Louis-Philippe as bishops to refuse office. Gregory was very anxious lest the new Government should be anti-clerical, and this seemed to him most mischievous. Priests were, therefore, told that they should not subscribe to the paper.

Montalembert believed that if the Pope really understood what seemed to him the truth about France he would withdraw his disapproval. He and Lamennais and Lacordaire therefore went to Rome, suspending publication of *L'Avenir* in November 1831. The Pope was greatly troubled by risings in the Papal States, and in February 1832 came the French occupation of Ancona.[2] He did not wholly refuse to see the 'Pilgrims of Liberty', as they called themselves, but entirely refused to discuss their ideas. Lamennais, very angry, went off to Germany; and in August 1832 appeared the papal answer in the form of an encyclical, *Mirari vos*.

The errors condemned by this document were political, not theological. The dangers to the Church from a free Press were stressed; a close connection between Church and State declared advantageous; princes were exhorted to defend religion. The three 'pilgrims' reacted differently to this official disapproval. Lacordaire and Montalembert at once submitted. They had not changed their views, but they recognised that further opposition to authority would do far more harm than any good that would come by continued propaganda. Montalembert wrote to Lamennais: 'The ideas we have propagated and defended are good or bad, true or false, divine or worldly. If they are worldly and false, we ought to bless God because He has prevented us from defending them longer. If they are true and divine, what better opportunity could there be for their future triumph, what more outstanding blessing from God

---

[1] Quoted by Debidour: *Hist. des Rapports de l'Église et l'État en France*, 1789–1870. Paris, 1898, p. 422.
[2] See *supra*, p. 202.

could they receive, than the sanction which would be given them by the practice of humility and Christian resignation?'[1]

Submission was what Lamennais could give only formally. Rome treated him with great consideration under the circumstances; a friendly letter accompanied the encyclical sent to him. He had hoped to persuade the Church to abandon old traditions and boldly to take a new line; such a course would have been hard for any such body at any time, but for Rome in 1831–32 it was practically impossible. He could not accept Montalembert's position, and in 1834 he brought out *Paroles d'un Croyant*, a powerful attack on the existing social and political order. His belief was no longer that of a Catholic. He had said his last mass in April 1833. He was never excommunicated, but by his own desire he was no longer a practising priest.

Very different was the reaction of Lacordaire. He threw himself into his priestly mission whole-heartedly, and his sermons in Nôtre Dame in Paris, in 1835 and again in 1843–51, as well as in many provincial cities, had an enormous influence. He was thirty-three in 1835 and the freedom, even passion, of his preaching brought, as de Falloux said, 'from the foot of his pulpit to the foot of the altar men, one might even say classes, who had kept themselves studiously aloof'.[2] He spoke freely of contemporary problems, but though some of his democratic views frightened the conservatives, his intense spirituality disarmed them.

Montalembert, a peer of France, naturally followed a different course. His only personal extravagance was his library; he bought books freely and had them beautifully bound. He believed that modern France was quite out of touch with the true Middle Ages and had much to learn from them, so he studied hard and produced a life of St. Elizabeth of Hungary, which began a whole new method of writing of the lives of saints by laymen, in which they appeared as real historical personages, not dummies with haloes. He was interested in the preservation of ancient churches and in the reintroduction of the traditional music of the Church when the Benedictine monastery at Solesmes was refounded in 1837. Numbers of young Catholics followed his lead; reviews and journals published their articles on history and on political theory.

He probably helped to inspire the powerful movement among young men towards genuine social work. Ozanam (1813–53), besides producing some brilliant work on Dante, threw his energies into the organisation of the Society of St. Vincent de Paul, whose members devoted themselves to personal assistance of the needy. He wrote in

[1] De Meaux: *Montalembert*. Paris, 1897, p. 42.
[2] De Falloux: *Mémoires d'un Royaliste*, 4th ed. Paris, 1888, Vol. I, p. 166.

1834: 'I believe in authority as a means, in liberty as a means, in charity as an end.'[1] A very large number of young men enrolled themselves in this work of direct investigation and amelioration of the living conditions of the poor, and the Society spread by degrees all over the Catholic world. The young legitimists found in practical social work, teaching apprentices, holding Sunday Schools for working men, in which lay and religious instruction were combined, and so forth an outlet for the activity which their principles prevented them from using in politics; the terrible conditions they learned of at first hand made them all the more antagonistic to the 'usurper' of July.

Montalembert himself felt it his duty to play an active part in politics. He would have liked to form a Catholic party, which could exert the same sort of influence as O'Connell's Irishmen. He had already in 1831 deliberately broken the law by opening, with the help of Lacordaire, a small school for poor boys. He was prosecuted and his rank entitled him to trial by the Peers, which gave him a good opportunity for setting out in public his demands for freedom in education. The rigid control of the law and of the University was attacked by both radicals and Catholics, but the feelings roused on both sides were very bitter, and the deputies on the whole were apt to dislike any extension of the influence of the Church more than they detested the policy of the University.

When Guizot became Minister of Education in Soult's cabinet in 1832 his department was separated from that of Religion, to which the Bourbons had attached it. He was an active Protestant, but by no means bigoted. Montalembert and his friends found that he as sincerely as they believed that all education must be based on religion. He had met and made friends with Lamennais' brother, who had founded a congregation of Christian instruction in Brittany, and he so much admired the work of the Christian Brothers that he wished to give the Cross of the Legion of Honour to their Superior-General, who felt it his duty to refuse. It was some time before Guizot was able to start full work in his department; he himself fell ill and the death of his wife in March 1833 was a very serious blow.

During 1833 he began a serious overhaul of elementary education. He did not want free and compulsory education; like a good nineteenth-century liberal, he felt that it was the right of parents to decide whether their children should go to school and to pay for them if they possibly could, though he admitted that the children of the really poor could be let off school fees. He also believed in

[1] Quoted O'Meara, K.: *Frederic Ozanam, his Life and Works*. Edinburgh, 1876, p. 102.

competition, and therefore wished private or Church schools to exist alongside those supported by the State. He thought two grades of primary education would be necessary—a general very elementary instruction for all children, and a further higher standard for the future artisans and craftsmen in the towns.

Teachers for the State schools should, he thought, be trained in Normal Schools, a rather primitive form of Teachers' Training Colleges; there were 47 such institutions in existence and he planned to organise them and increase their number. Local education committees were to be set up, and in spite of opposition Guizot insisted that the local priest or Protestant pastor should alway be a member. The payment of teachers was to be met from special local taxes, to which an addition might be made by the Ministry if necessary. The right of members of religious orders to teach without passing the State examinations was maintained. Before laying his bill before the Chambers, Guizot sent a draft of it for comment to all the 39,300 elementary schoolmasters, and was gratified that about a third of them wrote replies. He also chose 490 men, mostly officials of the University, who carried out a rapid inspection of schools all over France and drew up a report. Later the country was divided into districts, each with a permanent inspector of elementary schools.

Such careful preparation deserved and had success. The bill was passed, and Guizot could report that by 1847 the number of boys' primary schools had risen since 1830 from 31,420 in which 1,200,715 children were being taught to 43,514 in 1847 with 2,176,079 pupils. Teachers' Training Colleges had increased from 47 to 76.[1]

Secondary and higher education offered more serious problems. Guizot introduced a bill in 1836 which would have given greater freedom to private, which for all practical purposes meant Catholic, secondary schools, but the anti-clericals in the Deputies amended it so much that it was withdrawn in 1837. Meantime, he did what he could to lessen the opposition to the University by appointing vigorous men as professors. A new Chair of Constitutional Law was created to give a worthy position to an able Italian, Rossi, who had been lecturing in Geneva and who had been made Professor of Political Economy in one of the Paris colleges. There was opposition to this appointment, but it died down. The Minister for Education would very much have liked to establish residential colleges on the lines of those at Oxford and Cambridge, but this was not practicable; he had to be content with widening and improving the University and the Institute as opportunity offered.

[1] Guizot: *Memoirs of My Own Time.* Trans. Cole. London, 1860, Vol. III, p. 80.

There was a steady expansion in the number of monasteries and convents established during the July monarchy. In 1842 alone 220 new establishments of nuns were authorised; as almost all schools for girls were run by nuns, this involved a further expansion of educational opportunity. The question of secondary education was one which really needed settling, and another bill was introduced in 1841 by Villemain, who had taken over the Ministry in 1839. Inspection of Church schools was proposed as a condition of their recognition as legal, and this was strongly opposed by many leaders of the Church. Montalembert did his best to calm his co-religionists, but some very wild attacks were made on the University and on the whole system of State schools. On the other side, the Jesuit scare was raised again. After their formal expulsion, the Jesuits had opened schools just over the borders of France—in Belgium, Spain and so forth—and encouraged by their success had been quietly slipping back into the country.

Once again the Pope was appealed to, and Rossi, the Professor of Constitutional Law, was dispatched to Rome to ask Gregory XVI to bring his influence to bear on the Society of Jesus and induce them to keep the law, or at any rate not to break it too openly. So the situation dragged on, thoroughly unsatisfactory for everyone concerned, but insoluble so long as the Government depended on the votes of men to whom Catholicism and Bourbonism still seemed identical. So indeed they were, so far as some of the old-fashioned bishops and the old aristocracy were concerned, and it is certain that nothing but a complete surrender to the Church would have reconciled them to Louis-Philippe.

The liberal Catholics, too, were not reconciled, but for a very different reason. They were becoming more and more concerned with the social evils involved in the triumph of capitalism. Trade was expanding, in spite of the maintenance of tariffs which seriously raised the cost of living. Imports and exports nearly doubled between 1825 and 1847. To improve transport, 578 million francs were spent on the main roads by the July monarchy, and State subsidies paid to owners of post-horses to ensure an adequate supply came to 3 million francs a year. In 1833 a commission was appointed to investigate the pros and cons of railway building by private or State enterprise, and in 1837 a privately-owned railway was opened running from Paris to St. Germain. In 1838 the Government proposed to build three railway lines, but its bills were defeated. The capitalists expected great profit from new enterprises, but though companies were formed to obtain concessions they found it very hard to raise all the money needed for work which would bring in no return for some years, and also came up against the general problem of railway engineers: the fantastic price demanded for necessary sections of land.

In 1841 a law was passed giving the companies power to buy land at a reasonable price, but this did not prove sufficient encouragement, so next year a scheme was evolved by which the State should take over the land and build the permanent way, while private companies laid the tracks and provided the actual trains. The new plan was most attractive to investors, and in 1845 there was an outburst of speculation in the forming of railway companies and the buying of their shares, which led to a serious economic crisis. It so happened that there was a poor harvest that year, and the borrowing for speculation so raised the charges made for loans that many businesses were in serious trouble. This in turn involved unemployment and great distress among the workers.

A more flexible banking system might have helped to spread the burden, but local banks were kept weak by the rights given to the Bank of France, whose charter was renewed in spite of opposition. Though in theory they believed in competition, the great Paris financiers preferred centralised finance. Small local traders in the provinces, small farmers and manufacturers, found it very hard to borrow if they were in difficulties. They could hardly be blamed for keeping wages low and hours long, they felt, for only by selling very cheaply could they maintain their profits at a sufficient level to build up reserves.

Like Lord Shaftesbury in England, and moved like him by a philanthropy which sprang from sincere Christianity, Montalembert and his friends tried to secure laws that would protect the most helpless of the victims of the industrial developments, the children. In 1840 the House of Peers demanded a legal limit to the hours of child labour. A law was passed in 1841, but as the inspectors who enforced it were to be unpaid and to be manufacturers, it was a farce. By it, no child under eight was to be employed in a factory; those under twelve were to work only for a limited period and to attend school for part of the day; no one under seventeen was normally to work at night. There was no provision made for the part-time schools and the whole effect was deplorable; the shocking conditions were publicised but it was clear that no genuine effort was being made to amend them.

Louis-Philippe had failed to win the Catholics. The old Church-and-King group still held aloof in spite of Guizot's concessions; the new Church-and-Workers men were antagonised. They neither of them plotted revolution; but equally neither group would offer any resistance to a revolution because of their respect for the Government.

Chapter XIX

FRANCE IS BORED

'IT is not right to believe, because we are tired by the great movements which have convulsed this century and ourselves, that everybody is weary like us and fears the smallest movement. The generations which are growing up behind us are not fatigued; they want to act and get weary in their turn. What action have you allowed them? France is a nation which is bored.' So said Lamartine in a debate in 1839.

'What have we done since 1840? Nothing, nothing, nothing!' An otherwise undistinguished deputy, Desmousseaux de Givre, won fame by his outburst in the Chamber in 1847, one of those phrases so easily remembered and so expressive of people's thoughts. Men of very different capacity and outlook were united in opposition to the policy of the King's ministers, if in nothing else. Louis-Philippe could justly claim that they were very unfair; lots of activity had been going on and some real successes had been obtained. His ministers could ask precisely what sort of action they should have asked the new generation to undertake, and point out that a number of very exciting things had been happening to relieve the tedium of daily life. The truth was that the ordinary people were only rarely interested in these events; that the failures of policy had been more noticeable than the successes; that politics were felt to be controlled by a small group of men whose support or opposition were decided by motives more personal than national.

As the King and the wealthy electors had convinced themselves that any serious political and social reform was not only unnecessary but positively dangerous, policy took the form of one expedient after another to meet immediate needs. One line of action, which might have been expected to be popular, was that of overseas expansion. Population was growing, though not so fast as in other countries, and in the towns not in the countryside.[1] Output from the farms rose very slowly, and whenever a bad season came, food had to be imported. It was not so much a home for emigrants that was needed as a source of raw materials. Conquest of colonies would satisfy not

[1] See Morazé, C.: *La France Bourgeoise*. Paris, 1947, for an interesting survey of the demographic and economic evolution of France in the nineteenth century.

only material but spiritual needs by throwing glory of victory over the arms of France.

An obvious area for action lay in North Africa. At the very time of the July revolution French troops were trying to consolidate their position in Algiers. The coast which runs on the south of the Mediterranean from, roughly, opposite Cape Gata, where the Spanish peninsula swings up to the north-east, to a point south of Sardinia, is backed up inland by a series of hills and mountain ranges. Along the coast were a number of ports where local chiefs frequently engaged in piracy. Inland on the lower hills were various tribes, engaged in agriculture but also frequently in local warfare. Arabs wandered with their flocks and camels, foraging and trading far back into Africa, and in the towns the Arabs called Moors conducted often very thriving businesses. In the towns, too, were a good many Turks, remnants of the time when the Sultan was exercising authority over northern Africa. The people were Mohammedan, but detested the Turks almost as much as they did the Christians.

The new Government sent General Clauzel to complete the subjugation of Algiers. He was a rash and ambitious man of nearly sixty, and immediately began operations on a much larger scale than had been expected. He hoped to conquer Tunis, but this would have needed very large forces, and he was recalled. A series of administrators followed him, but no one had seriously thought out what their aim should be. Troops were sent out often, it seemed, as a sort of punishment if their discipline was bad or they were suspected of revolutionary ideas, and they suffered terribly, for their uniform and diet were wholly unsuitable for a hot country. Sickness was constant; in 1832 there were over 3,000 men seriously ill, and without any proper medical service.

In 1833 a commission of investigation was sent out and reported that no attempt should be made to hold more than the coast line. Energetic commanders, however, could not be expected to stay pent in unhealthy towns, subject to constant raids from the local peoples. Oran, well to the west of Algiers, was captured, and an attempt was made to come to terms with the leaders of the local Arabs. In 1834 a sort of treaty was drawn up with Abd el Kadr, the energetic chieftain of the Oran district, but soon he decided that he preferred independence and attacked the French with considerable success.

Clauzel was sent out again in 1836. He believed that so long as no attempt was made to show French strength inland, no permanent hold could be maintained on the ports. He therefore planned an assault on Constantine, a town in the mountains and a main centre of Arab power. The King had sent Nemours, his second son, with the expedition, hoping to associate the Orleans dynasty with the army; but the strength of the enemy and the difficulties of the country had been badly underestimated. A severe defeat nearly led to the wiping out of the French force; casualties were very heavy and guns and material lost. One of the junior commanders, Changarnier, showed ability of a high order in extricating the remnants of the troops and bringing them back to their base. Clauzel was recalled and in 1837 a new commander appointed.

General Bugeaud, the man who had acted as the gaoler of the Duchess de Berry, was a man of ideas. He envisaged Algeria as an extension of France and a powerful support for the army. First of all, the whole of the territory formerly under the Dey of Algiers, who had been dethroned in 1830, must be brought to complete sub-mission; then it should be occupied by new French settlements of soldiers and their families. This would, he thought, give such good prospects to men in the army that recruitment would be greatly stimulated and the military training of the settlers would secure them against Arab attack.

A certain number of settlers had already come over, but the civil organisation was very weak and inefficient. The Arabs were shocked by the entire absence of organised religion; there were no chaplains with the forces, no churches in the towns. This was partly remedied in 1838 when a bishop was appointed and nuns came and opened schools.

Conquest had to precede settlement, and the disgrace of Con-stantine be expunged. Nemours was again sent with the expedition which, after terrible fighting, secured the fortress. Joinville, the third of Louis-Philippe's sons, who was in the navy, came up with a support column and was horrified at the conditions he found. The mountain country was rugged and roadless; the weather fearful. 'Torrents of rain, rivers in flood, snowfalls, men dying of cold, stragglers whose shouts for help only brought us to them to find them lying headless on the ground, and, last of all, a terrible outbreak of cholera.'[1] So inadequate were the medical arrangements that it was discovered that the cesspools from a 'miserable hut' used as a hospital were leaking into the spring from which the force got its drinking water.

The town was captured after very heavy and costly fighting. The local ruler, the Bey, had been so confident of the impregnability of his mountain fortress that he had left his harem with over two hundred women inside its walls. The two young princes took the building over as their residence; the ladies were somewhat of an embarrassment. In the end, 'the authorities decided to get rid of all this human cattle and distribute it amongst the most well-to-do

[1] Joinville: *Memoirs*. Trans. Loyd. London, 1895, p. 84.

15

of the Mussulman population'.[1] Such an attitude was not likely to
endear the French to the Arabs, who also saw the appalling sight of
the evacuation of the sick and wounded in crowded waggons from
which corpses were flung out and lightly covered with soil and their
places taken by men sick with cholera.

To celebrate the victory, the heir to the throne, Orleans, went
to Constantine and thence on a sort of tour. This annoyed Abd el
Kadr; he had expected the French to remain on the coast and not
rule inland. He started raiding and in 1840 reinforcements were sent
to Algeria. There were nominally 60,000 troops in the country, but a
considerable number was always in hospital. In spite of the raids,
27,000 immigrants arrived during 1841, and by 1845 the number
had reached 75,000. They were not the farmer type whom Bugeaud
had wanted; nearly all were traders and lived in the coastal towns.
But a start was made in the construction of roads and the towns of
Philippesville, Orleansville and Nemours remain as permanent
records of the Orleans family.

Bugeaud was appointed Governor-General of Algiers in 1840, and
the impact of his forceful personality was at once evident. He moved
his troops out into a number of strong points scattered over the
country from which mobile columns could be quickly sent to counter
Abd el Kadr's raiders. This plan also gave a chance to junior commanders to act independently and most of France's best generals in
the later years had had their training in Algiers. Each year the army
grew larger; from 64,000 in July 1840 it rose to over 101,000 in
1847.[2]

Like the European settlers who had to deal with the Red Indians
in North America, the French in Africa found it very hard to sub-
jugate an active and warlike people in mountainous country with ill-
defined boundaries. Abd el Kadr's main base at Mascara was taken
in 1841, but he himself retired to the hills. Pursued from point to
point, in 1843 he took refuge with the Sultan of Morocco. This
involved a very awkward situation. Protests were made to the
Emperor, as he was politely called, but in vain. To extend the war
into Morocco would undoubtedly cause reactions in Europe, and
especially in England, who from her fortress at Gibraltar watched
the African coast with a jealous eye. Her commander at Gibraltar
from 1842 was Sir Robert Wilson, who with Michael Bruce had been
responsible for the escape of Lavalette[3] and had served a term of
imprisonment in France. He was not at all likely to help the French,
yet his neutrality at any rate was essential if any force was to be used.

1 Joinville: *Memoirs*. Trans. Loyd, London, 1895, p. 90.
2 Guizot: *France Under Louis-Philippe*. London, 1865, p. 118.
3 See *supra*, p. 62.

Prince Joinville was given charge of the rather delicate mission in 1844. The French navy was in many ways most up-to-date; in Toulon, when he was fitting out, Joinville experimented with an electric searchlight which was not taken into general use for more than forty years. He called on Wilson to explain the situation and promised that no action would be taken until the Sultan had definitely refused the French demands for the expulsion of Abd el Kadr. When acceptance was not forthcoming, Joinville with considerable difficulty arranged for the evacuation from Tangier of all European officials, while an English representative tried to make a peaceful settlement. In August he, too, left, and under the eyes of the British frigates and many other warships, Tangier was bombarded. The accuracy of the French gunnery was admirable; the fortifications were destroyed, but the town was not touched. The squadron then sailed through the straits and attacked Mogador, on the Atlantic coast of Morocco, the chief trading port of the Sultan. Its fortifications were on an island, which was taken by assault and occupied by the French, who made no attempt to hold the town itself. They took off the English consul and a few other Europeans, left an adequate force on the island and withdrew.

In September a treaty was signed by the Emperor of Morocco by which he pledged himself not to allow Abd el Kadr to enter his territory and to prohibit his own subjects from joining him. No one expected that this last point could be enforced, but the loss of official support greatly weakened Abd el Kadr. For the next two years he went on struggling, but was captured and brought to France in 1847.

It might have been expected that this story of fighting and victory would have pleased the people of France who were reading with such avidity stories of Napoleon. Instead, their reaction was on the whole unfavourable. For one thing, the stories told by returning sick and wounded men told of horrible savagery and terrible reprisals, of suffocating heat and the torments of fever. Then the costs of the war seemed out of all proportion to the immediate gain, and it was clear that millions would have to be spent before Algiers would be sufficiently developed to stand alone much less bring in some addition to the national budget. The idea of so close an association of the army with politics as was involved in Bugeaud's plan displeased very many people. Yet it was perfectly clear that though the traders of the towns might acquiesce in French rule which would increase their profits and offer careers to their sons, the Arabs of the hills hated their conquerors and would rise whenever a leader appeared.

When it was clear to Bugeaud that in spite of his being made a

Marshal and a Duke his colonisation plan would be rejected, and that, as he himself had agreed, the Governor of the future would be a prince, the Duke of Aumale, he resigned in 1847. In September Aumale went out to take up the post; he had been in Algiers for some time and shared in the fighting. Three of Louis-Philippe's sons had thus been associated with the African campaigns; all had done well, but it was inevitable that the criticism of the whole Algerian scheme should fall upon the King and his family as well as on the politicians.

The repercussions of the search for dominions overseas involved France with England not only in relation to Africa. For some years England had had a penal colony in Australia, and the idea of having a similar establishment for France led to interest being taken in the Pacific. In theory there was much to be said for taking criminals to a new environment and giving them genuine constructive work to do and, at the end of their sentence, if they chose, a permanent settlement far away from all the temptations of their past life and with great opportunities for the future. It was the difficulty of carrying out this theory in practice which brought penal colonies into deserved disrepute.

In 1839 a French company was formed to colonise New Zealand. Ever since 1815, however, small English settlements had been planted in the islands, and in 1840 English sovereignty was proclaimed. The Marquesas group of islands, ten degrees south of the Equator, and very roughly halfway between Asia and South America, had been visited by a French captain who had sailed round the world in a frigate, and who reported that since the original discovery in the seventeenth century no foreign colonists had gone there, so that they were, so to speak, free for occupation by a European Power. They had good harbours, a healthy climate and only a scanty native population. In 1842 a fleet was sent from France and took possession of the islands, making the usual treaties with local chieftains. A few missionaries had already gone there and prepared the way.

Some distance to the south-west lay another group, the Society Islands, of which the largest and finest was Tahiti. For some little time both English and French missionaries had been attempting to convert the people, and the friction between them led to incidents which greatly embarrassed the ruler, Queen Pomare. Admiral Dupetit-Thouars, after occupying the Marquesas, sailed on to Tahiti and demanded compensation for wrongs done to French priests and traders and guarantees for the future. The Queen, afraid, offered to place herself under French protection and signed a treaty with the Admiral in September 1842 by which she was to retain internal government, missionaries of all faiths were to be free in exercising their functions, but all relations with foreign Powers, port control and so forth would be in the hands of a person nominated by the French.

The situation was accepted by the foreigners on the island, including the British vice-consul, in the absence of Mr. Pritchard, who combined the functions of missionary and consul. When the Government in Paris heard of the Admiral's act, they were seriously troubled. English neutrality was essential for the Algiers operations, apart from other matters, and English missionaries had been on the island for a long time; the Tahiti mission had been one of the first efforts of the London Missionary Society started in 1795. Though legally a French protectorate was correct, politically it was certain to lead to trouble. Fortunately, the peaceable Aberdeen was at the time in the English Foreign Office, and on the assurance that the Protestant missionaries would have full protection, French control was acknowledged in 1843.

Soon two hot-headed men made mischief. Pritchard had been very angry on his return to find what had happened, and began to foment trouble for the French. Admiral Dupetit-Thouars returned to Tahiti in November 1843, declared that Queen Pomare had violated the terms of the treaty, and that henceforward the French would take over complete sovereignty of the whole group of the Society Islands. His action was disavowed by the French Cabinet in February 1844 and the simple protectorate declared to be still valid. But during the interval Pritchard had persuaded Pomare to resist the French, promising help from England and spreading anti-French articles from English newspapers. For some time the local French commander managed to keep order, but a junior officer left in charge during his absence was so angry at an attack on a French sailor that he placed the principal town in a state of siege and arrested Pritchard.

It was impossible for such an act to be ignored, though the responsible commander did his best. He released Pritchard, but put him on an English ship which sailed away from the island. When the arrest took place, Pritchard was no longer in an official position, but his story when he reached England made everyone very angry. Fierce speeches were made, but Lord Aberdeen was not anxious to make too great a fuss. A hint was dropped that an adequate payment in cash might calm down offended dignity. Louis-Philippe offered to make a large immediate payment out of his private purse to avoid a vote in Parliament, but was persuaded not to do so. His Cabinet had to meet, as was to be expected, strong opposition, but in the end sense prevailed. On both sides of the Channel passion had been roused to a point wholly disproportionate to the incident. It was the

French who suffered, not the English Government; the glory of obtaining territory on the other side of the world was wholly obscured under the storm of charges of cowardly submission to England.

Probably the real cause of dissatisfaction in France was not the Pritchard incident but a general dislike of a foreign policy which was largely attributed to the King himself. After the settlement of the Greek question the three Powers, Russia, England and France, who had assisted in securing Greek independence, took an active interest in the Near East. The Ottoman Empire had been revealed as often incompetent and its local officials as apt to use their semi-independence in ways that shocked western opinion. The great Powers had, however, very divergent views based on their national interests.

Russia had long been recognised as the protector of the Christians of the Orthodox Eastern Church and spasmodic persecutions gave her good cause to intervene on their behalf. She was as well rapidly developing her territories on the Black Sea, and access to the Mediterranean through the Bosphorus and the Dardanelles was of the utmost importance to her shipping. England, with her bases at Gibraltar and Malta, found it easier to have a weak Turkey to deal with when, as frequently happened, her merchants in the Balkans and Anatolia, the Levant and Egypt, had complaints against local officials and traders. France, with a lively interest in North Africa, had an immediate concern with the districts between Algiers and the Suez isthmus.

In 1831 Mehemet Ali, who had helped the Sultan against the Greeks, tried to extend his dominion in Egypt by conquering Syria. The Turkish army sent against him was badly defeated, and the Sultan appealed to the Western Powers for help. Only Russia was at all friendly, but pressure from England and France prevented her intervention. Turkey was compelled to allow Mehemet Ali to hold Syria, nominally as representative of the Ottoman Empire. The Sultan made a treaty with Russia at Unkiar Skelessi in July 1833 by which, in a secret clause, he promised to close the Dardanelles to all foreign vessels except the Russians.

Mehemet Ali proceeded to build up his power. He taxed his people heavily to pay for his armies; he had dreams of establishing industries from which he would draw all the profits. De Broglie, as Foreign Secretary, had cherished English friendship, as indeed did the King himself, but Louis-Philippe, seeking for royal partners for his children, was anxious not to be alienated from the other Powers towards whom England was sometimes apt to take a high hand. Talleyrand, resigning from the London embassy in 1834, had indicated that it was time that France got on to better terms with the absolute monarchies.

In 1836 a Cabinet crisis allowed the King once again to get rid of his Doctrinaire minister de Broglie. The Finance Minister, without previous consultation with his colleagues, spoke of the need for further reduction of interest on the debt by a conversion scheme when he opened the budget debate in January. The matter was hotly discussed, and de Broglie infuriated the deputies by his schoolmaster's style when he snapped out a refusal to introduce such a plan, adding: 'Is that clear?' This phrase with its suggestion of superiority was held to be responsible for an adverse vote that forced the Government to resign on 5 February. The majority against it was so small that the King could perfectly well have kept it in power, but he was delighted to be rid of it.

Another period of shifting Cabinets followed. Thiers was in office from February to September, and tried to help the King to secure an Austrian princess for his eldest son; the failure of the scheme led him to plan a reversal of policy and the King dismissed him. In September Molé, a man of fifty-five, whose experience had been administrative rather than political, took office; his most important colleague was Guizot, on whom he had to count as main orator for the Government. Neither man was happy, and no one was surprised when the Cabinet fell in April 1837. The occasion was a demand for a million francs as a grant to the King's eldest daughter, Louise, who had married the King of Belgium. This and another grant for the second son, Nemours, were rejected. Guizot left, and Molé carried on, strengthened by the creation of fifty new peers in October 1837 and elections in which the divisions among the opposition were made clearer than the solidity of the support for the Government. It had no particular policy, and so roused little opposition. A bride was found for Orleans in Helen of Mecklenburg, who in 1838 duly produced a son. When Austrian troops left the Papal States, the French left Ancona, and affairs looked like moving gently along with no particular embroilments.

Signs of coming trouble in the East appeared when Mehemet Ali threatened to declare himself wholly independent of Turkey. Molé's enemies were determined to throw him out; though by no means united on an alternative policy they felt that France's position in Algiers and her lack of any real ally were not adding to her reputation. Guizot wanted to develop his plans for educational reform. The attacks on the Cabinet when the deputies met in December 1838 came from all sides; Molé resigned and a dissolution gave the electors a chance to show their opinion. In the electioneering in February 1839 open attacks were made on the King, who was accused of trying, like Charles X, to carry on his personal rule under the forms of the constitution.

Molé was defeated in March 1839; he lost thirty seats. This was not a great enough swing to alter the situation fundamentally, and, in fact, to the ordinary well-to-do citizen the political issues were very far from clear. For three months manœuvres went on; one man after another tried to form a cabinet, but the divisions, largely personal, between the leaders of groups prevented success. Then in May a revolt in Paris led by one of the many secret societies, 'The Seasons', frightened the politicians and a cabinet was quickly formed. Soult, seventy years old but still active, took over both the offices of Prime Minister and Foreign Secretary; both Thiers and Guizot, the two main forces in the deputies, were left out.

Once again defeat came over a demand for money for the Royal Family. Nemours was marrying a princess from the useful Saxe-Coburg family and the demand for half a million francs for him was rejected. In January 1840 Soult resigned, and Thiers took office. Guizot was appointed Ambassador in London.

While France had been making cabinets and royal marriages, the situation in the Near East had been changing. In 1839 the East India Company had seized Aden; it was a high-handed action, due in part to the need the company felt for a secure port to the west of the Persian Gulf, in part to a fear of Russian influence over the Ottoman Empire. In the same year the Turks moved against Mehemet Ali's son, Ibrahim, in Syria and were defeated. An important section of the Sultan's fleet joined Mehemet Ali; a French fleet in which Joinville was cruising could have prevented this move, but remained aloof. The Powers began to be alarmed, and the Austrian Ambassador at Constantinople organised a Collective Note from the European representatives informing the Turks that it was hoped that no treaty would be made with the ruler of Egypt without their approval. This was presented in July 1839.

Thiers was by no means willing to follow the leadership of Austria or, for that matter, of England. He believed that it would very much strengthen France in Africa if an independent Power ruled in Egypt, separating the Moslems of Algiers from the Sultan in Constantinople. He knew that the army and even more the navy were very confident in their ability to deal with any enemy. English statesmen were having to deal with revolts in Canada; the East India Company was at war in Afghanistan and extremely suspicious of Russia's actions in Persia. It was known that the Cabinet was divided over policy in the Near East.

Guizot was therefore dispatched to London as ambassador. He had never been in England, but he knew the language well and his work on English history had made him a reputation as a scholar. That he was a Protestant might also help him in a strongly anti-Catholic society. Thiers believed that the Government which was showing itself friendly over the reburial of Napoleon might be co-operative over Egypt. His main aim was so to delay international action that Mehemet Ali might prove his superiority and make a favourable settlement with the Sultan without the Powers' intervention.

Unfortunately, he had based his plans on two erroneous assumptions. Mehemet Ali was in serious difficulties. The provisioning and maintenance of Ibrahim's forces in Syria were a tremendous strain, and the Syrians were proving more and more unwilling to submit to rule by a man whose sole claim to power was that of conquest. The other mistake was that he underestimated Palmerston. The Foreign Secretary of England was not in the least disposed to dally, or to see any growth of French influence in the eastern Mediterranean. He assured the Cabinet that there was a serious danger of independent action by Russia unless the Sultan were helped to deal with the Pasha. If he were not allowed to hurry on a settlement, he would resign. Neither the Queen nor his colleagues would have minded this, for his forceful personality made him an awkward man to work with, but they were well aware that he was immensely popular and that to allow him to resign on such a point would mean a storm in the newspapers.

In July 1840 Guizot warned Thiers that it was possible that France, which was insisting on Mehemet Ali being allowed to keep Syria, might be taken by the other Powers to be pursuing an independent policy, and that to continue delay in the hope of a direct settlement—ignoring the Powers—between Turkey and Egypt might be dangerous. On 16 July Thiers wrote to him: 'We must not be disturbed, and must hold our course steadily. The English are engaging in a dangerous attempt.'[1] On the very next day, 17 July, Palmerston informed Guizot officially that Austria, Prussia, Russia and England had signed a Convention by which they promised support to the Sultan unless Mehemet Ali accepted terms which excluded him from Syria.

French reaction was violent. Securities fell, shouts were raised for war in defence of Egypt. Communications were slow; weeks would elapse before the official Note reached Turkey, the Sultan sent an ultimatum, and Mehemet Ali replied. There was still hope, and the good offices of Louis-Philippe's son-in-law, Leopold of Belgium, with his niece, Victoria of England, were engaged. Leopold wrote on 26 July that he thought the signing of the Note of 15 July without

[1] Guizot: *An Embassy to the Court of St. James.* London, 1862, p. 207.

inviting French adhesion 'has had here a very *disastrous* effect'. 'There is a material difference between leaving a company from motives of one's own, or being *kicked out* of it.'[1] Victoria did not like Palmerston, but she also distrusted France and was not willing to provoke a crisis in her Cabinet. On 26 September she told her uncle that 'France is in the wrong, and *quite* in the wrong. Albert . . . is quite of my opinion.'[2]

During the autumn warlike preparations went on in France. A large scheme of fortifications around Paris was begun which had the useful effect of giving employment to some of the men who, lacking work, paraded the streets singing the 'Marseillaise'. French feelings had been exacerbated by the ostentatious movement of English warships to Beyrout, where the Syrians were urged to return to their allegiance to the Sultan, and then to Alexandria. On 11 September Beyrout was bombarded; Ibrahim had plenty of men but no ships, so had to look on powerless to intervene. The French navy could easily have retaliated, for it was probably much more than a match for the English Mediterranean squadrons, but this meant war. Orleans made no secret of his wish that England's bluff should be called, but the risk of involving the two countries in war was one which could be run only for a very important object. And Thiers and the French Cabinet were beginning reluctantly to suspect that they had misjudged the power and capacity of their Egyptian protégés.

Another attempt to assassinate the King on 15 October was a reminder, as the *Saisons* rising had been, that the régime was not wholly secure. When the King's Speech was being drafted for the meeting of the Chambers at the end of October, Louis-Philippe refused to allow warlike passages to be included and Thiers resigned. It seems likely that he was not sorry to do so; other people could now bear the blame for his errors. On 3 November Acre was taken by the British and Mehemet Ali forced to return the Turkish naval vessels to the Sultan. The estimates for the fortifications round Paris—150 million francs—brought home to the deputies what a very costly business war would be.

Mehemet Ali and the Sultan finally came to terms. Syria was restored, and the hereditary rule of Egypt assured to the rebellious vassal. In July 1841 France returned to the fold and joined the other four Powers in the Treaty of the Straits, by which the Powers guaranteed the integrity of the Ottoman Empire and the Dardanelles were closed to all warships. The victory was Palmerston's; Russia had lost her privileged position gained by the Treaty of Unkiar Skelessi in 1833 and France had been publicly humiliated.

[1] *The Letters of Queen Victoria*. Ed. Benson and Esher. London, 1908, p. 227.
[2] Ibid., p. 231.

Montalembert summed up the situation in a speech in the House of Peers in November 1840. 'We were deceived with regard to the Pasha of Egypt, both as to his moral worth and the material worth of his forces.'[1] A scapegoat had to be found, however, for the disappointment which had hurt the feelings of so many Frenchmen, and the obvious man was the King.

[1] De Meaux: *Montalembert*. Paris, 1897, p. 148.

Chapter XX

THE GATHERING STORM

LOUIS-PHILIPPE had not much liked Guizot. His air of superiority was annoying; even his very upright carriage, with his head thrown back so that he seemed to look over the heads of other men, predisposed people to resentment. Yet when he came into power, nominally under Soult but practically the head of the Cabinet, Louis-Philippe found in him the man he had been looking for. For seven years, from 29 October, 1840, until 21 February, 1848 —the longest continuous period of power for any minister of the constitutional monarchy—he had control of France. He had worked long at political theory, and his ideas were clear. Representative government was essential, but the representation must be only of those capable of sound thought and action. 'One must discover all the elements of legitimate power . . . and organise them into actual power',[1] he wrote. The main aim was, however, negative. 'Resistance not only to evil, but to the principle of evil; not only to disorder, but to the passions and the ideas which engender disorder— this is the paramount and peremptory duty of every government.'[2]

Guizot believed that the 'elements of legitimate power' were to be found in the middle classes, whose praise he had so eloquently expounded in two speeches in 1837 that 206 deputies had contributed to meet the cost of their printing. His definition of 'middle class' was a narrow one; he was content with an electorate of about 225,000 in a population of about 35 million. Men of proved worth should be deputies, and men who held office under the State had proved themselves valuable. Close co-operation could be secured between executive and legislature when administrators also helped to make the laws, and as deputies had to be re-elected when they accepted a Government post no infringement of the right of voters was involved. In 1842 complaints were made that of 459 deputies 149 held offices of one kind or another, but Guizot spoke strongly in defence of a system which gave a secure majority.

Support was also maintained by direct personal approach to deputies. 'During the sittings of the Chamber he too often left his

[1] Guizot: *Hist. du Gouvernement Représentatif*. Paris, 1880, Vol. I, p. 109.
[2] Guizot: *Democracy in France*. London, 1849 (5th ed.), p. 10.

ministerial seat to go to sit and whisper on the benches of the
Government supporters, without fearing the rumours that, in fact,
arose from such whispered colloquies.'[1] De Falloux, a conservative
who on the whole admired Guizot, thought this undignified. As in
eighteenth-century England, small State pensions were often given
to friends and dependents of useful politicians. A very odd example,
which shows how this use of State funds was accepted as natural, was
when the upright and respected philosopher Victor Cousin, Minister
for Education in Thiers' cabinet in 1840, secured a pension of 1,200
francs a year for his mistress, Madame Louise Colet, a writer of
inferior verse.[2]

The only opposition Guizot seemed to fear was that of the other
politicians, and few of them were concerned with basic reforms. De
Tocqueville, looking back over political life under the July monarchy,
saw it as a 'labyrinth of petty incidents, of petty ideas, of petty
passions, of personal views and contradictory projects'.[3] Men in
politics, he said, 'spent all their perspicacity in vain endeavours to
find subjects upon which they could seriously disagree'.[4] Even
administrative reforms were long debated and rarely accepted; for
example, in 1846 a plan was put forward for reform of the postal
system, which had long been criticised. The delivery of letters was
organised in a number of zones, each one with a special tariff, the
charge for a letter varying from about 3d. to 1s. 6d. The fee was paid
by the person who received the letter; it could be paid in advance by
the sender, but this was looked on as impolite for it assumed that the
receiver would find the payment irksome owing to poverty.[5] Guizot
strongly opposed any alteration, but in 1848 agreed to a reduction of
the maximum charge to 5d.

In such conditions it was unlikely that the radical social and
political reforms which alone could have made the government of the
Orleans family truly popular would be seriously considered, much
less effected. Accusations were constantly brought against Guizot
and his system, but had far more effect outside the Chamber than
within it. If the various groups, legitimists, radicals and personal
enemies, had co-operated he could have been defeated, but they no
more than he understood the situation. Each election was fought
mainly on personal and local issues, and the Government retained
its majority.

[1] De Falloux: *Mémoires d'un Royaliste*. 4th ed., Paris, 1888, Vol. I, p. 240.
[2] Enfield, D. E.: *A Lady of the Salons*. London, 1922, p. 34.
[3] De Tocqueville: *The Recollections of Alexis de Tocqueville*. Ed. 1948, Mayer,
London, p. 2.
[4] Ibid., p. 8.
[5] De Falloux, op. cit., Vol. I, p. 245.

Guizot was Foreign Minister until, in 1847, Soult at last retired and he had nominal as well as actual control of the Cabinet. This was, perhaps, unfortunate for him, for he was so absorbed in a variety of negotiations that he could not, even if he would, detach himself from day-to-day business and view the situation as a whole. The most important field for action lay in relations with Spain, for events across the Pyrenees, as in the eighteen-twenties, affected France on the ideological as well as on the practical side of life. Both Portugal and Spain were suffering from disputed successions and outbreaks of civil war. In Portugal in 1822 Pedro, the eldest son of King John VI, had been proclaimed Emperor of Brazil, which had declared its separation from its mother country. When John died in 1826 Pedro's daughter inherited the throne of Portugal and had to struggle for it against her uncle, Miguel. In 1831 Pedro abdicated, handing over Brazil to his son, and came back to Portugal to help his daughter. France was interested, but refrained from intervention as England's alliance with Portugal, which went back to 1703, was more or less accepted as giving her a kind of protective interest. Louis-Philippe, however, had his eye on the Portuguese royal family; he sent his son Joinville to Brazil on one of his cruises with the French navy and in 1843 arranged for him to marry the daughter of the Emperor. To such an indirect connection England could not object.

The Spanish question was far more complex. Ferdinand VII, who had been replaced on his throne by France, had married in 1829 his fourth wife, Christina of Naples, niece of the Queen of France. He had no son and was anxious that his brother Carlos should not succeed him. In 1713 the ancient law of succession by which a woman could inherit the throne had been set aside. It was restored in 1789, but the decree was not published until 1830. Before Ferdinand's death in 1833 Christina had borne him two daughters, Isabella and Marie Louisa Fernanda, so Isabella was declared his heir and her mother proclaimed Regent for her three-year-old daughter.

Carlos promptly claimed the throne, but his first efforts were defeated and he fled the country in 1834. International finance now began to affect the history of the unhappy country, not for the first time by any means, but in its modern guise. Both the pretender and the baby Queen's government badly needed money, and both approached the great international bankers, the Rothschilds, for funds. Each of the Rothschild brothers had an independent establishment in a different capital city, but they kept in the closest touch with each other. Nathan, in London, knew that the British Government favoured Christina; she was forced to depend on the more liberal elements in the country, and the parallel with Portugal made both young queens appear to the public in a sort of fairy-tale guise, fair maidens threatened by wicked uncles. A loan to Christina would be approved in England. This alone made the risk worth taking, in his view, but there was another potential gain. There were only two main sources of quicksilver in Europe, and scientific developments were increasing the demand for the metal. One was in Austria and was Rothschild property; the other in Spain. These mines were under-developed, and in February 1835 the lease was secured by which, for five years, the Rothschilds were to work the mines and pay the Spanish Government a fixed sum for every hundredweight of quicksilver extracted. Fifteen million francs were also loaned to the Government at a low rate of interest. It was therefore essential for the Rothschilds to keep Isabella on the throne.

That they were able to do so was due chiefly to the incompetence of her uncle, Carlos, who had wide support in the country but was unable to use it to advantage. Louis-Philippe at one time thought of supporting him, for Austria and the other Central European Powers were not at all pleased when Christina was forced in 1836 to re-establish the very democratic constitution of 1812 which had been overthrown by her husband Ferdinand. The failure of his marriage negotiations with Austria led to his dropping the idea, and when an English fleet helped to reduce Bilbao, held by the Carlists, in December 1836 the complete defeat and flight of the pretender made it plain that to help him would be a dangerous business. In 1839 Carlos came to France, and resigned his claims in favour of his son, another Carlos. The shocking misgovernment of Christina led in 1840 to another revolution, this time by the liberals. By October she, too, was a refugee in France; General Espartero, the leader of the opposition, was in power and in 1841 declared himself Regent.

This triangular struggle tore the unhappy Spain into fragments. Carlists, Christinists and liberals fought each other, and in 1843 Espartero in his turn had to fly. The constitutional vacuum thus created was filled by the declaration that Isabella, who was just fourteen, was of age and in full exercise of royal power.

It was inevitable that Louis-Philippe should see in the position of the Spanish royal family an admirable opportunity for a good marriage. That his son should be allowed by the Powers to marry the Queen herself was not to be expected, but her heir was her younger sister and that offered possibilities. In 1843 a sort of public reconciliation between England and France took place when Queen Victoria and her husband visited Louis-Philippe at his country estate, the Château d'Eu. Victoria already knew Louise, Queen of Belgium, her uncle's wife, and was predisposed to like her father,

Louis-Philippe, though she retained the suspicions she and her ministers had already formed about his Spanish plans.

All the chancelleries of Europe were buzzing with suggestions and counter-suggestions about the future husband of the child Queen. To a modern observer, the plan put forward by Austria that she should marry her cousin Carlos and so eliminate the dynastic struggle seems far the most sensible. To English statesmen this was anathema. The belief that a 'constitutional' monarchy must be best was genuine and strong and it was arguable that the position of the Queen of Portugal might be adversely affected if the Carlist party in Spain scored such a success. English financiers and even the English Ambassador in Spain were in favour of the 'progressive' party. By now, too, the French felt that a 'cordial understanding' with England was essential for their success in establishing control in Africa and the Pacific.

Throughout 1845 and 1846 discussions went on. The suggestion of another Coburg prince as a husband for Isabella was objectionable to France; that she should marry one of the Neapolitan Bourbons was not much liked by the Spaniards or Christina, who was on very bad terms with her family. In 1846 the situation in England was changed by the fall of Peel's government over the Corn Law crisis and its aftermath, and Palmerston replaced the amenable Aberdeen at the Foreign Office. He was told by Aberdeen of the long semi-private discussions that had been going on, but this was very different from having been engaged in them himself.

The precise reasons which led to the cutting of the knot by Louis-Philippe were very much argued over at the time and later. Whether directly or indirectly, there is no doubt that Palmerston's reappearance decided the matter. Before his influence could be fully exerted, Louis-Philippe and Christina acted. On 10 October, 1846, Isabella was married to her cousin, Francis, the son of her father Ferdinand's youngest brother and Carlota of Naples, her mother's sister. The kinship was very close; the bridegroom very unattractive and also generally believed to be incapable of having children. At the same joint ceremony, her younger sister, the heir to the throne, was married to Montpensier.

No enthusiasm was felt in France for what was felt to be a personal and not very creditable royal intrigue. The reaction in England was that France had acted in an underhand and almost treacherous way. Victoria was not at all placated by a letter from the Queen of France which announced the match a month before it actually occurred; the tone of her reply showed clearly that she disapproved, and that Louis-Philippe insisted on treating the marriage as a purely family affair and concluding it rapidly made her very angry. For once her sentiments and Palmerston's agreed, and she wrote to the King of Belgium that she could not understand '*how* the King *can* wantonly throw away the friendship of one who has stood by him with such sincere affection, for a *doubtful* object of personal and family aggrandizement'.[1]

This attitude was shared by many Frenchmen. The day had gone when such marriages were felt to be a national triumph; even if a son of the King of the French should eventually become the consort of a Queen of Spain, it would not make much difference to the ordinary merchant or landowner in France. Montpensier's wife brought him a very large dowry, and this was the aspect of the situation that most struck public opinion. Serious politicians were alarmed at realising that now France had no ally whatever and no prospect of one since the 'understanding' with England had obviously ceased to be 'cordial'. In fact, the only advantage gained by the King was the dowry, which secured his son an income. Isabella did, in fact, produce children; Montpensier in 1870 caused immense scandal by killing the brother of Isabella's consort in a duel. And Spain went on, misgoverned, torn by faction, undeveloped both economically and politically.

Louis-Philippe's family had suffered a serious loss when on 13 July, 1842, his heir, the Duke of Orleans, was killed in a carriage accident. He had been in every way the leader of his brothers; to him, as Joinville wrote, 'we turned for guidance always'.[2] His son was only four, his father the King was seventy. The Government asked that Nemours, the second son, should be officially appointed Regent for his nephew when the child inherited the throne. Nemours was not popular, as Orleans had been; he was looked on as very much a conservative. Odilon Barrot and the radicals wished the boy's mother to be official Regent; Lamartine thought this was the natural thing and the choice of Nemours emphasised the dynastic as compared to the constitutional aspect of the monarchy. The Government carried its plan. The tone of the debate, not its outcome, was what mattered; in the same year, 1842, plans for reform were put forward and rejected; unless they were whole-heartedly accepted, monarchy as Louis-Philippe understood it was unlikely to survive.

The death of Orleans roused genuine sympathy for a while, but opposition to the King and his Government outside the Chambers remained and increased, not so much in violence but in taking on a more positive tone, putting forward practicable schemes. The free-

[1] *Letters of Queen Victoria*, 1837–1861. Ed. Benson and Esher. London, 1908, Vol. II, p. 106.
[2] Joinville: *Memoirs*. London, 1895, p. 218.

16

dom of the Press was, especially after the laws of 1835,[1] no greater than before 1830 and, as then, attack was more amusing than support, so that owners and editors were constantly trying to evade the laws. In 1836 an attempt was made to popularise the Press by Girardin, who produced a paper for 40 francs a year, about half the usual rate, and introduced serial stories; these were such a success that most other papers had to follow suit. Before 1835 witty and satirical papers, such as *Charivari* founded in 1832, were full of cartoons attacking the King; after 1835, when direct criticism of the King and his family became an offence, the ministers and leaders of society were pilloried.

Guizot wrote in his memoirs that the series of Press prosecutions in 1833 'was an error, inevitable perhaps, in the existing state of parties and minds, but one which aggravated the mischief we were anxious to stifle'.[2] The 'error' he perpetuated while he was in power; there were endless prosecutions, followed in most cases by very heavy fines and imprisonment. In the prison of Ste.–Pélagie special quarters were set aside for the editors of four papers, so frequent were their visits. That the advertisement given to the opposition by these trials was of importance may be doubted; they were too frequent to attract much attention. The financial embarrassment caused by law costs and fines made it hard for papers without large financial backing to survive. There was no very great increase in subscribers to political journals; advertisements did not yield very much. Many papers had a very brief existence; the radical *Réforme* survived till 1848 only with great difficulty, for it had few subscribers; the *National*, constantly prosecuted, had very wealthy men behind it. The provincial Press remained weak and depended for news on extracts from Paris papers.

The favourite charge brought by the radical papers was that of corruption, and they had a field day in 1847 when a case brought before the House of Peers seemed to justify their charges. M. Teste, the President of the Court of Appeal, who had previously been in charge of the Ministry of Public Works, was accused of having, with the complicity of a general, received a bribe of 100,000 francs for favour shown to a mining company. He was found guilty and sent to prison for three years, and the general was fined 10,000 francs. Such a case allowed the opposition papers to hint that many such crimes must have been committed, though they had no evidence at all.

In August the same year the Duchess de Praslin was murdered by her husband. It was a peculiarly revolting murder, and the Duke

---

[1] See Collins, I. Article on 'The Government and the Press in France during the Reign of Louis-Philippe', *Eng. Hist. Review*, April, 1954.

[2] Guizot: *Memoirs*. Trans. Cole. London, 1860, Vol. III, p. 203.

committed suicide before he could be brought to trial. This case could be used to cast aspersions on all prominent people in society. Politicians were rogues; aristocrats, immoral—these were ideas very readily accepted, especially by workers to whom the class war was being preached by a new type of socialist.

Blanqui (1798–1854) never produced an orderly plan, as had the Utopists, but his articles embodied the fundamental ideas of the new Communism often in phrases eminently quotable. Much that Marx and Engels put into shape in the Communist Manifesto was to be found scattered through his writings. Such phrases as that capital 'is illegitimate for it is the produce of the work of others and cannot confer any rights'; that the majority 'have no liberty save that to choose their masters' and are condemned 'to forced labour for the profit of the possessing classes' were very effective.[1] Even Marx's most famous slogan, 'Workers of the world, unite!', can be found in a slightly different form, 'Workers, you are weak and unhappy because you are divided. Unite!', in the pamphlet written by a woman socialist, Flora Tristan [2] (1803–44), which appeared in 1842, part of which had appeared in a Fourierist paper.

United action was, however, very difficult for men without any surplus funds for organisation, whose immediate aim was actual employment at a reasonable wage. Such visions as those of Cabet (1788–1856), who in 1842 published his *Voyage to Icaria* in which he advocated complete ownership and control of all economic life by the State, were not likely to spur them to action. Proudhon (1809–65) published in 1840 a pamphlet on Property, which contained the famous phrases 'What is property?' 'It is theft'. He had no plan on which men could work, however; he was really an anarchist.

Far the most practical of the revolutionary writers was Louis Blanc (1811–82). He was a most skilful journalist, with a knack of clear and persuasive writing. His book on *The Organisation of Labour*, which appeared in 1839, was based not on theory but on fact, or so it appeared, and suggested a plan of reform based on contemporary conditions. He used statistics to show that not only was a man's wage inadequate to support a family, so that his wife and children were forced to work for long hours at fantastically low rates of pay, but that unemployment averaged four months a year. A budget of essential expenditure was used effectively to make his point. He calculated that three million people were starving. Such conditions led inevitably to crime and to the destruction of the very basis of society, family life.

[1] Quoted in Leroy, M.: *Histoire des Idées Sociales en France*. Paris, 1950, p. 409.
[2] See Puech, J. L.: *La vie et l'œuvre de Flora Tristan*. Paris, 1925.

The remedy lay not in any tinkering with the situation but in direct State action. 'What the proletariat lacks is the means of production—it is the Government's function to provide them.'[1] 'The State is the poor man's banker.' But he did not propose any immediate destruction of social institutions. He wanted first factory legislation, to impose decent conditions, and secondly, the opening by the State of national factories for the production of goods, equipped with first-class machines and paying good wages. He held that men had the right to work and the State the duty of providing it. The State factories would be so efficient that, he believed, their competition would gradually ruin private enterprises and eventually all production would be national. Low fixed interest would be paid on capital, but the control would be decentralised, each factory being eventually run by managers and foremen elected by the workers. Profits would be divided into three parts during the early stages of the experiment. One third would be distributed equally among the workers; one would go to a fund for sick pay and pensions, from which loans could be made to other factories; the last would be reserved for new machinery and development.

The contrast between Louis Blanc's ideas and other writers' lay in their apparent sobriety. No destruction was envisaged, no sudden overthrow, but a peaceful penetration by the method accepted as proper for capitalism, competition. There was nothing to offend the Christian reformers, who were well aware of the evils he analysed. The two main weaknesses were not clear to contemporaries—that he greatly under-estimated the power of the capitalists to resist, and that his plans, like those of most modern socialists, wholly ignored agriculture. The majority of Frenchmen still lived outside the towns and factories, and there was nothing to attract the peasant in the 'Organisation of Labour'.

Before State factories could be set up, those who believed in them must have political power. Manhood suffrage was the essential preliminary. The right to vote must be won before the right to work could be gained. That a very wide movement towards democracy was inevitable was held by other thinkers not at all socialist in outlook, such as de Tocqueville, who became a deputy in 1839 and joined the Opposition.

There were many men in the Chamber whose main aim was to get rid of Guizot, and by 1847 the various groups were sufficiently united to demand a large extension of the suffrage. They asked for all payers of 100 francs in direct taxes, and certain other worthy persons, to have the vote, which would nearly double the electorate, and also that, except for Cabinet ministers and a few other holders of

[1] Blanc, L.: *L'Organisation de Travail*. Ed. Marriott. Oxford, 1913, p. 14.

important offices, no Government employee should be a deputy. Guizot repeated his arguments against going too fast, and his obedient majority threw out the projects. Thiers restated his favourite maxim, that the King should reign but not govern, but both King and Cabinet felt safe in ignoring him.

In fact, they were safe, so long as the lower middle classes were convinced that the Government's policy was to their advantage. In the elections in 1846 Guizot had told the voters to 'enrich yourselves by thrift and work', a phrase which his opponents unjustly shortened to 'enrich yourselves'. By 1847 the advice seemed less practical to follow. Thrift was all very well, but so much of the nation's wealth was being absorbed by the Government. The Algerian and colonial expeditions had been costly; heavy expenses had been incurred on railways which were as yet no real help to traders and had led to waste of money in speculation. The yield from taxes had risen, but it by no means covered the annual costs of a Government which added to necessary expenditure the salaries and pensions paid to its supporters. Every year the deficit grew; in 1847 annual expenses had risen to 1,630 million francs as compared to the 1,015 million of 1829, and the average yield from taxation was only 1,138 millions. Constant borrowing was required; 1,355 million francs in loans had been raised during the reign of Louis-Philippe and 444 million more taken from the Sinking Fund, but in spite of this there was a deficit of 415 million[1] at the beginning of 1848 and the Government was negotiating another loan.

A large number of manufacturers and shopkeepers themselves wanted to raise loans, for disastrous floods had caused great damage and the textile industries, always subject to fluctuations in demand, were very short of orders. Unemployment and low wages checked the workers' demand for goods, and hit retailers badly. Under such conditions opponents of the Government were sure of a hearing if they could get some sort of propaganda organisation going, beyond their newspapers, which had a limited circulation and were always liable to prosecution. Political associations and public meetings were, however, illegal.

An ingenious plan was developed after Cobden had visited France in 1846 and told the story of Manchester's campaign against the Corn Laws. There was no law against holding dinner parties, even if the guests paid for their dinners. In the autumn of 1847 Thiers, who represented the more traditional politicians, and Odilon Barrot, the radical who had defended the men who damaged St. Germain de l'Auxerrois,[2] began organising Reform banquets. Thiers took no

[1] Figures from Garnier: *Traité des Finances*. Paris, 1872.
[2] See *supra*, pp. 188–189.

active part but Barrot toured the country. On 9 July, 1847, the more radical deputies appeared at a banquet in Paris attended by 1,200 people; the 'Marseillaise' and revolutionary songs enlivened the speeches. Lamartine, whose book on the Girondins had had a great success, made a fierce and eloquent speech, appropriately accompanied by a thunderstorm.

Barrot and Thiers did not want revolution; they wished for moderate reform but a maintenance of the constitution as it stood. Even Barrot refused to appear at a banquet at Lille when he heard the customary toast to the King's health was to be omitted.[1] The plan soon got out of control; the republicans and socialists began to organise banquets too. Toasts were drunk to 'The Rights of Man' or 'National Sovereignty' or even 'The Working Class'. 'Reform' was a mystical word used by speechifiers of every shade of opinion; no one translated it into a programme, it simply stood for opposition to 'Corruption', which was the national enemy.

'Reform' was certainly in the air. The English Government was dealing with serious unrest in Ireland; in Prussia the King had to grant a constitution; Hungary was demanding greater liberty from the Emperor of Austria; there was constant agitation in Italy. The new Pope, Pius IX, who succeeded Gregory XVI in June 1846, was experimenting with constitutional reform. Yet when the Chambers met in Paris in January 1848 the official Speech from the Throne held out no hopes to those who wanted social or constitutional reform. The King merely scolded the Opposition for fomenting blind and dangerous passions. A number of critical amendments to the formal Reply were defeated by Guizot's obedient majority.

On 29 January de Tocqueville made a remarkable speech warning the Government that it was in peril. He told them that though the workers were not actually rioting, 'they are gradually forming opinions and ideas which are destined not only to upset this or that law, ministry or even form of government, but society itself'. The revolution of 1789 came because 'the class that was then the governing class had become, through its indifference, its selfishness and its vices, incapable and unworthy of governing the country. Do you not feel—what shall I say?—as it were a gale of revolution in the air?' He finished by saying, 'In Gód's name, change the spirit of the Government; for, I repeat, that spirit will lead you to the abyss.'[2]

No one believed him.

[1] Lamartine: *Histoire de la Révolution de 1848*. Paris, 1859, Vol. I, p. 26.
[2] *The Recollections of Alexis de Tocqueville*. Ed. Mayer, London, 1948, pp. 12–15.

Chapter XXI

FAREWELL TO MONARCHY

Paris in 1848 bore a very different aspect from the Paris of to-day. Most of the streets were narrow and crooked, though there were broad boulevards with trees, and wide spaces with little sentry boxes before most of the important buildings. On the right bank of the Seine stood the great palace of the Tuileries with its gardens alongside the river, and near it the Louvre, with the broad Place de la Carrousel between them. A short walk away on the same side of the Seine, opposite the island on which stood Nôtre Dame, was the Hôtel de Ville, centre of the city government, where Lafayette had embraced Louis-Philippe. Across the river were the Palais Bourbon and the Luxembourg, which housed the two Chambers of Parliament.

Around and beyond, on both sides of the river, stretched the twelve *arrondissements*, the administrative districts, each with its mayor. There were great palaces and buildings which had survived the Revolution; churches and monasteries with open spaces round them; in some streets were smart new shops and restaurants and cafés, but hemming them in were the old congested narrow streets. The outer districts, especially the twelfth *arrondissement*, were dense masses of ramshackle tenement houses, factories and workshops.

The Prefect was normally responsible for keeping order in the city as a whole, though each mayor had his own organisation. Besides the ordinary police there were the gendarmes, who carried weapons, and a special and very unpopular municipal guard. There were always soldiers on duty outside the royal palaces, the Government offices and the Houses of Parliament. Louis-Philippe had restored the Paris National Guard, for which he had an affection; it was drawn from the middle class, in which he placed his confidence. It was organised on military lines, with infantry, cavalry and some artillery, all in theory ready to act as a disciplined force whenever summoned.

In such a city the guardians of order were always at a disadvantage. Narrow streets could easily be blocked and there were many points which had to be guarded. Armouries, barracks and stores were placed at various key points, but men passing between them in times of trouble could be attacked by stones or even gun-fire from the roofs and windows beneath which they had to pass. It might have been expected that Louis-Philippe, who had gained a throne because of the collapse of the defences of Charles X, would have ensured that precise plans were always ready for action in time of trouble. The comparative ease with which mobs had been subdued during his reign, and the unjustifiable confidence he had in the loyalty and even affection felt for him by the business men and shop-keepers, probably explain the extraordinary inadequacy of the resistance of the Orleans monarchy when faced by large-scale demonstrations.

In January 1848 some radical politicians and officers of the National Guard planned to hold a Reform banquet in the working-class area of the twelfth *arrondissement*. The liberal politicians of the so-called 'constitutional' Opposition refused to support it, and Guizot prohibited the plan. Whether he had a legal right to do so was debated at length by the deputies, but he carried his point, though with a smaller majority than usual. The Opposition now determined themselves to hold a banquet on 22 February in order to force the Government to prosecute them and test their rights before a law court.

On 21 February the *National* and other Left-wing papers which had taken great interest in the banquet scheme published an announcement that the guests would proceed to their meeting place in a procession; they would include officers and men of the National Guard and students, as well as deputies and Peers. No banners were to be carried. Odilon Barrot and the others responsible for the banquet were taken aback; they had not even been consulted about the newspapers' announcement. They did not need the authorities to tell them that such a procession was quite clearly illegal except with Government permission, so their main point in arranging the banquet—to test whether it could lawfully be prohibited—had been thrown away. Even Louis Blanc was opposed to open flouting of the law, so the opposition felt that it would play straight into Guizot's hands unless the whole scheme were postponed. The local committees, which had been very busy organising a monster demonstration of speechifying, were, however, very reluctant to give up their plans.

The morning of 22 February was very wet and cold, which must have pleased the authorities as tending to discourage crowds, but have been very uncomfortable for the municipal guard which had been called out to disperse any demonstrators. Troops were ready, but except for a few infantrymen remained inside their barracks. In spite of the bad weather, crowds began to collect early in the day;

by 9 a.m. the Place de la Concorde and the open spaces near the Madeleine church were full of people, among whom groups of students were conspicuous. They were good-tempered; they chaffed the soldiers; they wandered into the Chamber of Deputies, but withdrew when some troops appeared. The 'Marseillaise' was sung from time to time, but no serious demonstration was made.

As the day drew on the crowds grew larger. Unemployed men assembled in the Champs Élysées; some gun shops were broken into and weapons seized. Barricades began to rise in the workers' quarters; speeches were made outside the offices of the radical newspapers. Guizot was not seriously worried; his political opponents seemed to be refraining from fomenting trouble, and he hoped that by nightfall the people would go home and the weary soldiers and police have a rest.

During the night, members of secret societies began to meet, but there was no concerted plan for using the situation. It seems as if everyone who had a grudge against the Government felt that this was a good chance to proclaim it. Next morning, 23 February, the crowds again collected, and the ministers decided to call out the National Guard. To Louis-Philippe's consternation, the senior officers reported that a number of the companies could not be trusted; they were already shouting for Guizot's dismissal.

When faced by the weapons of assassins, the King had shown remarkable bravery, and he still had great faith in Guizot and in his own hold over his people. Yet that strange timidity and uncertainty he had shown in the crisis of 1830 again overcame him; he could face an immediate danger, but lost his head when faced with an uncertain future. Thiers had said the day before to de Falloux, 'The National Guard is going to give a good lesson to Guizot. The King has a quick ear, he will listen to reason and give way in time.'[1]

Thiers was right, so far as he went, but both he and the King misjudged the position. This was already more than a ministerial crisis. The deputies met as usual on the morning of the 23rd, all the approaches to the Chamber being guarded by infantry, but no real business was transacted. At two o'clock the King sent for Guizot. The deputies sat on, whispering and wondering; at three o'clock Guizot returned. He entered, so de Tocqueville wrote, 'with his firmest step and his loftiest bearing, silently crossed the gangway, ascended the tribune, throwing his head almost back from his shoulders for fear of seeming to lower it, and stated in two words that the King had called upon M. Molé to form a new ministry.'[2]

Molé meant nothing whatever to the crowds in the Paris streets.

[1] De Falloux: *Mémoires d'un Royaliste*. Paris, 1888, Vol. I, p. 265.
[2] De Tocqueville: *Recollections*. Ed. Mayer, London, 1948, p. 31.

To get them to disperse, as everyone except the King and his friends realised, something much more sensational would have to be done. All through the evening and for most of the night there was a coming and going of potential ministers till at last, at 6 a.m. on the morning of 24 February, Louis-Philippe yielded and Thiers and Barrot were empowered to form a government. By then it was far too late.

In the night the news of Guizot's fall had become known and many worthy citizens illuminated their houses. Outside the Foreign Office the crowds were shouting for his punishment, milling about and pressing close up to the weary troops standing guard. An officer's horse took fright and plunged about; a shot went off— whether fired by a soldier or by someone in the crowd will never be known. The soldiers, cold, wet and tired after their long vigil, believed they were being attacked and fired on the crowd. Several people were killed, and an angry mob seized a coach and, placing the bodies on it, began to parade the streets, below, in some places, the cheerful illuminations of those who thought the trouble was over. Rumours were flying everywhere; people were shouting that the Government was massacring the men of Paris.

At 2 a.m., in the midst of his Cabinet-making, Louis-Philippe decided that a strong man must be put in charge. Most unwisely he chose Bugeaud, who had shown in Algiers that he could act with decision, but he was very unpopular. In any case, it was too late for him to do anything effective. He found the troops he was to command were not, as he had been told, 50,000 strong but only 35,000, many of whom had already been on duty for forty-eight hours in the mud and the cold.[1] Moreover, the King had told him that on no account were the soldiers to fire except on a direct command from a superior officer. The only plan he could make was to try to organise four strong columns, to pull down the barricades and make movement possible.

On the morning of the 24th, de Tocqueville, on his way to the Chamber of Deputies, noticed the curious character of the situation in Paris. In one street all the shops were closed, and 'neighbours stood talking in little groups at their doors, with subdued voices, with a frightened air'.[2] Farther on, along a boulevard, he watched how 'the great trees along the curb came tumbling down into the roadway as though of their own accord. These acts of destruction were the work of isolated individuals, who went about their business silently, regularly and hurriedly, preparing in this way the materials for the barricades which others were to erect. Nothing ever seemed

[1] Lamartine, A.: *Histoire de la Révolution de 1848*. 4th edition. Paris, 1859, Vol. I, p. 110.
[2] De Tocqueville, op. cit., p. 37.

to me more to resemble the carrying on of an industry, and, as a matter of fact, for the greater number of those men it was nothing less.' 'I would rather have met in the same place a furious crowd.'[1] Later on his way back he saw the barricades being erected in the same competent and business-like way while the onlookers watched quietly.

These well-planned and solidly-built obstacles were not easily overthrown save by gun-fire or a large body of men. To bring up cannon was in many places impossible, and the commanders of Bugeaud's columns found it hard to destroy them without firing on the crowd that thronged around them. One such column was held up near the Chamber of Deputies; others were scattered by the simple pressure of the people and any isolated soldier was immediately 'seized, embraced, disarmed and sent back'.[2] Forbidden to fire, officers tried haranguing the crowd, but often without much conviction and always without result.

On the morning of the 24th, Thiers and Barrot were trying to convince the people of Paris that Guizot was gone and that they would introduce all the desired reforms. The difficulty was to get at the people; there were so many focal points, and the crowds were growing larger every hour. If any of the officers commanding troops had had the enterprise to act without explicit orders some of the key positions could easily have been cleared; that none had was in itself a sign of the weakness of the King and the 'spirit of routine' which pervaded all branches of the Government service. A proclamation written out by Thiers was given to an officer to read out to the crowd outside the Chambers, but someone tore it from his hand and in any case no one would have listened. A new commander of the National Guard was appointed, but by now it was quite impossible for him even to make contact with the majority of the men.

The chief difficulty was that there were no leaders of the people, nor did they seem to have any definite aim. The Left-wing papers displayed placards demanding 'reform' and various orators addressed the crowds proclaiming their own individual solutions for all problems. More and more weapons were being taken from disarmed troops or by capture of the armouries of the police, but even these were haphazard and individual efforts. The mob outside the Hôtel de Ville met no resistance from the soldiers on guard there; when they decided to enter the building the troops stacked their guns and retired to their barracks, and the municipal authorities were reduced to impotence.

The quietest region was around the Tuileries. There were 4,000

1 De Tocqueville, op. cit., p. 41.
2 Ibid., p. 41.

soldiers there and a substantial contingent of the National Guard. At
11 a.m. on the 24th the King and Queen sat down to their usual
luncheon with Nemours and Montpensier and the rest of the family.
Two deputies, Duvergier de Hauranne and Rémusat, came to the
door and asked to speak to Montpensier. They told him that the
danger was acute, for some of the soldiers were going over to the
people. When he heard this, the King cried: 'It is impossible!'
but an officer standing by said: 'I saw it myself.'[1]

The only plan that occurred to the King was to encourage the
troops near-by by holding a review. He and his sons and some of
the available generals hastily donned their uniforms and mounted
their chargers. They rode out on to the Place de la Carrousel and
began the formal parade, first of the troops, whose attitude seemed
correct though not cordial. From the National Guard came shouts
of a distinctly unfriendly kind; the King now realised for himself
that he was faced by a revolution. Not wishing to evoke open opposition, he went back to the palace.

He now heard that some of the unpopular Municipal Guard had
been killed while guarding the Ministry of the Navy. Thiers came in
to own that he could do nothing, and suggested that Barrot be given
full control. Louis-Philippe agreed to this, and also decided to
replace Bugeaud by Gérard, who was more popular. To think that
such rapid changes in command in the midst of a crisis would be
helpful is an indication of the confusion of mind of Louis-Philippe
and his friends.

Deeply depressed, the elderly monarch began a series of interviews with people of various kinds; sounds of firing could now be
heard inside the palace from the Château d'Eau, not far off. Soult
and Gérard remained silent when he asked if military action could
still save the situation. The word 'abdication' now began to be
heard. A newspaper man, Girardin of the *Presse*, produced a scheme
for the King to abdicate in favour of his grandson and declare the
child's mother, the Duchess of Orleans, Regent. The existing
Chambers should be dissolved and an amnesty declared for all involved in the revolution. Montpensier urged his father to abdicate;
the Duchess and Bugeaud begged him to stand firm.

Many observers thought, at least when they wrote down their
accounts of those tense days later on, that if the King had immediately publicly announced his abdication and shown his
daughter-in-law and her little son to the people a wave of sentiment
might have been created that would have saved the monarchy. It
certainly seems to be true that any clear lead from someone in
authority would have had a good chance of success. Louis-Philippe

[1] Lamartine, op. cit., p. 98.

took the fatal course. He signed a solemn act of abdication, but declared that by law his son Nemours must be Regent. This man of thirty-four, correct in manner, had no popular appeal whatever; as Regent he would have symbolised the maintenance of the existing system, not a dramatic change. Nor would the King face the people; his wife had earlier suggested it, but he refused. Instead, in the most commonplace sort of way, he and the Queen left the palace in an ordinary cab and drove to St. Cloud, followed by Nemours' wife and her children in a second cab.

Meanwhile, Barrot had been trying to convince the people that as head of the Cabinet he would see that everything went well. De Tocqueville saw him and a colleague coming into the Chamber of Deputies, where members had been waiting all day for something to happen. The crowd was cheering them, but they were in a strange condition for popular victors, 'their hats crushed down over their eyes; their clothes were covered with dust, their cheeks looked hollow, their eyes weary; never were two men in triumph so suggestive of men about to be hanged.'[1] They told him of the abdication, but said they were not worrying about the Parliament: 'What good or harm can it do?'

While they stood outside, they heard that the Duchess of Orleans with her two children and the Regent, Nemours, had come to the Chamber of Deputies. This German princess showed far more sense than the Orleans family or than the constitutional politicians. Dressed in mourning, pale, with traces of tears on her face, she was an appealing figure. She sat with the two children on the steps below the tribune from which the orators spoke, with her brother-in-law standing in his uniform stiff and upright beside her. A messenger was sent to bring in Barrot, for there was no one with authority to speak. Then the doors of the Chamber were forced and a crowd rushed in; the Duchess was taken to the topmost benches, where politicians of the centre-Left usually sat.

Marie, a lawyer, not very prominent in politics but generally popular, spoke, saying that, though by law Nemours was Regent, the Duchess had been acclaimed as the natural Regent for her son. Under the circumstances, he thought a small provisional government ought to be appointed. Another lawyer, Crémieux, supported him, and the deputies agreed to set up a committee of five. The Duchess herself was anxious to speak, but was advised not to. Barrot at last appeared, out of breath, and declaimed that 'The crown of July rests on the head of a child and a woman.' The deputies applauded, the crowd remained silent.

Two more troops of men, bearing flags and very excited, now

[1] De Tocqueville, op. cit., p. 48.

burst into the Chamber. The whole situation changed in a flash. Ledru-Rollin, a man of forty-one, who had been associated with some of the secret movements against the Government, now declared that what was needed was a republic, to be proclaimed at once, and a provisional government to summon a Convention to make an entirely new constitution.

Lamartine now went to the tribune. It was a great occasion for a famous poet to show his power over people, and he was listened to by everyone. His own account of the occasion shows how very conscious he was of playing a great part in a great drama. Most people expected that he would plead the cause of the mother and child, but instead, after referring to them in a sympathetic way, he came out strongly in favour of a republic. He was loudly applauded by yet another group of invaders, men who having found their way into the Tuileries had been seizing and destroying the furnishings. With the Chamber full of wild men shouting for a republic, it is not surprising that those near the Duchess hustled her and Nemours and the children out of the hall by a back door. They got separated in the turmoil; the elder boy was attacked but was carried out; the younger was missing for some time, and the poor mother, half fainting, was in despair till they were brought to her and all three pushed into a carriage and driven away. Nemours managed to evade the crowd, borrow some clothes to replace his uniform, and make his escape.

It seems quite possible that Lamartine's speech was the turning-point in that odd day. He had for some time been in opposition and though his reputation was with the upper classes not the workers of Paris, he was capable of making that great emotional appeal which could under such conditions have had more than a temporary effect. He had while writing his book on the Girondins become steeped in the story of the 1789 revolution, and it looks as if he saw himself playing the part of a Danton. To patch up and amend the existing constitution would be much less satisfactory than striking boldly out for a radical change.

The Royal Family, by devious routes, made their way to the Channel coast, where they got in touch with the British Consul at Havre. He arranged their transport to England; a long letter which he sent describing the flight was passed on to Queen Victoria by Palmerston, who commented that it was like one of 'Walter Scott's best tales' and that the consul 'has also probably rendered a good service to the Provisional Government, who would have been much embarrassed if their Commissioner had arrested the King and Queen'.[1] Guizot, too, got away and reached London safely. By the summer yet another group of royal exiles had settled down in Eng-

[1] *Queen Victoria's Letters*, 1837–1861. London, 1908, Vol. II, pp. 156, 163.

land ; the chief difference was that owing to Louis-Philippe's prudent investments the latest party was better off financially than the Bourbons. Two years later, in August 1850, the ex-King died at the age of seventy-seven.

Palmerston's judgement was, as usual, shrewd. The Provisional Government in Paris certainly had enough worries without having to decide how to deal with the Orleans family and their friends. Its composition was of the oddest, for it was formed in a haphazard way during a time of utter confusion. The deputies had voted for a committee of five, but this was before the declaration of a republic. When names were actually put forward, the deputies who remained in their Chamber were far outnumbered by a crowd of excited men who had no respect for any constitutional authority and particularly disliked the members of the Chamber who had formed the Government party.

The people who were mainly responsible for turning the demonstration of 23 February into a revolution were the editors and writers of the radical newspapers. It was they who had precipitated matters by planning a procession ; they had constantly inflamed the crowd by violent speeches. Their attitude to the future was on the whole not that of revolutionaries ; they were as much astounded as the Orleanists at the collapse of the monarchy. What they had aimed at was to get rid of Guizot and his system and by a substantial increase of the electorate to eliminate for the future the personal power of the King in the government of the country.

The fighting had been done mainly by the unemployed workers, and many of them had quite different plans for the future. The socialist Louis Blanc had not only proclaimed that they had a right to work or maintenance, but had drafted an apparently practicable scheme of national workshops or factories through which regular employment would be provided. They had overthrown the King and Guizot; they would not be content with a new government which still consisted of their employers.

Three different sets of claimants for power, mutually antagonistic, were by force of circumstances obliged to combine in the new Provisional Government which had to restore order in Paris and think out the plans for an Assembly to make a new constitution for France. The liberal deputies wanted merely a modification of the existing system; the republicans wanted a political change far more profound; the socialists wanted an entirely new economic as well as political structure.

All three groups were represented in the Chamber when names were put forward for the new rulers of the country. Dupont (de l'Eure to distinguish him from all the other Duponts), Garnier-

Pagès (who owed his position largely to his dead brother's popularity), Marie and Crémieux, two lawyers who had spoken up when others were silent, and Marrast were radicals who were republican rather by force of circumstances than conviction. To them were added Ledru-Rollin and Flocon, journalists and revolutionary republicans, while the shouting workers demanded that Louis Blanc and Albert, a working man, should be added to the list.

Such an odd collection of men and views needed an outstanding person as its head if any reasonable allocation of duties and overall scheme of action were to be devised. The only man whom all were willing to have as President was Dupont, and he was eighty-one years old. As Barrot said, his popularity and his white hair were useful for the speech-makers,[1] but as a controlling force he was negligible. Lamartine was a wonderful orator but no organiser. The man who might have dominated the situation was Louis Blanc, for he stood for the real revolution and had the workers of Paris behind him. His experience and personality were not adequate for such a tremendous task.

Throughout the afternoon, evening and night of 24–25 February these new rulers struggled in the Hôtel de Ville to make some sort of decision. People of all sorts were rushing in and out; Jerome Bonaparte and his son, who happened to be in Paris, offered their assistance in restoring order, but this was refused. Louis Blanc's first defeat came when he urged that the red flag should replace the tricolour; an emotional speech by Lamartine led to his having to accept instead red badges of office for members of the Government. On the other hand, he succeeded on 25 February in getting the Government to issue a decree by which the right to work was recognised and the creation of national factories promised.

If this meant anything, then he should at once have been empowered to set to work on his own plans. This was not at all what his non-socialist colleagues wished. Nor was he allowed to create a new Ministry of Labour. Instead, he was persuaded that a special Parliament of Labour should be set up where the workers themselves would discuss plans and of which he should be the head. He, therefore, allowed himself to be side-tracked; in the Luxembourg, where the workers met in very large numbers, there were plenty of ideas for discussion but no power available for putting any of them to the test. Marie, the lawyer who had been made Minister of Public Works, admitted that Blanc had been deliberately put in a position where 'he could disorganise labour only in theory and not in fact'.[2]

---

[1] Barrot, O.: *Mémoires*. 3rd ed., Paris, 1875, Vol. II, p. 30.
[2] Thomas, E.: *Histoire des Ateliers Nationaux*. Ed. Marriott. Oxford, 1913, p. 142.

The two leading figures in the Provisional Government were Lamartine, who made himself Foreign Secretary, and Ledru-Rollin, who was Minister of the Interior. Administration was carried on with great difficulty, especially in the early days when the Hôtel de Ville was incessantly invaded by various deputations demanding action of all kinds. A new National Guard had been instituted on 25 February, but it was recruited from very young men attracted by the pay of 1½ francs a day and was not much use in keeping the streets clear. At intervals the Government was forced to issue decrees which made substantial changes in the law, although in theory they were merely carrying on until France had expressed its wishes through a Constituent Assembly.

On 29 February the most unpopular indirect taxes, on salt, the stamp duty on newspapers and so forth, were abolished, and on 1 March the licences required by sellers of alcoholic drinks were also withdrawn, so that anyone who chose could open a shop or public-house. Also on 29 February it was declared that no newspaper would be prosecuted for political reasons and a week later the greater part of the Press Law of 1835 was repealed. On 1 March it was decreed that in future no civil servant or other Government employee would be asked to take any oath of loyalty. Slavery was finally abolished on 4 March; imprisonment for debt was forbidden by a proclamation on 9 March; next day all persons who had been imprisoned for offences against religion were released, and on the 12th corporal punishment was prohibited. In April the local 'octroi' taxes on meat and wine were abolished.

The duty of enforcing these regulations was largely in the hands of the prefects. Ledru-Rollin dismissed most of those who had served under the Orleans monarchy and replaced them by his own republican friends or by small commissions of two or three people. In some areas such commissions had already been created by local people, and these were mostly allowed to remain. Crowds of applicants for Government posts besieged the ministers, and they were genuinely shocked at the light which was thrown on the job-hunting technique which had been developed under Guizot. The schools were circularised and told that the children must be instructed in the principles of true citizenship; this meant to Ledru-Rollin extreme democratic republican ideals, and he in turn was accused of using his official position for political ends.

The provinces as a whole accepted the news of the abdication of the King and the declaration of a Republic quite happily. In the manufacturing towns in the east and south there was jubilation, and in many places Trees of Liberty were planted in the revolutionary tradition. They were usually poplar trees, sometimes even fully

17

grown ones, dug up and decorated with flowers and ribbons and replanted in a public place with speeches and singing and dances. One marked difference from the first great revolution was that in very many villages and small towns the local priest played a prominent part in these ceremonies.

The Church in France as a whole hastened to accept the new Government. The legitimist clergy had always looked on Louis-Philippe as a usurper; the more liberal Catholics hoped for greater freedom. Many bishops and archbishops issued letters declaring that the Church believed in no special form of government, but did uphold liberty, equality and fraternity. The prayer after high mass now asked for salvation for the Republic, not for the King. This lead of acceptance was followed by almost all minor officials; and even the royal princes, Aumale and Joinville, who were with the forces and whose popularity would have enabled them to stage a counter-revolution, quietly accepted their dismissal.

In some of the industrial areas there were riots and machine-breaking. New textile machines that were blamed for unemployment were broken and Englishmen, who had been brought over to demonstrate them, were attacked. The barely completed stations on the new railways were in some places burnt down by the transport workers of the roads and the river, who feared the competition of the trains. Steam printing presses in Paris were damaged for the same reason; fear as usual led to violence. Peasants living near the State forests broke in and helped themselves to the timber, and the local tax offices were destroyed with all their records in a few towns. Louis-Philippe's house at Neuilly was burnt as a demonstration; Rothschild and others of his friends had their property seriously damaged. A few religious establishments were attacked, and some Jews ill-treated. There was a great deal of confusion everywhere; there was rioting and destruction in scattered districts, but there was very little serious violence and nowhere that bath of blood which was dreaded by the students of 1789.

The constitutional revolution began with a decree on 4 March which proclaimed that henceforward every Frenchman would have the right to vote at the age of twenty-one if he had resided for six months in one place. Men of twenty-five were eligible as deputies. At one stroke all the elaborate property qualifications had gone. The Constituent Assembly was to consist of 900 deputies; the detailed regulations distributed them among the departments according to population, including four for Algiers and twelve for the other colonies. From having under a quarter of a million voters, France now would boast of over nine million active citizens.

The organisation of such an election was not at all easy. At first it was planned to hold it on 9 April so that the Assembly could meet on 20 April. The republicans were opposed to so rapid an ending to the provisional system; they suspected that France as a whole was more conservative than they. Ledru-Rollin sent circulars to officials which bore a melancholy resemblance to those used by governments under the Restoration, urging them to bring their influence to bear so that the right type of man should be elected. His action led to an open breach with his more conservative colleagues. The practical difficulty of making out lists of electors, a task entrusted to the mayors all over the country, made a postponement necessary. The new date was 23 April, Easter Sunday; some Catholics suspected that it had been chosen to prevent people attending church services. If, which is dubious, there were any such aim it was easily defeated; the bishops gave leave for the hours of mass to be altered if necessary, and in many places the priest marched to the poll at the head of his flock.

The method of election had to be simple. All the voters were to attend in the chief town of the district; it was arranged that as a rule men from the same village should all vote in turn to help the officials to check the lists. Their names were called aloud and each man marched up to receive a paper on which the names of all the candidates were printed. He put his mark against one and withdrew. Anyone who could not attend with his neighbours was allowed to come forward later. Under such conditions no plan of second ballots could be permitted; the candidate who received most votes became the deputy.

Elaborate electioneering was also impossible. There was no Orleanist party, but the 'legitimists' still hoped that a return to the elder branch of the Bourbons might be possible in the future. They met openly at Angers and drew up a list of candidates.[1] The more revolutionary groups, very active in clubs, also tried to put up a large number of candidates. But there was no time to organise anything like regular parties to which people would give their adhesion, still less to draw up any rival programmes. The election was of necessity of individuals who were known to the voters either in person or by reputation.

As might have been expected, especially when it was announced that deputies would receive 25 francs a day during the session of the Assembly, the number of men standing for election was immense. No one had an idea of what a very large number of votes would be required for success; inevitably they thought in the familiar terms of hundreds when now thousands were required. Considering the novelty of the whole affair, there was surprisingly little trouble on

[1] De Falloux, op. cit., Vol. I, pp. 293 ff.

that Easter Day. There were riots and some fighting in Limoges and in Rouen, but in most places the people marched to the polls in a very orderly manner. Over 84 per cent of the electorate registered their votes. On the night of 24 April, when the last ballot papers had been collected, it could truly be said that for the first time the whole of the men of France had had and used the right of free choice of their representatives.

Chapter XXII

THE EMPIRE IS MADE

THE obvious cause of the collapse of the Orleans monarchy was the economic condition of France. The dissatisfaction of the lower middle class had led to the Reform movement; the unemployed of the new industrial system had conquered Paris. The urgent need was for the factories to reopen, but the very circumstances of the time made this almost impossible. All over Europe political upheavals made normal trade slow down; fresh orders for French goods on a scale large enough seriously to affect the situation were exceedingly unlikely. Even the employers who could have done so were unwilling to resume production, for they dreaded the revolutionary and socialist attitude displayed by the demonstrators. In Paris and in many other towns business was at a halt.

Financial institutions were already under strain. The Stock Exchange was reopened, but closed again for lack of business. The Provisional Government announced a ten-days' moratorium; debts due within that period need not be met till its close. This gave a breathing space, but creditors, not unnaturally, wanted payment, and all over France people went to the banks drawing out their money. Everyone wanted cash, solid gold and silver coins, and it was, of course, quite impossible for the banks to repay immediately the whole of their deposits. Most of them had to close. Still less was it within their power to advance money. Even the savings banks underwent the same strain, and as their deposits were on loan to the Government the State itself was affected.

The first man put in charge of finance resigned in a few days. The Government had very little cash at its disposal and the position seemed quite desperate. No one was buying goods; those who tried to raise money by selling their carriages and horses or even their houses had to accept a fraction of their recent value. Garnier-Pagès, who took over the Exchequer, announced the floating of a large loan and planned to sell immediately the Crown jewels and forest land. The savings banks were ordered not to pay any depositor more than 100 francs in cash; the rest would be in the form of Government stock at its face value, although the market price was well below par. The great men in finance who really had some money were not at all attracted by such arrangements; they waited to see what would happen. Only some of the better-off workers came with their small savings and even little gifts to the help of the State.

By 15 March to provide for immediate needs it was necessary to declare bank notes to be legal tender and to permit their issue up to a sum of 350 million francs. Special discount banks were opened in Paris and the larger provincial towns to provide loans for business men. The confiscation of the Orleans family estates was proposed, but the plan was dropped lest all owners of property should be alarmed and antagonised. The decrees abolishing some indirect taxes had lowered the national revenue, so the direct taxes were increased.

These financial troubles lay behind the urgent and immediate danger of the great mass of unemployed men who, hungry and wretched, had nothing to do but parade the streets. The Ministry of Public Works on 28 February promised to find work for all and subsistence until actual jobs were found. The only Government department that could immediately give work was the Roads and Bridges organisation, but it already had its own body of labourers and its officials were not very enterprising. On 2 March, in answer to the workers' demands, the setting up of national factories and the enforcement of a ten-hour working day were promised, but as the government was quite determined not to allow Louis Blanc to make any attempt to put his ideas into practice, the only plan open to it was that of some sort of relief work suitable for unskilled labourers. Meantime, men were told to apply at one of two offices, newly opened, where they would be paid 2 francs a day if they were given an actual job and 1½ francs subsistence money if they were not. As there were no jobs, crowds thronged in drawing their 1½ francs; no proper register could be kept and chaos resulted.

Émile Thomas, a manufacturing chemist aged twenty-six, lived near one of these offices. He was himself a first-class organiser and he rapidly worked out a plan which on 3 March he submitted to the Minister of Public Works, Marie. He had no sympathy whatever with Louis Blanc and socialist ideas, so to open actual factories for the manufacture of goods did not enter into his schemes; in any case, at that moment, to create such organisations would have been very hard indeed. What he suggested was that a large building on the outskirts of Paris should be given the name of National Factory; that men should be enrolled, divided into squads under officers whom he would recruit from the technical colleges, and sent out to work on such things as levelling of open spaces, repair of damaged property and so forth. The men were to register in the first place at their local mayor's office and the municipalities were to find the necessary money for their pay.

Thomas was hailed as a saviour by the Provisional Government and given the old royal palace and park of Monceau as his head-quarters. Soon he found he had to open his own registers, for those provided by the local authorities were impossible to check. By 15 March he had 40,000 men under his command due to receive pay or work. The collection of funds from local authorities on such a scale proved impossible, so very reluctantly the Exchequer made grants. Thomas' main problem was to find the jobs. The Roads and Bridges officials were extremely unco-operative; they were jealous of Thomas' young officers. Soon it was necessary to arrange that men worked only on certain days, mostly on shovelling earth to level ground and making embankments along the river, so as to allow all some employment.

That genuine and satisfactory work should be given was Thomas' main aim, but he was thwarted in every direction. He asked that factory owners should be given credit so that they could employ their former workers, but this plan was turned down; it would, in fact, have been difficult to work and certainly have led to complaints and jealousy. He wanted to send men out of Paris to do highly necessary work on the main roads. This the Government rejected, fearing lest the provinces should be infected by Paris revolu-tionaries. He wanted to build workers' houses; this was an invasion of private enterprise. Though opposed in theory to Louis Blanc's plans, he did, in fact, open tailoring and bootmaking shops, where the men could buy clothing, of which they were in desperate need, at cost price on the instalment plan. He also opened a clinic, where kindly doctors attended for nominal fees to treat the sick and injured.

According to Thomas' own account[1] an extraordinary communal spirit seems to have developed among the men of the Parc de Monceau. They were used to military service; low though their pay was it did allow them and their families to survive; they felt that the whole organisation was for them and not for employers' profit. Louis Blanc at the Luxembourg with his seven hundred or so members of the workers' parliament was not unnaturally angry at the building up of such a quasi-military organisation under the name of his National Factories. When his men and Thomas' met in the streets or at the continuing workers' demonstrations, there was always a danger of fights. More and more men were attracted to Thomas' centre; they came in from villages or even in some cases from abroad. When finally the scheme was closed, there were over 100,000 men on the books.

The Government, too, became alarmed. Providing money for the

[1] Thomas, E.: *Histoire des Ateliers Nationaux*. Ed. Marriott. Oxford, 1913.

wages and expenses of such an organisation was very difficult;
Thomas was always in difficulty because of the spasmodic and
inadequate amount of Government grants. Revolutionary clubs
developed rapidly among the men and leaders were emerging.
Thomas himself seemed to be in sympathy with the Bonapartists,
who were already beginning to appear as a factor in politics. On
4 May the new Assembly had met in a hastily built hall about 120
feet long, where perched on steep rows of benches the deputies of the
nation heard, with difficulty because of the shocking acoustics, the
reports of the Provisional Government and appointed a new
executive committee. One of this committee's major problems would
be to deal with the National Factory organisation.

The choice of men for this Government, which closely resembled
the Directory of 1795 in consisting of five individuals under whom
were the ministers, indicated that the revolution was to be regarded
as finished. Arago, Garnier-Pagès and Marie, men of the milder
liberal group, got the most votes. Lamartine was fourth, this was
probably because he refused office unless Ledru-Rollin, too, was
chosen, and he and his friend came at the bottom of the list. The
Paris workers kept up a series of demonstrations, and on 15 May
members of the clubs and delegates of the labourers invaded the
Assembly, demanding not only work and food but that help should
be sent to the revolutionaries in Poland. For about three hours the
tumult went on; then the demonstrators pulled the President out of
his seat and declared the Assembly dissolved. They then went to the
Hôtel de Ville.

The National Guard was called out to clear the streets and many
of the men's leaders were arrested. The workers' clubs were closed,
and next day, on 16 May, Louis Blanc's Workers' Commission at the
Luxembourg was declared at an end. The men who had been attending its meetings now joined up with the rival organisation under
Thomas, where they now received 8 francs a week wage in return for
two days' work. Thomas himself was more of a problem; no one
could deny that he had served the Government well and had organised his men into a coherent and comparatively effective force.
This was, in fact, his undoing; it was felt that, now the old rivalry
had ended, the organised workers were too powerful.

On 25 May the Ministry of Public Works announced the setting
up of a committee of enquiry into the administration of the National
Factories and next day it asked for a list of seventeen particulars with
regard to every individual man, to be produced within twenty-four
hours. Such a request was obviously impossible to satisfy, and
Thomas resigned. There was no excuse for arresting him, but something not far off that was arranged. He was told to go to Bordeaux

and design a canal; when he said he was a chemist, not an engineer, he was answered that for his own safety he should go. He was not even allowed to go and see his mother, but was hustled into a carriage with two policemen and driven away.[1]

Naturally, his men were furious and the people sent in to do his work found it impossible. His subordinate officials resigned, and all was chaos. On 12 June some of the newspapers published his letter of protest, which still further embittered the men who had trusted him. On 21 June the younger men were ordered to enlist in the army or leave the Parc de Monceau organisation; the medical help was stopped and the price of goods supplied to the workers raised by 50 per cent, the rise to apply to goods already supplied. Next day Paris again saw masses of men marching through the streets demanding redress.

It is clear that the Government had decided to end the social revolution of 1848. When on 23 June a great crowd assembled round the column of the Bastille, Cavaignac, in charge of the army in Paris, was ready. He had about 50,000 men under his command and used them not in detachments but as a massed force. Arago spoke to the crowds and asked them to disperse; when they did not, the troops attacked. Heavy fighting went on all next day. Efforts were made to induce the workers to surrender; the archbishop addressing the crowds was shot, probably by a soldier by mistake, but the tragedy made many people believe that wicked revolutionaries were setting out on a campaign of murder. On 26 June a deputation from the demonstrators asked Cavaignac for an armistice, but he demanded unconditional surrender and the slaughter went on till all possible resistance was over.

The terrible Days of June left very bitter memories behind them. Those who had preached class warfare seemed to be justified; those who had hoped for genuine social reform were in despair. How many men died is not known; 900 of the Government forces were killed and over 2,000 wounded; the police estimate of 1,460 rioters killed is certainly very much too low. The hopes of the workers were drowned in a sea of blood.

Over 15,000 men were arrested, of whom over 6,000 were later released. The men considered to be leaders were tried by courts martial; a few were executed but the others sentenced to simple imprisonment or to forced labour. The great mass of the prisoners was deported; at first it was planned to send them to distant French colonies, but consideration of expense led to their being shipped to Algeria. Louis Blanc was not among them; he had escaped to England.

[1] Thomas, É., op. cit., pp. 289 ff.

*17

One effect of the tragedy of the Days of June was to rouse among the members of the Assembly a dread almost amounting to hatred of the workers. The liberal Catholics had been working out a plan of social reform ameliorative rather than thorough, but which would have given substantial help to the poorest and weakest. This scheme had to be dropped; it had no support at all. Another result was the elevation of Cavaignac to the rank of saviour of the nation. The Assembly invested him with full executive powers, so the Commission of five resigned. The General, who was no politician, appointed ministers from the moderate republican majority in the Chamber, and ruled France with their help until December 1848.

Meantime, the new constitution was being drafted. A committee of eighteen was empowered to carry out this task. Three major principles had emerged from the events of February—France was to be a republic, manhood suffrage was accepted, and the right to work or maintenance had been recognised. These were stressed in a lengthy preamble to the formal constitution which was debated in September and October and finally promulgated on 4 November, 1848.

The question which raised most interest was that of the President of the Republic. Inevitably, more than theoretical arguments influenced members of the Constituent Assembly. Several leading politicians hoped that they might themselves hold this high office and therefore approved of the plan that the President should nominate the ministers, although their responsibility was to the Assembly. On the other hand, no one was willing to give him much real power, and it was decided that he should hold office for only four years and not be re-eligible.

It was over the question of how he should be appointed that the most vital arguments took place. If he were to be chosen by the Assembly itself, then it was felt he would inevitably be bound to a political party or group of parties, but he was to represent the whole of France. Finally it was decided that he must be a Frenchman, who had never lost his citizenship, aged thirty or over. He was to be chosen by the direct vote of all electors; their votes would be checked by the Assembly and the man who had an absolute majority would at once be declared President. The date of 10 December was fixed for the election.

Universal suffrage was maintained, but the method of *scrutin de liste* was reintroduced for the election of deputies, whose number was fixed at 750. No deputy could hold a paid Government office. Elections were to take place every three years. The third point of the February demands, the right to work, was whittled down after stormy debates to a vague statement that the State should, within the limits of its resources, ensure work for the citizens and help those unable to work.

Between June and December no radical changes could be made nor any serious political programme be carried out. Secret societies and political clubs were banned; the Press was restrained by the re-introduction of caution money. The radical republicans once again, in September, began holding banquets; these and a proposal by Cavaignac to send emissaries into the provinces to rally republican sentiment, were plainly preliminary moves towards the elections of the future.

When the first elections to the Constituent Assembly took place some of the Bonaparte family had stood as candidates. The question was raised whether they were entitled to stand, as all members of the family had been deprived of French citizenship. The Assembly, feeling that this had been a royalist move, allowed them to be elected.

Louis-Napoleon, the only active politician of the Bonapartes, showed very great ability in his conduct. He had made a dramatic escape from his prison at Ham in May 1846, and was living in England in 1848. He returned to France after the revolution, but did not offer himself as a candidate in April. In May additional elections were held for some vacant constituencies and he then came forward, as did Thiers, who had not been successful in April. A great many of the Paris workers voted for Louis-Napoleon since Émile Thomas gave him his support. Lamartine and Ledru-Rollin opposed the legality of his election, but the majority of the Assembly held that as others of his family had been allowed to sit, there was no ground for excluding him. As before in Switzerland, Louis at the right moment declared that, rather than be the cause of dispute, he would resign. The applause that resulted from this decision greatly strengthened his position in the country, and when at the end of August additional elections had to be held for thirteen vacant seats, he once again stood. No less than five departments put him at the head of the poll.

He played very little part in the debates. He spoke with a strong Swiss accent and was not at all eloquent; once, when the question was raised as to whether any member of a family that once had reigned in France could be President, he spoke briefly and awkwardly. The effect was to diminish the fears that many people had felt when he had first appeared on the scene.

Thiers, Barrot, Molé and other politicians of the 'constitutional' party gradually came to the belief that it would be wise to support Louis-Napoleon as a candidate for the Presidency. Cavaignac was the main rival and they disliked the idea of his continuing to lead the nation. They gave him practical help by revising his electoral manifesto, which began by stressing that the name Napoleon symbolised order and security, and then went on to vague promises designed to meet the desires of various groups. Ledru-Rollin, Lamartine and Raspail all offered themselves as candidates.

During the days of 10 and 11 December, 1848, 75 per cent of the adult men of France went to the poll. The result came as a shock to the politicians. Lamartine secured less than 8,000 votes; his dreams of statesmanship were ended. Raspail did little better. Ledru-Rollin, who had counted on the republicans, gained over 370,000, or about 5 per cent of the total votes cast. Cavaignac had nearly a million and a half, under 20 per cent; to too many people he was known as the man who had carried out the terrible slaughter of the Days of June. Louis-Napoleon Bonaparte had five and a half million. The politicians had been thinking in terms of Paris, but the bulk of the voters lived in the provinces. For them the only familiar name was Napoleon. The first Napoleon, according to the propaganda of the 'forties, had saved France from anarchy and ruin. The politicians had made a mess of things; the legitimists had not even produced a candidate; the Orleanists were discredited. How else could they cast their votes?

The Empire was made. Though for many months the struggle went on between the Assembly and the President, there could be no doubt of the final issue. One man could claim to represent all classes, all aspirations; the deputies stood for groups and interests, divided amongst themselves. The very limits of the President's power helped him to lay on others the blame for anything that went wrong. That he would quietly retire in four years no one could believe. It was simply a question of how soon and on what grounds the final decision would be made and the Second Republic like the First become an Empire.

The causes of a failure of an organisation, especially one so complex as a political system, are inevitably difficult to discover. No assessment can be wholly objective; the date at which an analysis is made and the outlook of the person conducting it will lead to the stressing of some factors at the expense of others. Contemporaries tended to account for the two revolutions which shattered constitutional monarchy in France in terms of personalities alone. Later writers have often tended to go to the opposite extreme and deal with abstractions, such as national character or economic forces. Can a foreigner, writing more than a century after the period between the two empires, hope to understand? At the best, one can only offer suggestions.

Constitutional monarchy is a hybrid type of political organisation whose chief advantage seems to lie in its flexibility. Even a written constitution like the Charter could be modified both by law and by custom. In the early nineteenth century it was thought of as based on a balance of political forces; a national tradition of personal rule represented by the monarch; constitutional recognition given by an Upper House to the economic and social powers of wealth and family; a more or less flexible representation of other classes through an electoral system. Such a constitution cannot endure unless, preferably almost unnoticed, harmony is maintained by a gradual shifting of control between its organs of government to correspond with changes in the social evolution of the nation.

England was the model of the constitution makers, and during the nineteenth century she herself made changes which amounted to a constitutional revolution in effect if not in name. Both by law and by accumulative modifications in procedure the Crown lost direct control and the powers of the non-elective hereditary chamber were weakened as it grew in size. Such changes may be resisted, and here the personal factor comes into play; monarchies survived in those states where the sovereigns recognised that their part in national life was to be something quite other than the making of political decisions, and where privileged classes gradually abandoned their exclusive rights. France had but one generation in which to make such adjustments, yet it could be argued that she had her chance in 1830.

In 1789 and the years that immediately followed France broke with her long tradition of kingship, only to replace it under pressure of war and disorder, by a new type of monarchy. The Empire differed in more than name from the kingdom of Louis; though in many respects the system it employed was a development of the old organs of royal power, it was based on the revolutionary principle of public consent. Louis XVIII dimly recognised this fundamental change; his successors did not. Both Charles X and Louis-Philippe could have saved the constitutional monarchy had they been willing to accept radical changes. Both were old men, who could remember the revolution of 1789. It was psychologically impossible for them to act with such wisdom and such courage; unjustifiable confidence was replaced by unreasoning fear.

It could be argued that it was not the general scheme of a constitutional monarchy but the narrow basis of suffrage on which it rested that led to its collapse. In 1814 a wide franchise would have been impossible; France was a defeated country and the victors were afraid of the common people. In 1830 the situation was different; a bold acceptance of the truth that the Orleans monarchy was the result of a popular revolution was possible. It was the politicians, drawn from a narrow section of society, who were not willing to risk a change in the system with which they were familiar. When in 1848 they were forced suddenly to expand the electorate they could not adjust themselves any more than the monarchs could. The counter-revolution of the Days of June killed the Second Republic. The experienced men in politics, many of them able, honest and sincere, were too preoccupied with their fears and hopes, for their country as well as for themselves, to look with open eyes upon the people of France and their needs and their longings.

BOOKS FOR FURTHER READING
In addition to those referred to in the text

A list of authorities, original and secondary, will be found in Lavisse, *Histoire de la France Contemporaine*, Vols. IV and V, by S. Charléty.

Bullock and Taylor, *A Select List of Books on European History, 1815–1914*, Oxford, 1949, contains a short list of books on the period.

Some recent books may be mentioned:

A series of short studies on different aspects of the Revolution of 1848, published by Presses Universitaires de France, 108 Boulevard, St Germain, Paris, from whom a full list of the series *Collection du Centenaire de la Révolution de 1848* can be obtained.

In the series *De Quoi Vivaient-ils?* interesting brief studies, including Aubert, *De Quoi Vivait Thiers?* and Dumont et Gitan *De Quoi Vivait Lamartine?* have recently been published by Deux-Rives, Paris.

Leroy, *Histoire des Idées Sociales en France*, Paris, 1950, is a full and interesting account of minor as well as major thinkers between Babeuf and de Tocqueville.

Robin-Harmel, *Le Prince Jules de Polignac*, Avignon, 1950, throws light on the fall of the Bourbons.

De Sauvigny, *G. de Bertier, Le Comte Ferdinand de Bertier (1782–1864)*, Paris, 1948, contains much interesting material on the extreme royalists.

Collins, I., articles on de Villèle and on the Press under Louis-Philippe in the *English Historical Review*, Vols. LXVI and LXIX.

INDEX OF SELECTED SUBJECTS
AND PLACES

ADMINISTRATION
  System, 7, 41
  Changes in personnel: *1814–30*, 18,
    72, 74, 84, 102, 109, 118, 126, 133,
    140, 159, 161, 165, 170; *1830–48*,
    185, 210; *1848*, 257
AGRICULTURE, INDUSTRY, TRADE, 2, 3,
    195–6, 221–3, 245, 261
ALGIERS and MOROCCO, 158, 167, 224–
    228
ALLIED ARMIES OF OCCUPATION, 62–3,
    71, 79, 83, 93–4
ALLIED POWERS
  Policy *1814* onwards, 18, 20, 26, 42,
    45–7, 52, 65, 67
  Holy Alliance, 71, 75, 82, 103, 171
  Congresses: Vienna, 32, 35; Aix-la-
    Chapelle, 93; Verona, 124–5
ARMY, 6–7, 25, 33–5, 38–9, 51, 52, 74,
    77, 79, 91
  Plots in, 118–19, 121, 124
  In Spain, 128 ff.
  Law of *1824*, 138–9, 141, 150
  In *1830*, 173–4, 198–201, 202–3,
    224–7
  In *1848*, 247, 248, 250–2, 265
AUSTRIA. *See* Allied Powers

BANKING, FINANCE, SPECULATION,
    3–4, 13, 31, 40, 43, 79, 94, 121,
    125, 136, 137, 145, 172, 184, 194,
    222, 261–2
BANQUETS: Political, 200, 245–6, 248
BELGIUM, 165, 172, 185, 202. *See also*
    Leopold
BONAPARTE FAMILY, 18, 75, 206, 256,
    267. *See also* Napoleon; Napoleon
    Louis-
BONAPARTISTS, 26, 33, 35, 47, 57, 70,
    102, 104, 111, 114, 174, 214, 264.
    See also Napoleon; Napoleonic
    Legend
BORDEAUX, 10, 42, 54, 146, 162, 170,
    264
BOURBON FAMILY, 8, 12 ff. *See also*
    Louis; Artois; Angoulême; de
    Berry
  Spanish. *See* Spain; Ferdinand
BUDGETS and TAXATION, 30, 104, 114,
    119, 120, 139, 144, 152, 161, 163,
    169, 188, 245, 257

CABINETS
  1814, 23, 32; *1815*, 47, 64–7; *1816*,
    76; *1817*, 86, 90; *1819*, 94–5,
    105; *1820*, 106, 112; *1821*, 114,
    117; *1822*, 126; *1824*, 138, 139,
    1827, 155; *1828*, 157, 159; *1829*,
    162, 164–6
  1830, 170, 184, 187; *1831*, 189,
    1832, 209; *1834*, 210; *1835*, 211,
    1836, 231; *1837*, 231; *1838*, 231,
    1839, 232; *1840*, 232, 234, 236,
    1848, 249, 266
CHURCH
  And State, 5, 28, 54, 76, 80, 90–1,
    113–14, 139, 142, Ch. XIII
    pp. 147–53, 167, 225, 258
  And People, 5, 6, 32, 54, 57, 115,
    119, 149, 150, 153, 170, 174, 188,
    203, 218, 259, 265
  Gallicans, 5, 147, 216
  Ultramontanes, 5, 6, 147, 160, 215,
  Liberal Catholics, 214–19, 266
  Religious Orders, 148, 221
  Jesuits, 139, 147, 150–5, 160, 174,
    221
  And education, 75, 103, 140, 160
  Congregation, 54–5, 117, 151–2
  Knights of the Faith, 55–6, 108,
    115, 118, 140, 149, 153
CONFISCATED LANDS and COMPENSA-
    TION, 31, 73, 76, 79, 87, 102, 104,
    114, 136–8, 142–3
CONGRESSES. *See* Allied Powers
CONSTITUTION
  Of First Empire, 7: additional
    Act *1815*, 43; Charter of *1814*,
    11, 15, 17–18, 22, 26–30, 40, 47,
    68, 71, 75, 76, 82–3, 142, 144,
    168; amended *1830*, 181, 183,
    188
  Second Republic, 254: Provisional
    Government, 255–7; Constituent
    Assembly, 258–9, 264; Constitu-
    tion, 266
  See also Council of State; Deputies;
    Elections; Peers
COUNCIL OF STATE, 7, 17, 25, 43, 49,
    50, 140
COURTS and JUSTICE, 28, 33, 73, 78,
    152, 154

INDEX OF SELECTED SUBJECTS AND PLACES 273

DEPUTIES: procedure, 28–30, 96, 113, 120; trial by, 151; group system, 70, 72; hold government posts, 143, 151, 163, 189–90, 236–7, 245; in revolution of *1830*, 178; in Revolution of *1848*, 249–255
See also Elections

DOCTRINAIRES. *See* Liberals

EDUCATION: organisation of, 6, 75, 148; university, 6, 75, 103, 108, 119, 120, 148, 155, 173, 219, 220; secondary schools, 6, 148, 153, 219–20; primary schools, 6, 75, 148, 219–20

EGYPT, 158, 230–5

ELECTIONS
Electoral Laws, 27, 49, 81, 84–6, 105–6, 109, 113, 135, 137, 154, 183, 190, 259
Elections: *1815*, 49–50, 64–5; *1816*, 81; *1817* (partial), 91; *1818* (partial), 93; *1819* (partial), 104; *1820* (partial), 111; *1821* (partial), 113, 116; *1822* (partial), 120, 122; *1824*, 134–5; *1827*, 156; *1828* (by-elections), 159, 161; *1830*, 170; *1830* (partial), 187; *1834*, 210; *1837*, 231; *1839*, 231–2
Character of elections, 237; *1848*, 258–60, 267
Of President of Republic, 266–8

ÉMIGRÉS, 1–4, 7, 31, 35, 46, 49. *See also* Church; Confiscated Lands

ENGLAND: relations with France, 42, 67, 115, 125, 126, 130, 131, 134, 165, 167; after *1830*, 185, 226, 234, 238–41. *See also* Allied Powers; Wellington; Palmerston; Victoria

FINANCE. *See* Banking

FLAG: White, 15, 34, 69; Tricolour, 15, 34, 39, 41, 45, 47, 69, 129, 175, 181, 256; Red, 256

FOREIGN POLICY, 113, 115, 134, 158, 165, 202, 209, 230–5, 238–40. *See also* Congresses; Allied Powers; England; Spain

INDUSTRY. *See* Agriculture

JULY REVOLUTION, 170–84

LIBERALS, 46, 70, 83, 84, 93, 96–7, 102, 118, 135, 142, 145, 146, 147, 154, 156, 159, 162, 166, 168–70, 176–8, 183, 244, 251, 255

LYONS, 38, 77, 87–9, 120, 165, 170, 195–201

NAPOLEONIC LEGEND, 115, 207–8, 227, 268

NATIONAL DEBT, 4, 30, 31, 51, 71, 75, 86–7, 93–4, 104, 126, 136–7, 143–145, 161, 163, 166, 245

NATIONAL FACTORIES OR WORKSHOPS, 244, 256, 262–5

NATIONAL GUARD, 16, 63, 74, 77, 80, 88, 92, 127, 155 (of Paris, disbanded), 169, 187, 188, 190, 198, 247, 248, 249, 251–2, 257, 264

NAVY, 131, 158, 227

ORLEANS FAMILY, 14, 141, 180 ff., 203, 231–2, 238, 252, 258. *See also* Orleans; Chartres; Joinville; Nemours

PARIS
In *1814*, 9, 10, 16, 18, 32; *1815*, 37, 41, 45, 46; during Restoration, 63, 79, 108, 144, 170
In *1830*, 171 ff.; during Orleans Monarchy, 187, 195, 201, 203, 232; fortifications, 234; in *1848*, 247 ff.

PEERS
Creation of, 50, 69, 103, 133, 156, 166, 209, 231
As Law Court: 58, 110, 187, 201, 207, 211, 219, 242

PLOTS
Revolutionary, 70, 77–9 (Didier's), 87–8 (Lyons), 108, 109–10 (Bazar Français), 118–19 and 121 (Army), 206–8 (Louis-Napoleon)
Royalist, 88, 89 (Tuileries Garden), 112, 204–6 (Duchess de Berry)

POPES: Pius VII, 55–6, 90–8; Leo XII, 150, 160; Gregory XVI, 163, 202, 217, 221; Pius IX, 246

PORTUGAL, 123, 125, 130, 238

PRESS
French National, 18, 32, 33, 51, 60, 87, 91, 93, 97–101, 105, 119, 141, 149, 150, 154, 155, 159, 166, 169, 172, 177, 200, 242, 248, 251, 255, 257
Provincial, 101, 242
Censorship, 32, 83, 97, 99, 108, 141, 150, 155
Foreign, 88–9, 91, 167

PROTESTANTS, 5–6, 54, 108, 149, 188

PRUSSIA. *See* Allied Powers

RENTES. *See* National Debt

REPUBLICANS, 8, 70, 111, 174, 176, 181, 198, 200, 255

REQUIEMS and FUNERALS, 26, 33, 56, 146, 150, 156, 188

RIOTS
In Paris, 63, 103, 120, 155, 156, 170, 173, 187, 188–9 (St. Germain l'Auxerrois), 203, 264
In provinces, 87, 103, 119, 258, 260
ROMANTIC MOVEMENT: influence, on politics, 69 ff., 214; on society, 213 ff. See also Chateaubriand; Lamartine
ROUEN, 149, 165, 170, 260
ROYAL GUARD, 51, 63, 108, 172
ROYALISTS. There are too many references to quote for the period 1814–30. After 1830, 189, 196, 259
RUSSIA. See Alexander; Allied Powers

SECRET SOCIETIES: Knights of the Faith, see Church; Carbonari, 109, 113, 115, 121, 196, 200, 216; others, 196, 200, 232, 249

SOCIALISM, 191–4, 214, 243–4, 255
SPAIN, 123–32, 158, 161, 170, 238–40
Spanish colonies, 134

TAHITI, 228–30
TAXATION. See Budgets
TRADE. See Agriculture
TREATIES
1815, 64, 70–1
1818, 93
1841, 234

WHITE TERROR, 52 ff., Ch. VI passim.
In Spain, 130 ff.
WORKERS
Control by Livret system, 3, 199
Conditions, Ch. XVI, also 79, 195, 222, 234, 249, 262
Organisation of, 196, 200
Social Reform, 218, 222, 223, 237
In 1848, 255–8, 262–5

INDEX OF IMPORTANT PEOPLE

Abd el Kadr, 224–7
Adelaide of Orleans, 178, 186
Alexander of Russia, 8, 10, 17, 18–20, 21, 42, 66, 70, 133
Angoulême, Duke of, 13, 14, 15, 42, 82, 92, 94, 127–32, 139: becomes Dauphin, 141, 144, 150, 156, 157, 163, 164, 174, 175
Angoulême, Duchess of, 13, 22, 42, 82
Artois, Charles, Duke of: character, 13, 15 ff., 33, 38–40, 47, 64, 74, 75, 80–2, 87 ff., 105–6, 112, 116–17, 126, 128, 132, 138–9; becomes King Charles X, 140–1, see thence to 175, especially as constitutional king, 145, 154, 156, 158, 161, 163; plans coup, 171; defeat and flight, 171–5, 204

Barrot, Odilon, 189, 241, 245–6, 248, 250, 253, 256, 257
Bellune, Duke de, 117, 127 ff., 132, 133, 139, 144, 164
Berry, Duke de: character, 14, 32, 34, 79, 82; murdered, 105–6
Berry, Duchess de, 79, 105, 111, 112, 204–6
Bertier, Count Ferdinand de, 55, 74, 79, 140
Beugnot, Count Claud, 16, 24, 32, 38, 48
Blacas, Duke de, 20–1, 24, 40, 47, 87, 90
Blanc, Louis, 243–4, 248, 255–6, 262–5
Bourdonnaye, de la, 127, 159, 160, 164–6
Broglie, Duke de, 22, 60, 96–7, 119, 159, 184, 209, 210, 211, 230–1
Bugeaud, Marshal, 295, 225–8, 250–2

Canuel, 87–9, 127, 133
Cavaignac, 265–8
Cayla, Madame du, 116, 124, 132–3, 139, 140, 155
Charles X. See Artois
Chartres, Duke of: character, 180; becomes Duke of Orleans 1830, 199; 203, 231, 234, 241
　　Orleans, Duchess of, 231, 252–4
Chateaubriand, Viscount de, 68–9, 73, 82, 83, 89, 98, 101, 112, 114, 118, 124: Foreign Minister, 126–38, 143–5, 149, 154–7, 161–3, 165, 168, 181

Constant, Benjamin, 43–4, 143, 163
Corbière, 107, 112, 117, 139
Corvetto, 66, 86, 94

Dambray, 23, 48, 76, 86
Decazes, Élie: described, 49, 64, 66, 70, 73, 74, 78, 80 ff.; Dessolles-Decazes Cabinet, 95 ff.; fall of, 106, 113
Dessolles, 95, 104, 105
Donnadieu, 77–9, 88–9, 117–18, 127, 133, 155

Ferdinand VII of Spain, 115, Ch. XI passim, 238
Fouché, Joseph, Duke of Otranto, 4, 17, 40, 43, 48, 52–3: fall of, 64
Foy, 126, 139, 143, 146
Frayssinous, Abbé de, 120, 152–3, 157

Guizot, François, 76, 82, 84, 86, 97, 102, 121, 166, 168, 181, 184, 186, 189, 209–10: educational policy, 219–21, 231–3, 236–8, 242, 244–5, 248–50, 254

Joinville, Prince de, 180, 208, 212, 225–7, 232, 238, 241, 258

Lacordaire, le Père, 216–8
Lafayette, Marquis de, 91, 93, 108–9, 111, 115, 119, 121, 145–6, 165, 176–187
Laffitte, 44, 51, 121, 137, 146, 163, 177, 187, 189
Lainé, 76, 82, 85, 133, 160, 168
Lamartine, Alphonse de, 115, 213, 223, 241, 246, 254–7, 267–8
Lamennais, Félicité de, 151–2, 161, 215–18
Lavalette, Count de, 61–2, 76
Ledru-Rollin, 254, 255, 257, 259, 267–268
Leopold I of Belgium, 186, 233–4, 241
Louis, Baron, 24, 30, 48, 66, 94, 95, 105, 184, 189
Louis XVIII, 9, 12: as King of France, p. 20 forward, references frequent; as constitutional king, see especially 23, 51, 61, 64–7, 76, 80, Chs. VII and VIII; death, 140
Louis-Philippe. See Orleans

275

Manuel, 93, 113, 119, 126–7: death and funeral, 155–6
Marmont, Marshal, Duke of Ragusa, 40, 88, 167, 171–5
Martignac, Jean-Baptiste de, 119, 129, 142: in office, 157–64, 187
Molé, Count, 90, 184, 231, 249, 267
Montalembert, Count de, 216–18, 235
Montesquiou, Abbé de, 17, 23, 41
Montmorency, Duke de, 117, 124–6

Napoleon I, 1, 7–10, 19, Ch. IV passim.: death, 114; reburial, 207–8
Napoleon, Louis-, 206–8, 267–8
Nemours, Prince de, 186, 224–6, 232, 241, 252, 253–4
Ney, Marshal, Prince of Moskova, 35, 38: trial and death, 58 ff.

Orleans, Louis-Philippe, Duke of, 9, 14, 35, 41, 42, 72, 78, 115, 146, 148, 168, 170, 175: becomes king, Ch. XV forward to p. 254; as constitutional king, 186, 211; relation with the people, 203, 211, 235; abdication, 252
Orleans, Duchess of. See Chartres
Ouvrard, 125 ff., 139, 144
Ozanam, 218–19

Palmerston, 233–4, 240, 254
Pasquier, Duke de, 48, 66, 73, 86, 95, 97, 105, 113, 149
Périer, Casimir, 189, 197, 202, 203
Peyronnet, Count de, 117, 154, 163, 170, 173
Polignac, Duke de, 150, 156, 162: in office, 164–74, 184, 187

Richelieu, Duke de, 48–9: first ministry, 65, 95, 102, 105; second ministry, 106–17
Rochefoucauld, Sosthènes de la, 116, 132, 139, 140, 145
Rothschilds, 13, 43, 114, 137, 238–9, 258
Royer Collard, 84, 96, 117, 119, 151, 168

St. Cyr, 49, 52, 90, 91, 94, 104, 105
Serre, Count de, 76, 86, 95, 96, 105, 113, 117
Soult, Marshal, Duke of Dalmatia, 34, 38, 187, 189, 197, 199–210, 232, 236, 238, 252

Talleyrand, Prince of Benevento, 4, 7, 9–11, 15–17, 20–6, 35, 43, 47, 51, 62: fall of, 64–5, 67, 75, 78, 106, 110, 155, 178, 185–6, 230–1
Thiers, Adolphe, 99, 101, 172, 177–8, 209, 231: in office, 232–4, 245, 249–250, 252, 267
Thomas, 262–5, 267
Tocqueville, A. de, 214, 237, 244, 246, 249, 250, 253

Vaublanc, Count de, 66, 71, 74, 76
Victoria, Queen, 180, 186, 209, 211, 233–4, 239–41, 254
Villèle, Count de, 23, 72–3, 105–7, 112 ff.: in office, 117 ff.; Prime Minister, 125 ff.; decline in influence, 153–5; fall, 156, 158, 161, 169, 171
Vitrolles, Baron de, 15, 17–19, 24, 26, 40, 45, 52, 66–7, 88–9, 133, 166

Wellington, Duke of, 1, 10, 35, 45, 47, 59, 62–3, 125, 185